Whatever next?

Whatever next?

Reminiscences of a journey through life

Earl Ferrers

First published in Great Britain in 2011 by
Biteback Publishing Ltd
Westminster Tower
3 Albert Embankment
London
SE1 7SP

Photos of 'Two Back' and Staunton Harold © Steve Bond.
All other photos from the personal collection of Earl Ferrers.
Cartoons reproduced by kind permission of Matt Pritchett.
Every reasonable effort has been made to trace copyright holders of
material reproduced in this book, but if any have been inadvertently
overlooked the publishers would be glad to hear from them.

ISBN 978-1-84954-091-9

10 9 8 7 6 5 4 3 2 1

A CIP catalogue record for this book is available from the British Library.

Set in Adobe Garamond Pro
Printed and bound in Great Britain by
TJ International, Padstow, Cornwall.

To Annabel
who is everything

Contents

Acknowledgements

To my grandson, William, for having badgered me, remorselessly, to write this book.

To so many people, members of my family and others, who have also encouraged me to write this book.

To Jane Wickstead whose diligence, determination and patience has shown no bounds in having translated my indecipherable handwriting on to a computer, and then being prepared to alter it all over and over again. It was a tour de force – and she always managed to smile!

To my publishers, who went out of their way to be kind, understanding and co-operative to the New Boy, and for not having been driven to distraction by his constant procrastinations.

To myself for being so stupid as not to realise – and therefore be deterred by – what a Magnum Opus all this was going to be.

Preface

I ALWAYS THOUGHT that it would be an impertinence to write a book about my life. I have made no spectacular achievements, and I have never kept a diary to help me to remember what happened and when. I have plodded through life meeting anything which 'chance' happens to throw in the way with, I hope, enthusiasm.

But then I realised what a huge privilege life is, just being alive and experiencing the world. One tends to think that one is like a piece of flotsam on the river, moving this way and that way depending on the curves of the bank, the rocks and the currents. One tends to think what has happened would have happened anyhow – but it might well not have done. Maybe one has experienced things which, at the time, may have seemed insignificant, but which, in their totality, have made up one's life – for better or for worse. Despite my inevitable grumblings and groanings, I have been indescribably lucky, and I have hugely enjoyed life and the experience of it.

For life is an experience. Why are we here? Who sent us here? Where are we going? What are we supposed to do? What happens afterwards? These are basic questions, all of a pretty fundamental and philosophical nature, which everyone asks of themselves but for which no one has the answers. We are given the seven senses of man – the abilities to see, hear, touch, taste, smell, think and reason. But there are other senses with which we are not endowed such as the ability to answer the basic questions of why are we here, who sent us here, where are we going and what happens afterwards? We have not got the senses to understand or to provide the answers to the questions, so stop worrying and stop trying to answer the unanswerable.

But few of us do. A body, a 'soul', a life is made at conception when a sperm meets an egg. I have often wondered what would have happened if one of the other of the six million or so sperm which are supposed to compete for the fertilisation process had won the race, and not the one which did, whether 'I' would still be here – with possibly a different personality, different looks, different height, different academic achievements but basically the same 'me' who thinks and talks as I do. Would one have the same soul? Or would one just be a totally different person, as a brother is to another brother or sister? Would the 'person' I am now not be in existence? I never have existed? Nor one's soul either?

I find this pretty frightening stuff – pretty confusing stuff and pretty awesome stuff, too. If the latter premise is correct, it is pure chance – one in six million – which has enabled me to live and experience life at all and even to experience, if one believes such things as I do, another life after this one. If one of the other sperm had got there first, what would have happened? Would I never have been born, never have experienced this life and would never experience what happens afterwards? What would there be instead? Nothing? Never existed? Quite frightening, really – and unanswerable. And it is the same for everyone.

Chance? Pure chance? No design? No one in charge? That in itself is pretty unthinkable, too. When one looks at the human body with its bones and muscles and arteries and nervous system, and when one realises that, on the whole (barring a few exceptional aberrations) everyone is born with two arms and two legs and two lungs and one heart, one realises that there must be some overall 'person' in charge.

How is it that the fertilised egg knows how to multiply continuously and yet to change the form of multiplying when the heart or the lungs, for instance, have become big enough? Stop multiplying there, and direct your efforts to some other part of the anatomy! And how is it that the cells of the spinal cord know how to multiply in such a way that it contains, in each person, that myriad of nerves and blood vessels and tissues? How is it that, when a surgeon opens up anyone's body, he always – with, of course, a few exceptions – knows exactly where to find the pancreas, the Islets of Langerhans, the heart, the spleen? In everyone, all over the world. They are all the same.

If you stop thinking about the astonishing wonders of the human body, look at the horses, the cows, the dogs, the squirrels, the flies. They all have a skeletal and a nervous system too, one which is similar, but which is peculiar to each species They also have this remarkable make-up, but they all are different.

In my later life I have found an interest and peace in ducks – ornamental ones. The different varieties of ducks have different varieties of colourings. A male meets a female – and they almost always mate with their own breed – an egg is produced from which a duckling appears. In the fullness of time the duckling produces feathers, white ones, brown ones, golden ones, black ones. They all appear in the right place, with black and white diamonds down the back, or with a golden stripe in a particular place near the wing. How does the individual cell know whether to – or how to – produce a black feather or a white feather or a golden feather? Yet they do. Always in the right position. And when the ducks moult, automatically another feather emerges, the same colour, the right colour and in the right place. How is it all achieved? And the same goes for every other bird or fish or animal in the universe.

All these things are impossible to fathom. It forces the inevitable question. Why are we here? Is no one in charge? I take great succour from what a wonderful Roman Catholic Priest said to me, Father Valentine Elwes, who married us. Because I am an Anglican and because I was about to marry a Roman Catholic, I had to have, as the Catholics say, 'instructions' so that as a non-Roman Catholic one should understand a little of what makes one's wife-to-be adhere to her religion.

He said a fundamental thing, which I have never forgotten. There is always someone greater than what you see who has created whatever it is that you see. If you admire a beautiful picture, someone has painted it. If you admire a magnificent house, someone has built it. If you admire a lovely car, someone has designed it. If you admire a beautiful garden, someone has created it. If you admire all that one sees in this world, someone must have created that too. It cannot have appeared – in all its beauty and unbelievable complexity – as a result of just a big bang.

I have always found that of huge comfort, but even the most devout Christian cannot give you the answers to many of these fundamental questions. In the Creed, we say 'I believe.' We do not say 'I know.' A dash of humility? A dash of uncertainty? – oh yes! Humility is essential. Uncertainty is inevitable.

We have been used to saying in church 'World without end.' There is no end. Life in this world comes to its end in death, but life in the Hereafter is without end. I can just about get my feeble mental processes around that concept even if I cannot understand it, but I have recently been totally knocked sideways by the concept that, if life has no end, then it has no beginning either. How on earth does that make sense, one's bewildered and oh-so-limited thought processes ask? If the world is here, physically, there must have been something here beforehand in which, as it were, to plonk the world. Something, somewhere, must have a beginning even if it has no end.

But, if it does have a beginning, something must have been here before 'it' began. What?

But here am I asking all the questions, which I said at the start that it is absurd to ask, because we cannot answer them and we do not have the ability even to consider how to answer them.

For all that, they are fascinating questions. For all that, it makes one realise what a privilege – yes, a privilege – it is to have been chosen to experience, or at least to have found oneself experiencing, life. The other six million participants in the sperm race never had that.

I, therefore, felt that I should jot down some of the experiences and happenings in my life, not that they will be of wild interest to many others or that they will become a bestseller – I doubt if many will ever read them – but because, simply by the nature of things, life has unfolded for me, as it does for everyone, in a unique way.

This is not an autobiography. That would be too pompous in thought. It is more in the nature of reminiscences or memories, a little piece of this and a little piece of that, as one remembers life unfolding. The dates, the figures – even the facts – may not be entirely accurate, but I have no reason to believe that they are far from the truth.

FERRERS FAMILY

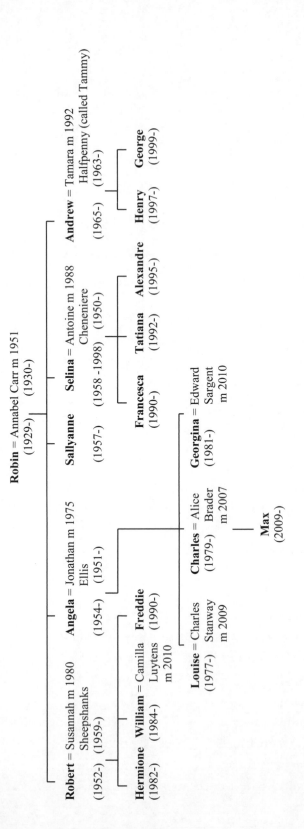

Robin = Annabel Carr m 1951
(1929-) (1930-)

Robert = Susannah m 1980
Sheepshanks
(1952-) (1959-)

Angela = Jonathan m 1975
Ellis
(1954-) (1951-)

Sallyanne
(1957-)

Selina = Antoine m 1988
Cheneniere
(1958 -1998) (1950-)

Andrew = Tamara m 1992
Halfpenny (called Tammy)
(1965-) (1963-)

Hermione   William = Camilla   Freddie
(1982-)   (1984-) Luytens   (1990-)
                    m 2010

Louise = Charles
Stanway
(1977-) m 2009

Charles = Alice
(1979-) Brader
         m 2007

Georgina = Edward
Sargent
(1981-) m 2010

Francesca   Tatiana   Alexandre
(1990-)   (1992-)   (1995-)

Henry   George
(1997-) (1999-)

Max
(2009-)

Family

IT IS SOMETIMES helpful to have the names of a family, because otherwise any potential reader can become easily confused and lost, so I am enclosing a summary – I hope accurate! – of both Annabel's and my families.

Annabel's father was **Brigadier William Carr**, always called **Bill**. He was born in 1901. He inherited the estate at Ditchingham when his father died on 28 January 1925, when Bill was in his twenties. He was in the 12th Lancers during the war. He was a superlative horseman, winning all the point-to-points in his youth. He was in the British team for the Olympic Games in Berlin in 1936.

Annabel's mother was **Donna Nenella Carr Salazar**. She was an Italian lady from Naples who was first married to General Sir Foster Newland, by whom she had a daughter, **Antonella**. Nenella married Bill Carr in 1927. They had one child, **Annabel**, my wife. Nenella always said that she had to spend nine months in bed waiting for Annabel whilst she was pregnant. I never knew whether that was strictly accurate – or whether it included a little Italian poetic licence.

Antonella Lothian, Annabel's half sister, was always called **Tony**. She married **Peter Kerr**, who later became the **Marquess of Lothian**. They lived at Melbourne Hall in Derbyshire, which was three miles away from my old home at Staunton Harold and where Annabel used to come and stay.

To confuse things a little, Peter Lothian's mother, **Mrs Andrew Kerr**, (not Carr) more usually known as **Marie Kerr**, was Annabel's godmother and, separately, she was also one of my mother's greatest friends. As my mother and Marie Kerr, who was then living at Melbourne Hall, were

L: My grandfather, Camfer, 11th Earl Ferrers; R: My grandmother, Gaga

close friends, therefore their children must be friends, too. We were not. We thought **Peter** and his brother **Johnny** insufferable.

My father, because he was Viscount Tamworth, was always known, even by my mother, as **Tam** – short for **Tamworth**. He went to Winchester, where he contracted polio, which left him for the rest of his life with a considerable walking disability. He had a younger brother, **Andrew**, who was a scholar at Winchester. My father went to India in the 1920s to try and earn some money. He and my mother married there. They came back to England and my father went into the Stock Exchange in London with George Henderson and Co. They lived at 35 Victoria Road, which was built by my grandfather, an architect, **Walter Knight Shirley**, later **11ᵗʰ Earl Ferrers**.

I had two sisters, **Betty and Penelope**. Betty could never say Penelope. It became transmogrified to Nepalie, and then abbreviated to **Neppy** which was the name by which she has always thereafter been known. They both went to school at Downe House in Berkshire.

After leaving Downe House Betty went in to the WRNS, which made her feel that she was a real woman-of-the-world (I don't think

L: My father, 12th Earl Ferrers – 'Tam'; R: My mother, Hermione

really that she was!). After the war she worked as a secretary for the Georgian Group, where she was paid £5 per week, and later for the Coal Board which was less intellectually stimulating, but paid about £1 per week more.

She married **John Luttrell** in 1959. John worked in the oil business in Qatar when Qatar was just developing from being a desert.

They had one child, **Robert**, who went to Winchester College, and afterwards became a Catholic and married **Pauline Roddy,** an Australian. They both, with their children **Madeleine**, **Lucy** and **Prudence**, live in Sydney, Australia.

Neppy became engaged at the age of sixteen when she was still at school to **Maurice Robson**. Maurice was thirty-two and was in the Army as a Chaplain to the Forces. He was chaplain to the soldiers who were stationed in Staunton Harold.

Neppy and Maurice were married in the Chapel at Staunton Harold in 1944 at three days' notice because Maurice did not know when he would be allowed leave.

After the war, Maurice's first incumbency was at Bamford-in-the-Peak in Derbyshire where the stipend was £360 per year, £90 per quarter. Paid in arrears.

He then took on the living at Brailsford and Shirley in Derbyshire, of which my father was the patron. They later retired to Southrop in Gloucestershire, when Maurice was seventy-three and Neppy only fifty-five. Neppy now lives near her daughter in Cornwall.

Neppy and Maurice had two children, **David** and **Phillida**. After having been in the Merchant Navy, David married **Josephine Manwaring-White**. They have two children, **Oliver** and **Jonathan**. They live in Surrey.

Phillida married **James Jermain**. He is mad keen on sailing and became Editor of *Yachting Monthly*. They now live in Cornwall. They have three children, **Katie**, **Abigail** and **Eleanor**.

Annabel was twenty-one when we were married in July 1951. I was twenty-two and was 'in Statu Pupillari' – an undergraduate – at Magdalene College, Cambridge, having completed the first of three years' work on a degree course in Agriculture.

Robert was born in December 1952, when I was an undergraduate. He went to a pre-prep school at Town Close in Norwich, then a prep school at Farleigh House, near Basingstoke. From there he went to Ampleforth. Robert did not like school. He wanted to farm. I was not keen on the idea (in the same way that my father was not keen on me doing it, either.)

Robert went to Kenya for his gap year which was organised by the Church Missionary Society, with whom we were put in touch by Simon Barrington-Ward, who later became the Bishop of Coventry. Robert married **Susannah Sheepshanks** on 21 June 1984. Susannah's father was **Charlie Sheepshanks**. He ran Sunningdale Preparatory School in Berkshire. His wife, **Mary**, was the sister of David Nixon who joined up in the Army with me in 1948. She writes, including poetry.

Robert and Susannah lived in the Old Vicarage at Shirley where my mother used to live, with their three children, **Hermione**, **William** and **Freddie**. Robert and Susannah and their family came to live at Ditchingham Hall in 2004 when we moved out to Park Lodge.

Robert, with **Jonathan Ruffer**, started up an Investment Management Firm, more usually thought of as Private Client Stockbrokers, in

1994, called Ruffer LLP. There were the two of them and two secretaries. Some fifteen years later, they employ 135 people and look after funds of over £10 billion. It has been the most astonishing success story, and I feel hugely proud of Robert for that which he and Jonathan have achieved.

Since Annabel and I moved to Park Lodge, Robert has been responsible for the running of all the farm and the estate at Ditchingham. So he has come back to doing what he wanted to do in the first place, but with the added and wider success of having been in the business world and all which goes with that.

Robert and Susannah have three children. **Hermione** always wanted to be a physiotherapist. She did a three-year course at the University of London, for which the National Health Service paid. When she passed her exams, the National Health Service said that they had no vacancies for physiotherapists.

There is something bizarre about the National Health Service training people for a job and then saying that they do not require them. I suggested that Hermione tried for a placing in the private sector, but private hospitals will not take on physiotherapists unless they have had experience in the public sector. Snookered again. She has now given up thoughts of being a physiotherapist and is working as a Personal Assistant to a headmistress of a school in London.

William went to Sunningdale where Susannah's father had been headmaster, although he had died by the time that William went there. William went on to Eton where, in the middle of his time there, be became an Oppidans Scholar. We felt very proud. He went to Christ Church, Oxford, where he obtained a first-class degree in Economics and Management. He then became a banker (sensible fellow). William seems to have everything – brains, intelligence, good manners, good looks and a great sense of twinkling fun. And he now has a very attractive and lovely girl who has just become his wife – **Camilla Lutyens**, known as **Millie**.

Freddie went to Sunningdale and then to Stowe. He did well there and enjoyed it. He has a mad passion for all the things which make one squirm – like snakes, and bats, gorillas and all sorts of creepy crawlies. He worked in the same school in London as Hermione for a while and taught, amongst other things, tennis, of which he is a trained coach. He then went to Oxford Brookes.

Angela, our no. 2 and first daughter, was born in 1954. She had red hair and was sometimes, not very originally, called Carrots. Despite the passage of time she still has red hair, albeit not so vivid – but she is no longer called Carrots. She went, as later did her sisters, to the Convent of the Sacred Heart at Woldingham. I am an Anglican and thought that a Convent education might be restrictive. I could not have been more wrong. It is the fullest education of them all. They have not only academic work and physical work and discipline, but they were brought up to be lovely ladies.

The girls always used to curtsey to the nuns in those days, and to other girls' parents too. There was a Mistress of Discipline who used to say at the beginning of the Prize Giving – and I loved this – when the girls all paraded with a hint of a self-satisfied grin on their faces, 'Glory be to God alone.' In others words, 'However, proud you may feel, get back in your box.' It was a wonderful de-bouncer and leveller. There were sufficient nuns in those days for each nun to have six specific girls for whom she would pray. The Headmistress was a wonderful lady, so gracious, courteous, understanding and holy, Mother Stanley who is now 106 years old. Almost unbelievable.

We were so impressed with what Woldingham 'did' for their pupils that Annabel and I always said that, in later life (and that means after they had left school), you could always tell a Convent Girl. They had a serenity about them.

Angela went to learn typing and then went to work in the Conservative Research Department, a place which turned out to have a great camaraderie about it, and the girls love going back for reunions and, as Angela says, 'seeing my mates again'.

Like Annabel, at the age of twenty-one, Angela was married – to **Jonathan Ellis**. He had to go to the Channel Islands to be crammed for his accountancy exams, and then became a senior partner of Larking Gowan in Norwich. They live near Holt in Norfolk. Jonathan is a real countryman and loves and knows all about wildlife and shooting. Now, at the age of sixty, he has retired – still a mere baby!

Angela and Jonathan have three children. **Louise**, who works in Robert's firm of Ruffer Investment Management, which is now called Ruffer LLP, of which she is now a director. She had a 'boy friend' at Durham University, **Chaz Stanway**. He went into the Royal Navy as a submariner. That was not the best of occupations in which to get married, with six months spent underneath the sea and the other six months in Glasgow. So they remained great friends. When Chaz had ended his career in the Navy, some fifteen years later – by which time he had risen to the dizzy height of Lieutenant Commander – they got married!

Charlie is Angela and Jonathan's second child. Like his father, he has become an accountant. At the age of twenty-eight in 2008, he married **Alice** who is Austrian. She is a pretty and lovely girl and, on top of that, speaks *seven* languages – English perfectly. They now live in Hong Kong where he practises accountancy and they have a son – our first great grandson – **Max**.

Georgina, who is always known as Beanie, is tall, striking, beautiful and with a glorious and gentle character. Anyone who marries her will be lucky! As it happens, she has now married **Edward Sargent**. Like her sister Louise, Beanie went to St Mary's Convent, Ascot, which helped to bring them up beautifully. She has always been mad on travelling in Africa. She now works with a travel agent firm, Cazenove Loyd, specialising in, guess where? … Africa. She likes to go on safari looking at animals and even gorillas. Not my scene.

Sallyanne is our third child. She has always had trouble with reasoning. She has the kindest and most helpful nature. She is exceedingly strong and will do anything – provided that she feels in the mood. If she is not, then, like litmus paper, it turns from pink to blue and Sallyanne will pursue her own course determinedly. She has become very set in her ways – but aren't we all? – and, when this happens, she can be quite difficult to dislodge. She now lives in a house of her own in Holt, and carers come in to help look after her. Angela has been wonderful and has taken over the responsibility of looking after Sallyanne.

Selina is our fourth child, bright, pretty, sparkling eyes, hugely attractive both in personality and looks. She was fifteen months younger than Sallyanne and always felt smothered by her, especially at school when

Sallyanne was finding it difficult to keep up to the mark and was usually late for everything. Selina tended to take the rap. When Selina left Woldingham she took off for America and went to Washington. She loved art and worked in Sotheby's and Christie's and made wonderful friends. An American friend of ours, fulminating over Selina, said, 'She is the best Ambassador for your country that you have. She has made lots of friends, good friends, nice friends, the right kind of friends, and she has not hitched up with the wrong ones. And she has chosen them all on her own.'

After two years Selina came back to England, a lovely, confident, beautiful girl whom everyone just loved. She married **Antoine Cheneviere** in 1988, when she was thirty. He was in the Art World, with his own firm, Cheneviere Fine Arts, and he specialises in Russian furniture. So they shared a common interest. Antoine is half Swiss and half Bulgarian and he is a person of whom I am very fond and whom I greatly admire.

Not long after Antoine and Selina were married, they were staying with us at Ditchingham Hall and Selina was pregnant. She said to me in a way which indicated quite a knowledge of life, 'You know, Daddy, it is very easy to become pregnant.' I said, 'What are you telling me that for? I should know. We had four children in six years. Yes, it is very easy.'

Selina and Antoine had three children. **Francesca**, known as Cheski. She was born in 1990. Quiet, deep thinker, beautiful and spookily like Selina, not just in looks but in mannerisms too.

Tatiana was their second child, born some eighteen months apart. Tati is much taller than Cheski, blonde like her mother, full of fun. Does all the wrong things, like smoking. Is always late and has an air of vagueness to life through which she paddles at her own unpredictable but charming pace, but she is a really lovely girl. Both Cheski and Tati were educated, like Louise and Georgina, at the Convent at Ascot.

Alexandre is the youngest of their three children. His name was always spelt in the Swiss way of Alexand*re*, not the British way of Alexand*er*. In order to emphasise the correct spelling, I always called him 'Rrrrr', which became truncated to Rooer. He is now, very Englishly, called Alex. The school and his friends find it easier. He went to the Westminster Cathedral School in London and he is now at Sevenoaks boarding school, which he likes very much and where he seems to be doing quite well.

This lovely happy family, where Love went round and round and outwards too, fell onto the rocks when, in 1998, Selina got cancer and died. They thought that she had an ulcer and then, on further investigation, they found the cancer underneath. It was in the duodenum. The oncologist told Selina that it was a very rare place to have it. He had only seen it in the duodenum three times in his medical career, and two of these were in old ladies of eighty. Yet, here was Selina aged thirty-nine, preparing for her fortieth birthday party. My doctor, Dr Bushnell, who is in the same partnership with Selina's doctor, Dr Wheeler, said that Selina would either die before her fortieth birthday, or the excitement of the anticipation and the preparation of it would keep her going, and she would die immediately afterwards. She did not make her fortieth birthday.

When I asked Dr Bushnell, when they had first discovered the disease, what the prognosis was he said with hideous clarity, 'Months rather than weeks. And months rather than years.' He was right. It was about nine months.

Andrew is the last of our five children – an 'afterthought' as people tend to say. I am bound to say that, when Annabel disclosed to me that she was pregnant again some seven years after I thought that the shutters had come down, I was appalled – nappies, screaming children, prams, whatever next? I thought that that had all been relegated to the history books. But no, that was right back in the frame.

The curious part about all this – and this is in no way unique – although one was apprehensive, almost dreaded the appearance of Number 5, when he came, I found that I had an extraordinary capacity to love that child in a way which I had not experienced with the others. It did not mean that I loved him more than the others. Some said, 'Well, you have more time now,' or 'You have got the experience which you did not have before.' I do not know what it was. I only know that I was deeply grateful to be able to discover a love that I did not know that I had. What was it? The love *for* Andrew himself, or the love of one's own offspring which one has had in later life? I think that it is probably the latter, but if Andrew had been an odious child – and, mercifully, he was the reverse of that – I doubt if this burgeoning of now fresh love would have been quite so forthcoming. Whatever it was, it was quite an experience.

There is always a hazard with having an afterthought. People say that you always spoil the youngest child. I am not sure whether that is entirely true. I was the youngest of three, and I did not think that I was at all spoilt! Others may have a different view. But there is no doubt that, on the whole, the youngest one does tend to get spoilt. 'That's not fair. I was not allowed to do that,' say the older ones. One can hear it all.

Having a second son, whilst bringing so many advantages, brings its own peculiar problems too, especially what one can conveniently call 'Second Son-itis'. Particularly is that so when funny things like titles and land are concerned where, if the larger part is to be retained of which the owner is merely a tenant for his life, it tends to be passed down to one person.

Once you start dividing it up, why restrict the division to sons? Why not daughters too? Once you start on that course, in two generations there is nothing left. Over these responsibilities, where it is often thought of as *my* land or *Charles'* land, or whatever, it is actually the preservation and the continuation of the *land* which is important and not the interests of the temporary *owners*. It is all very complicated stuff, loaded with trip wires and elephant traps and unexpected dramas of which 'it is not fair' summarises most of them. But life is not fair, and the sooner that we all realise that the better.

Andrew's prep school was, like Robert's, Farleigh House, near Basingstoke. At one point the Headmaster was in a state of distress as the cook had left and he had no cook for all these boys. Andrew said, 'Shall I ask **Marguerite** (Mary Robinson's daughter)?' The answer was yes and Marguerite went to become the cook at Farleigh House. The Headmaster was so pleased that he asked Andrew in and said, 'I would like to give you a present for this. What would you like?' That was a pretty wide canvas. Andrew did not know what to say – a car or a biro? He got a biro.

Andrew followed Farleigh House with Ampleforth which, unlike Robert, he enjoyed. Andrew always wanted to farm but, as with Robert and my father beforehand with me, I tried to dissuade him. Andrew has many qualities, of which a mildly stubborn streak is one, and he was not dissuaded. So it was arranged for him to go to the Royal Agricultural College in Cirencester.

In the summer holidays between Ampleforth and Cirencester, Andrew went to get some farming experience at Sandringham. He suddenly announced to Julian Loyd, who was the agent at Sandringham, that he wanted to leave because he wanted to go to Ampleforth and become a monk. Julian could not believe his ears. He let him go before the end of his allotted course even though it was inconvenient as harvest was approaching and Julian was particularly relying on Andrew to help. Julian said, 'You will never make a monk. You like the gin and tonics and other worldly things too much. You will be out in six months.' So he was. Thereafter, Julian has always referred to him as 'The Drunk Monk'.

Andrew did not like Pardon and Penance, where you got on your knees in front of the Abbot and apologised for being late. The obstinate streak coming out again. I thought that it was very good for him.

The prospect of Andrew becoming a monk put the cat really amongst the pigeons. Annabel, despite her deeply held loyalty and convictions to the Catholic Church, was mortified. There was her little one going into a Monastery. 'Happy Birthday, Darling Mummy. This is the last present which I will be giving you.' The tears cascaded down. On it went.

Andrew went into the monastery, but was out again about six weeks later.

After Andrew had left the monastery, Cirencester was back on the rails. Later, he joined the Country Landowners' Association as a member of the staff. He has been there for nearly twenty years and has found it interesting. He is now considering standing for Parliament, but there are so many people doing that, that he probably will not get in – eighty applications for one Constituency, 150 for another. He did not make it.

In 1992, Andrew married **Tamara Halfpenny**, who is usually called **Tammy**. It is quite confusing when Robert is called Tamworth. My father was called Tam, and now the daughter-in-law is called Tammy. Andy and Tammy were married at Staunton Harold, my old home. I felt so proud. I love that place, and it took one back years. It then belonged to the Ryder Cheshire Foundation. They had gone to so much trouble to make the gardens look beautiful but, on the day, it just poured and poured with rain. Such a pity. I said to Andy, 'If you see your old Dad crying, don't think that it is because you are getting married. It will be because he loves Staunton and cannot bear the fact that it is no longer part of our lives.'

They have two boys, **Henry and George**, charming children but like most young children – they are now eleven and fourteen – they fight like cats. They always have – not nasty fighting, but it usually ends with one hitting the other – then away we go. The screams start. It is so exhausting. I am amazed how the parents cope, but all parents say that of their own children.

Mary Robinson was not a member of the family, as such, but she came to us as a helper with a six-week-old daughter and she stayed with us for thirty-eight years until she died. Although she could cook nothing when she arrived, not even a boiled egg, she became a superb cook and total family confidante. She cooked, cleaned, looked after the children. When they grew up, the children used to tell Mary everything, months before we ever got a look in.

Mary came with a daughter, **Marguerite**, aged six weeks. 'There you are,' I said to Annabel. 'If she comes with a child and she is no use, you are lumbered. You will never be able to get rid of her.' Mary could do nothing. We were lumbered, but what a lumbering. She turned out to be a huge success. Father Edward Cruzet, the Parish Priest at Bungay, said that Mary was the nearest thing to a saint which you are likely to see in this life. We were very privileged.

Mary had nothing. The only thing which she had in this life was Marguerite. Yet she had the capacity to love all of our children without favour and without jealousy – even though they had more than her daughter did. It was truly a remarkable experience.

Marguerite loved playing with our children and spent most of the time with them. It was quite a delicate balancing act. She had to be with her mother because she was her mother's daughter, but not to play with other children in the house would have been intolerable. Marguerite trod the delicate path quite beautifully, giving happiness to everyone on the way – again, no offending. No jealousy. It was wonderful. And so it goes on.

Marguerite married **Peter Akister**, who was in the Parachute Regiment. He then left and went into business. They have two sons, **Edward** and **George**. They are now about nineteen and seventeen. They are quite charming and have the most beautiful manners.

Chapter 1

Childhood

I WAS BORN in 1929. My earliest recollections are of when we lived in London at 35 Victoria Road in Kensington and I was aged about five. My two sisters, Betty and Neppy, were older than me. Betty was six years older. Neppy was four years older. So, whenever I ventured to give an opinion, usually on nothing more profound than whether the jelly tasted nice, I was met with the rejoinder 'You are the youngest. Your opinion does not count. So shut up...' So generous.

Betty once went off to have her bath early, leaving her blancmange on the table. Fearful that the always avaricious Neppy would consume it whilst she was away, Betty left a note saying, 'I have licked this.' That, she thought, would be enough to see off any potential predators. It did not. It was eaten. Brothers and sisters, especially when young, are so charming to each other. We all fortunately got on very well together and family love was a great bedrock.

In those days – the mid 1930s – we had a cook, Edith Ruffhead, who was paid the princely salary of £25 per year and a wonderful cook she was. She always used to go regularly on Sundays to St Martin-in-the-Fields. It was the church of her choice and she loved it.

We had various nannies of whom the last, Winne Bug, I remembered best. She came to us when Neppy was four. I must have been nought. She was with us for my formative years as a child. She was a lovely, kind, understanding person. Neppy still sees her. She is well. In 2010 she was ninety-five.

Winnie was fourteen when she came to us. She was paid five shillings per week. After six weeks she went home for the weekend. In the train she was looking at this glorious £1-10-0 which she had earned. She felt so proud of it, and then … the pound note flew out of the window. Can you imagine it? It must have been devastating for the poor girl. But she survived!

My father had had polio when he was a boy at Winchester – a particularly horrible disease in those days – and he was left with a permanent and substantial lameness. He always walked with a stick. I never knew what my father did for a living – how could I at that age? Whenever I asked him what he was going to do today, he used to say 'I am going off to work the Bread and Butter machine.' My father had a unique ability to talk in a language all of his own, which was not always readily understood by others and especially not by a little four-year-old son.

I imagined that he literally went off and turned the handle of a machine, rather like a mangel-cutter which one might see on a farm, and then out came bread and butter. What my father actually meant was that he went to work as a stockbroker in the City in order to earn a living so that we could all have something to eat – including bread and butter. How could one have known that?

Sunday was, quite rightly, a special day and we would all go to church at St Mary Abbots in Kensington. My father always wore a tail coat and top hat, and grey spats on his shoes. You never see spats anywhere nowadays. He was always very smart, with a stick in one hand, and the other hand placed in the small of his back, for balance, I suppose.

Daddy used to put our weekly pocket money on the hall table on Saturdays – sixpence for my sisters. Then it went up to a shilling for them and sixpence for me.

Another example of my father's looseness of expression came in 1945 when it became clear that the War would soon be over. There would be great jubilation everywhere. Villages all over the country were preparing for VE Day (standing for Victory in Europe, the war in Japan was not yet over).

At Staunton a committee was set up of which my father was the chairman – even in those days you always had to have committees – and, as food was rationed, everyone round the table had been saying, 'I can give some sugar,' or 'I can give some tea,' or something else.

My father noticed that one of his tenant farmers, Horace Dunnicliffe, had kept his mouth shut and had offered nothing. So my father said, 'Horace, you can beg, borrow or steal something can't you?' The farmer was so shocked and insulted that he walked out and resigned from the committee.

My mother kept a wonderful, happy home. She was one of those people who emanated love from every pore to everyone who came within her range, but that did not stop her from having very high standards and from being hugely critical of anyone who fell below them.

My sisters both went to Kensington High School, the 'Ken High', which they quite liked. I went to Wagners, a pre-prep school at 48, Princes Gate. It was Mr Wagner's son who many years later, as Sir Anthony Wagner, became Garter King of Arms. Jeremy Morse, who was a brilliantly clever person, and who became Sir Jeremy Morse, was a great friend in later life. He was also at Wagners. So also was John Sainsbury who became Lord Sainsbury of Preston Candover. I do not remember him there and it only transpired that we had been schoolmates when we were both near eighty! My time at Wagners does not form a great part of my memory other than the fact that there were two masters, Mr Fry and Mr Le Froy, which at the age of six I found totally confusing, and also that there was a mistress – one who seemed elderly to me at that age, but who I suppose was only fifty – who said to me, when I was being slow in tying up my football boots, 'Come on fatty.'

I was profoundly wounded by that remark, even though there may have been some truth in it. It is odd how, in life, it is often the small things, in themselves of no consequence, which nevertheless imprint themselves into your memory, as if they had been branded there to the total exclusion of everything else. The poor mistress, whose name I have forgotten and who must long since be dead, would have been horrified to think that such a passing remark was to remain in the mind of the poor hapless recipient for the rest of his life, and that any other contribution which she may have made to the school and to his upbringing went down the sluice of life.

It all goes to show that you never know the effect which you have on others. We each, though, have a tremendous effect on other people the whole time – by what we say, by what we do, and by how we behave. You are what you are because it is natural to you. You behave in the way in which you do because it is natural to you. If you smile, that affects others. If you are sad, that affects others. If you sing in a beautiful choir, that affects others. If you sing in the street in the middle of the night, that affects others. If you drive at 90 mph, that affects others. If you drive at 30 mph in the middle of the road, that affects others.

In all of life, what you do affects others, but, of course, so often you are blissfully unaware of that, because it is natural to you. If a person were to bring a skunk into the room, everyone would know it was there because of the appalling smell. The poor skunk would not be aware of the effect which it was having on other people because the appalling smell is natural to it.

Which all goes to show that, whoever and wherever one is in life, one should never underestimate the effect one has on other people – good or bad.

***

Summer holidays were spent at Littlehampton on the Sussex coast where my parents used to rent a house. We loved our holidays there, playing, walking down the streets to the beach, calling in at the shops to buy kites and toys with the cousins, going riding, eating juicy pears, doing all the things which children do and, of course, the excitement of going for speedboat rides in the sea – at 6 pence a time in old money.

Betty hated wasps. Therefore they always chased her. They would. We would all sit down for a picnic on the beach and a wasp would appear. Betty was terrified of them and ran around us all like a crazy windmill. She usually got stung. Nobody else did!

My mother's sister and her husband, Christine and Eric Hussey (known as Auntie Chrissie and Uncle Eric), lived in Littlehampton with their two children, Helen and Dukie.

Helen and Dukie became very close to us all – especially Dukie. We were young. It was the summer holidays at Littlehampton. Beaches. Swimming. Ice creams. Tea parties in the garden. Hide and seek. Dumb

Crambo. It was all good, youthful and happy. We were cousins and we were all very fond of each other.

We had some other cousins who used to come and stay at Little-hampton, the Troutbecks. He became Sir John Troutbeck and was later Ambassador in Prague. They had two daughters, Mary and Clare. Clare's birthday was a week after mine, mine being on 8 June, Clare's on 19 June. So, whenever my sisters wished to crush me into oblivion with the remark, 'You are the youngest, so you don't count,' I could always come up with the remark, 'No, I am not. Clare is younger.' It was not a very stout defence, but it was the best that I could do.

One summer before the war, when I suppose that Mary and Clare were about eight and ten, they had a French au pair (although they were not given such names in those days) to help them to try and learn French. Her name was Blanche. Mary and Clare also tried to teach her tennis. It was an uphill struggle. They could not get poor Blanche to understand the basic principle that, between serves, the server and his or her partner changed sides on the court. The constant cry of 'L'autre côté, Blanche. L'autre côté' still rings in my head. Blanche must be ninety now.

Chapter 2

Staunton Harold

BACK WHEN WE were children, parts of our holidays from London were spent with my grandparents at Staunton Harold in Leicestershire. They were memorable – if somewhat imposing – occasions.

My grandfather was the 11ᵗʰ Earl Ferrers. He was an upright person, both in physique and attitude and carried a fabulous but well-trimmed beard, a proper beard, not one of these miserable, whiskery things all daintily created, which one sees nowadays. We used to call him Camfer which, I suppose, was grandchild-speak for grandfather. I remember kissing him on one occasion and exclaiming 'ouch' as the bristles of his beard gently imprinted themselves on to my then tender face. He frequently wore a stiff winged-collar.

My grandmother was always known as Gaga. We thought that to be a perfectly normal name but, of course, you could not really get much more insulting if you tried. But that was her choice. She liked it that way. We liked it that way, too.

She was a lively and very competent person who ran a very well ordered house with a butler, cook and many domestic servants. Her happy peal of laughter used to ring around the house.

She was always a great do-er. She used to get up at 6 o'clock in the morning and go down to the dairy, which was an out-house from the huge house, just opposite the kitchen door. The cowman would bring the milk down from the cowshed on a trolley which he pulled down a hill for about 800 yards, and which, presumably, he had to pull 800 yards back up the hill again afterwards.

The trolley used to have a large wooden cross attached to the floor. As a young boy, I always thought that this was some sort of religious emblem. It was nothing of the sort. It was merely a basic mechanical device, which fitted into the bottom of the milk churn – which in those days was a conical object with a round base – to prevent the churn from tipping off the trolley on its way down the bumpy road from the cowshed to the dairy. Very sensible.

In the dairy, my grandmother used to make cream cheeses – and very good they were, too. Nowadays, what is called a cream cheese is little more than a milk cheese. But these were the real works – good, thick, yellow cream. I have never tasted cream cheese better. She used to send them to customers all over the country in very smart waxed cartons emblazoned in green with a coronet and the words 'Earl Ferrers' Dairy' printed on them.

The milk was put into a 'separator'. The handle was turned and cream came out of one spout and skimmed milk, which was subsequently fed to the pigs, came out of the other. It was slightly more complicated than that because the separator consisted of about twelve cones which fitted one above the other and the mechanism was highly geared so that the cones, over which the milk dropped, spun round at a great speed throwing the lighter skimmed milk out to the edge and through a spout, whilst the heavier cream went out through a separate spout.

If I was lucky – and privileged – I used to try and help my grandmother separate the milk. It was not an easy task because the gearing was so great that turning the handle became a very heavy business especially for the arm muscles of a six-year-old boy.

Gaga was remarkable as I think that she must have been the only Countess to have had a Hawker's Licence which enabled her to go from house to house selling things.

Staunton Harold was a lovely, handsome, magnificent Georgian house with a church alongside it and a lake in front of it. For some curious reason, the Church was always called 'the Chapel'. In fact, it was a full-blown, free-standing, beautiful Church which is historically both important and unique.

The estate and house at Staunton Harold was originally owned by a wealthy gentleman called Harold Staunton. One of his descendants,

Margaret Staunton, married Ralph Shirley in 1423. Her brother died as a boy and therefore she became the heiress of Staunton Harold. That is how the house and the land subsequently merged into the Shirley family.

The Shirley family originates from a little village in Derbyshire, near Ashbourne, called Shirley. They held land there at the time of the Magna Carta. Of that land only some 250 acres of it still remain in the Shirley family. But remain it does.

When William the Conqueror came to England in 1066, he brought with him from France one Henry de Ferrers, to whom he gave land at Chartley in Staffordshire and who subsequently became Baron Ferrers of Chartley.

Some people used to say to my grandfather, with a certain amount of pride and amazement, 'Of course, your family came over with William the Conqueror, didn't they?' This used to infuriate my grandfather, who replied 'Certainly not. We were here to greet him.'

The Shirley family used to be a very wealthy family owning, at one period, land in seven counties. They have produced over the years some remarkable people – remarkable in both ways. One was killed at Shrewsbury because he was dressed up as the King in order to deceive the enemy. He did this very well – resulting in the King remaining alive and Sir Hugh Shirley being killed. The Shirley coat of arms is still emblazoned in the Battlefield Church at Shrewsbury.

One was Grand Falconer to Henry IV and is mentioned in Shakespeare. Three brothers, Sir Anthony, Sir Robert and Sir Thomas Shirley were traders and adventurers. One taught the Persians how to use gunpowder. Another spent so much time in Persia that he married a Persian lady and ended up by coming back to England as the Persian Ambassador to the Court of St James.

It is slightly doubtful how he came to be Persian Ambassador. There is one source which said that the then Persian Ambassador had a party in London at which some of the guests did too well and that, when they were nicely 'in their cups', Sir Anthony had a fight with his host and won. After this he became Ambassador. In other words a 'putsh'. Other sources say that the route was more conventional.

The most revered member of the Shirley family was Sir Robert Shirley.

He built the Church at Staunton Harold in 1653 and was prevailed upon by Cromwell to build some ships. 'If you can build a church, you can build some ships,' said Cromwell. Sir Robert, being a staunch Royalist, refused to do so and he was put into the Tower of London where he died at the age of thirty-two suspected of having been poisoned.

Charles II, who was then not yet Charles II because he was in exile in Belgium at the time, wrote to Lady Shirley a moving letter, which is still in our possession, on hearing of the death of Sir Robert. On commiserating with her over the loss of her husband, Charles concluded 'If ever it should be in my power to remember the loyalty of your husband you will see that I bear a great part with you in your affliction by the care which I shall have of you and all your family.'

When Charles returned to England and became King Charles II, he gave Sir Robert's son a peerage, a Barony, and he decided to resurrect the name of Ferrers in the title. Earlier, a separate barony, the Barony of Ferrers of Chartley, had become extinct but a daughter of the line of Baron Ferrers of Chartley had married a Shirley. Thus it was that, now, the two families – the Shirleys who were in England and the Ferrers who had come over with William the Conqueror – became united and the title of Ferrers was resurrected. This title was then uplifted to an earldom in 1712 by Queen Anne for whom Lord Ferrers had been Chancellor.

The first Earl Ferrers was quite a fellow. Not only was he Queen Anne's Chancellor, but he founded a Regiment, the King's Liverpool Regiment. It had as its special Regimental tune 'The Ferrers Gallop'. It was this Regiment which, by chance, came to be billeted at Staunton Harold during the War. It is curious how the unexpected often seems to happen.

The first Earl was a vigorous procreator too. He had twenty-seven children – legitimate ones. And fifty-one illegitimate children. He is even entered into the *Guinness Book of Records* as having the most illegitimate children of anyone. I suppose that that is an achievement of some sort. But I often wonder how the *Guinness Book of Records* knows that to be true.

He was married twice. The first Countess was married at sixteen and died at thirty-six whilst in the process of giving birth to her seventeenth child – and there were no twins. That was pretty staunch work. She had seventeen children in twenty years. It was from this marriage that

Camfer and all of us descended. Staunton Harold and the estate went to this part of the family.

The first Earl then married again, and had a number more children. Ettington, the Shirley's House in Warwickshire, went to this part of the family which was until recently owned by John Shirley and is now owned by his son Philip.

Another Earl, the 4th Earl, probably the most notorious member of the family, shot his steward. The Earl had fallen out with his wife and had made a financial settlement for her. He made his steward one of the Trustees. The Earl thought that the steward was looking more favourably on his Countess's interests than he was on his master's.

So, one Sunday summer afternoon, he sent all the servants out from Staunton Harold. He drank some port, found a revolver and sent for his steward, Mr Johnson. The Earl raged at Mr Johnson's disloyalty, and told him to get on his knees. This Mr Johnson did. The Earl said 'I am going to shoot you.' He picked up a revolver and shot him in the stomach. The poor man collapsed.

He then had to find some help. Word had got round that Johnson had been shot and one lady ran all the way to Lount, a village about two miles away, to summon help. A band of about six men appeared carrying staves because they were told that his Lordship was in his cups and had drunk a bottle of port, by which time he had. All the staff were, not surprisingly, scared stiff of going anywhere near the Earl.

They waited until the Earl was asleep, and Johnson was later taken to what is now 'Maggie's Cottage' and was laid down by the window. It did not seem to be a very bad wound but the bullet was lodged in his stomach and it proved fatal. Dr Timothy Kirkland came from Ashby to minister to him.

Maggie, the most recent inhabitant of the cottage when we were at Staunton and after whom the cottage was named, used to wash and starch my shirts. She was a typical old village lady, charming and superb at her work. I sometimes remind my accountant of what happened in a previous generation to one who did not look after the Earl's money properly with the rejoinder 'Be careful because these things can run in the family'. It has an electrifying effect!

The 4th Earl was tried by his fellow peers and was told to say that it was a mistake and that he did not mean to shoot him. He said that he would say no such thing. It was not a mistake. He had intended to shoot the steward.

Then he was told that he must plead insanity. Understandably, he was reluctant to do this too. But eventually he decided to do so, and he did. He pleaded his case so well that his fellow peers concluded that he could not possibly be insane. So he was sentenced to death, and hanged, legend has it, by a silken rope. He wanted to be hanged – if he had to be – at the Tower of London and not at Tyburn, which is now Marble Arch, because Tyburn was the place to which 'common fellons' go. But the Powers that Be said 'No.'

As was the form in those days, on his journey from Tower Hill to Tyburn, the coach in which Lord Ferrers rode was followed by another coach containing the coffin into which the poor fellow was going to be put. It must have been a very macabre sight, and it must have created a most uneasy feeling. The Earl, though, must have had a sense of humour, because he wore a very smart white suit which he had worn for his wedding. He did not wear it for any romantic reason but simply because, as he put it, 'the day of my wedding and the day of my death were the two unhappiest days of my life.'

When they arrived at the scaffold and Lord Ferrers had mounted it ready for this terrible death, he remained strict to protocol and he went to tip the hangman. Unfortunately, though, he gave the 'pour-boire' to the wrong man. He gave it to the hangman's mate. They both, the hangman and his mate, had their heads hooded, like some modern day terrorists and, thereafter, there ensued an undignified harangue, the hangman claiming that the money was his, whilst the mate said that the money was given to him.

The trial of Lord Ferrers is by way of being a classic as it is one of those trials which, I am told, legal students used to have to learn. Whether they do so now or not I do not know.

It is memorable because the hanging of Lord Ferrers was the first time that the dropping floor was used. Previously, the wretched individual had to stand on the back of a cart with his head in the noose, and the cart was driven forward so that he was left dangling, and the hangman would pull on his legs to expedite the severance of the neck and put the man out of his misery. With Lord Ferrers' hanging, there was no cart, just the floor suddenly dropped eighteen inches. The rest of the procedure was not, I think, dissimilar, taking about four minutes before death took over.

The other notable fact about the trial is that a Peer of the United Kingdom could be hanged for a criminal act in the same way as would be an ordinary commoner. That was not so in other countries. That is considered by some as one of the reasons by which England was spared the indignation and upheaval which France experienced with the Revolution and it is, some people surmise, one of the reasons why the English aristocracy survived whilst those of other countries did not.

Another notable figure was 5th Earl Ferrers, Admiral Washington. He was Lord Warden of the Cinque Ports and, as my father used to put it, 'got Versailles-itis'. As a result, in 1760 he enlarged the relatively small and manageable Hall at Staunton Harold into a colossal, majestic and formidable building, very much the same as it is seen today, copying what had happened after Versailles and other buildings in that period of European history. It was this huge enlargement of the Hall which, some 200 years later, was responsible for the sale of Staunton Harold. It was just too big to use and to fund.

The 10th Earl was, in my father's day, called 'Two Back' for the very simple reason that my father was the 12th Earl – and the 10th Earl was two back. He had no children. He lived like a Lord. He went shooting. He had his own pack of hounds and his own golf course. In the old days, the now famous Quorn Hunt used to be the Ferrers Hunt. If there was any money, he spent it. And, if there was not any, he spent that, too. The 10th Earl married Ina White, the rich Irish heiress and daughter of the Countess of Bantry in Bantry Bay. Regrettably, it was not a happy marriage. He loved her but, unfortunately, she did not love him. She missed Ireland. They had no children and much of her life was spent in a wheelchair.

Some generations earlier there had been some family feud between two parts of the family which had, as things have a wont to do, the destructive capacity of continuing for decades and even for centuries long after the cause of the original frisson had been forgotten.

As the years went by, Two Back thought that he had better meet the middle-aged man from this disagreeable line of the family who was to become his heir and who would inherit the title, Staunton Harold and everything else.

He accordingly invited my grandfather, Camfer, down to stay at Staunton. Two Back was pleasantly surprised to find that my grandfather was not a disagreeable, pugnacious or odious character, but that he was a cultivated man, who had been educated at Winchester, was a man of modest means, and was an architect by profession. He was Mr Walter Knight Shirley. He lived at 35 Victoria Road in Kensington.

Two Back, meanwhile, having had no direct heir and having had no particular love of that part of the family which was going to carry the baton after his death, had lived the life of Reilly. He kept a superbly elegant household with an indoor staff of eighty – and the debts mounted up. There was a description of life at Staunton Harold in those days in a book called *Bricks and Flowers*, written by Katherine Everett in 1951. I find it amazing that, even in those days, there should still be alive one who remembered Staunton in its high days.

In her book she described teatime:

At that moment a procession arrived, consisting of the butler and three powdered footmen, one of whom put out a tea-table, while another laid a fine lace cloth on it, and a third put a silver tray with teapot and kettle on it. The ritual was perfect, one man replacing another automatically, while canary-coloured china appeared and a quantity of varied foods – rich cakes and plain cakes, scones and biscuits, thin bread and butter, white and brown – and when all was completed the butler announced: 'Tea is served, my lady' – a fact we could scarcely have failed to know. This statement was the only active assistance he had given to the performance, and then the procession withdrew.

When Two Back died in 1911, my grandfather became, as it were, the Lord of Staunton Harold and all which therein lay. This was a role to which Camfer was not accustomed nor was it one to which he had aspired or to which he had been brought up. Nor did he anticipate debt after debt after debt which was built in to this magnificent estate. It certainly took the gilt off it and left everyone – my grandfather and, particularly, my father – wracked with worry during their years of tenure. Debts, mortgages, Death Duties and Income Tax at 50 per cent during the war. How could anyone cope?

It was to this lovely house and this lovely estate that we used to come during the holidays. It was a change from our home at 35 Victoria Road. In those days, if you wanted an ice cream, you placed a large card, almost the size of a small window pane, with a W printed in bold black, in the window. The Wall's ice cream bicycle man would stop and ask your requirements. An ice cream was 6d or 3d, but a triangle-shaped water ice, like a Toblerone, was 1d.

We used to watch the muffin man walk down the street carrying a tray of muffins on his head and ringing a hand bell. The knife-grinder would call with his portable grindstone on a tricycle. He would then ask if there were any knives to sharpen, and he would sharpen on the pavement all the shapes and sizes of knives which he had been given from the kitchen, and sparks would fly all over the place as he peddled the grinder. I wondered why nothing caught fire. Each night the lamplighter used to walk down the road, with his long pole, ready to go up to a lamp, stretch his pole up to the glass and switch on each gas street lamp one by one.

On special occasions, and for a real treat, we would have an early tea in the nursery, and I would go with Winnie, my wonderful nanny, to King's Cross to watch the Silver Jubilee train leave for Edinburgh. It was a magnificent train and it was a real treat just to go and see it. It was built in honour of King George V's silver jubilee. The train was futuristic in design with beautiful sweeping lines in the front of the engine, not dissimilar to the Eurostar shape of today, and the train and the engine were all painted silver.

How I enjoyed it, going all the way up the platform, imbibing every bit of the beauty of the train, to stand at the end of the platform and watch this superb machine leave the station. There were, I think, six different engines each with exotic names like Silver Link, Silver King,

Silver Mink and Silver Fox. No wonder one of my childhood passions was to become an engine driver. There was pride in those days.

It was from all of this that we escaped to go and stay with my grandparents at Staunton Harold. We always travelled by train. We went by taxi to St Pancras, the luggage with those huge, frantically heavy leather trunks, went by lorry.

At Leicester we changed on to a small local train. The small train went out of the station in the same direction from which the big train had come. 'Look,' we used to say. 'We are going back to London,' but the branch line took us in a different direction. We passed through such magical-sounding stations as Kirby Muxloe, Desford, Bardon Hill, Swannington and Coalville, until we came to Ashby-de-la-Zouch. There we all decamped from the train with the luggage, and we crossed over the railway track to the platform the other side. Can one imagine doing that kind of thing nowadays? What would Health and Safety have to say?

We were met by a chauffeur and a car – or two. The luggage was collected by a horse and dray, which had plodded all the four miles from Staunton to Ashby just to collect our luggage and to return again. The dray's driver was called Ripon. He was lame, and he had what was obviously a very uncomfortable walk.

I was always a trifle frightened about staying at Staunton. It was a huge house with a formal atmosphere to accompany it, even though Camfer and Gaga always extended a great welcome to us. But formality was the order of the day back then.

Every day started with prayers in the Dining Room. The servants – all thirteen of them – came into the Dining Room with the Butler bringing up the rear and closing the door. They all sat on a long bench at the end of the Dining Room. Camfer used to take the prayers and he read the lesson, which he had read in Greek to himself beforehand.

After that, we sat down to a hearty breakfast. It is astonishing how much people ate in those days and how much there was to eat. There was porridge and, if I remember correctly, a choice of bacon and eggs, fried or scrambled, or fish. A ham was always on the sideboard. Then followed toast (or scones) and butter and jam, or marmalade. No one went hungry.

This huge house had no electricity in it. It was all lit by lamps and candles. My grandfather was given a quotation for bringing the electricity down the Ashby drive, a distance of about a mile, for £70. He found that too expensive and so Staunton was left without electricity, until the War came and the house was taken over by the military. The military installed electricity. But then, helpfully, they took it out again at the end of the War.

So, the house was lit by oil lamps and candles. The really smart lamps were Aladdin lamps whose glow emanated from a mantle, a fragile cone-like structure, which broke with the greatest of ease if you so much as put a finger near it. They gave off a lovely mellow, soft glow. The majority of lamps, though, had ordinary flames emanating from a wick. Woe betide anyone who turned the wick up too high, especially if they then left the room because not only was there a major fire hazard (which fortunately never turned into reality) but you sooted up the glass of the lamp. This resulted in the lamp not giving out any light, but worse, it covered the room and the tables and the cloths with black soot too. No brownie points there.

Each morning the lamps throughout the house were collected and taken to the Lamp Room, which was near the Dining Room. There the wicks were trimmed, the glasses cleaned and the lamps re-filled with oil. In the evening, all the lamps were taken back around the house again to their respective positions and each one was lit. Looking back on it, it was an astonishing and time-consuming ritual. But that was life in those days.

We children had to make do, mostly, with candles. They, of course, flickered and made it all very ghost-like and we were perpetually, and inevitably, dropping candle-wax all over the place. Daddy used to say that the advent of electricity had reduced the amount of ghosts no end. The shadows and spooky feelings had gone, as had the inability to see that it was your dressing gown cord which was bumping down the steps behind you and not something supernatural.

One Christmas before the war, in Camfer's time, we were all staying at Staunton and Mummy dressed up on Christmas Eve as Father Christmas and walked down the Spring Passage. This was a long, narrow, dark passage. A young girl, who had just started work as a housemaid, saw this apparition coming down the passage. And screamed. And fled. Mummy was so upset that she had so frightened the young housemaid that she ran after her to try and console her. Even more screamings and even more fleeings.

The housemaid left her employment. She did not come back any more. That was hardly the easiest thing for a person to explain to her mother-in-law on Christmas Eve.

Despite the size of the house, there were, I think, only three downstairs lavatories, three on the main landing where the bedrooms were and two on the top landing where the servants' quarters were. Likewise there were three bathrooms on the bedroom floor and one on the servants' floor. The central heating was virtually non-existent. Despite this, there were two huge boilers below ground which had to be stoked every day. They had avaricious appetites.

There were 'bunkers' on each landing up to which coal had to be brought and where it was stored. As children, we never had a fire in our bedroom unless we were ill – and then it was quite a perk. It was particularly romantic to wake up in the middle of the night and to see the flames dancing around the walls. We enjoyed that. It had the added advantage of enabling one to see, with any luck, whether the fire would still be going in the morning and so could be continued.

The house used to use about 400 tons of coal a year. That didn't matter too much, as it was built on top of a coal mine, and coal was quite cheap – £1 per ton or so. But the coal had to be carried everywhere – up to the bunkers on the landings and in to the rooms.

There was, of course, no running water in the bedrooms. A maid would bring up a 'ewer', a brass watering-can-like object containing hot water, which would be put in the circular basin in the washstand in the corner of the bedroom and covered with a towel in order to keep it warm.

The estate had its own water supply, which sounds very exotic but it was not really, because it frequently broke down. It was powered by two Rams. Despite the efforts of all my school masters to inculcate some form of learning and understanding into my head at a later date,

I never understood how Rams worked. They can best be described as a self-perpetuating pumping system which required no engine or fuel, but which succeeded in pumping the water around the estate – by water.

All the laundry of the house was done in the laundry cottage. This was found at the far end of the Park. Mrs Charles lived there and, with help, she did the laundry. Her son, Stanley, who married Mary, went to live in the Melbourne Lodge at the top of the Melbourne Drive and, subsequently, they went with my mother to look after her house and garden at Shirley.

One used to see each Tuesday a horse and cart slowly walking across the park with hampers of dirty clothes and sheets. They were boiled in a copper and ironed with a flat iron of which there were four. Three rested on a special rack against the fire to get hot whilst the fourth was used to iron.

I remember old Mrs Charles giving me, when I first went to school, a lavender bag with a message in which she said that she hoped that I would have 'right happy school days'.

Everyone changed for dinner. Of course, at that age, I never went to dinner, but I remember my mother saying that she was a little apprehensive of staying with her parents-in-law and remembered how at lunchtime, Gaga would say 'Tonight ladies, we will wear our lace.'

There was an outside bell on the roof of the house. It was called a Toxin. To this day I do not know why. I thought that a toxin was a disagreeable thing which you had in your stomach if you were unlucky. The Toxin would be rung at 7.30 p.m. to alert the members of the household to go and change and it would be rung again, at five minutes to eight, to alert them to the fact that there were only five minutes left before they had to be on parade in the Drawing Room.

When dinner was ready, the gong would be sounded by Stone the butler, not with a great big bang, but with a crescendo of little hits, which made a beautiful resonant noise. Camfer would lead the way into the Dining Room with a lady on his arm, and all the other ladies would go in on the arm of a gentleman. Very elegant it must have been. How much we have lost.

Sundays were always special days. The Church stood proudly about

200 yards from the front door. It was built by Sir Robert Shirley and has
over its West Door the epitaph:

In the yeare 1653
When all things Sacred were throughout ye nation
Either demollisht or profaned
Sir Robert Shirley, Baronet,
Founded this church;
Whose singular praise it is
To haue done the best things in ye worst times
And
Hoped them in the most calamitous;
The righteous shall be held in everlasting remembrance.

'Do the best things in the worst times and hope them in the most
calamitous.' I have always thought that that was not a bad motto for
the whole of life. Do the best which you can and, when events gang up
against you to such an extent that life seems intolerable, then hope for
the best. And don't despair.

It had always been the custom, which my grandfather inherited, that
Lord Ferrers had his own private Chaplain on the estate, who lived in the
Parsonage, a house into which, during the war, my parents and all our
family moved. Lord Ferrers had to pay the Chaplain – in those days £50
per year – and he was allowed to live in the Parsonage. Lord Ferrers had
to pay for the upkeep both spiritual and material of the Church, bricks
and mortar, the lot. In Two Back's day, the Chaplain spent his Sunday
locked in the Church and his meals were brought over from the Hall
for him to consume in the vestry. I do not think that the modern cleric
would think too much of that.

There were usually three services on a Sunday held at Staunton, but
not necessarily all on the same day: Holy Communion at 8 a.m., Matins
at 11 a.m. and Evensong at 3 p.m. The main service was Matins at 11
a.m., and this was the one which, as a young boy, I was obliged to attend.

There was quite a ritual attached to it. The Chapel had a quaint custom,
which had existed since Jacobean times, of the men sitting on the right

hand side of the Nave and the ladies on the left. Families were therefore separated – but everyone took that as par for the course. Lord Ferrers and the male members of his family, and any male guests who were staying in the Hall, sat in the front pew on the right-hand side and spilled over, if necessary, into the second pew. Lady Ferrers and the female members of her family and any female guests who were staying in the Hall did likewise and sat in the front pew on the left-hand side, spilling over, if necessary, to the second pew.

Each senior employee of the estate and Hall would have his own particular pew – the agent, the head gardener, the Chaplain's wife, the housekeeper, the cook, the butler, they all had their special pews, with their wives on the other side of the aisle. Other employees or tenants or visitors would fit in as and where they could although, as in good Church of England practice, they tended to gravitate towards a pew in which they normally found themselves, thereby claiming some form of squatter's rights over it.

The party from the House itself would gather in the Hall and, at two minutes to 11 o'clock, they would set off to the Church with my grand-father in front. Once inside, my grandfather and grandmother would go to their pews, with the others filtering into their pews. The door was then locked and the key was carried up on a velvet cushion to my grandfather.

That custom still existed until we left Staunton in 1954. The door was always locked although the key was not brought up on a velvet cushion. I used to carry it in my hand.

The Church is beautiful in its architecture. It has a lovely and serene atmosphere. The ceiling is a complex painting of the beginning of Creation. There is a beautiful Father Schmidt organ, over which the cognoscenti drool. It stands in the choir loft. In our day, the air for the organ was produced by some poor character, sometimes me, pumping a lever behind the organ and watching a little lead weight go up and down. One could not afford to relax because, if the organist were to pull out an extra stop or, in modern day parlance, to switch up the volume, the lead weight would leap up to the top, and there would be a hideous noise like bagpipes deflating.

Each pew had a door attached to it, and in front of Lord Ferrers' pew was the place from which the Chaplain took the service. It was the Jacobean Triple-Decker pulpit – unusual for these days but not, I suppose, for those days. As its name implies, there were three tiers to this structure. The lower one, on ground level, was the Clerk's Reading Desk, where the Clerk sat. He gave the responses as people were not very educated in those days and he may have been the only literate member of the congregation. Others might join in from memory. In the absence of the Priest the Clerk would take the service. In the olden days services were often from there. As this faced north and was immediately in front of Lord Ferrers' pew, few could see what was happening. So the service was usually conducted by the Priest, in the analogy of the Car Park, from level 2. The top pulpit – level 3 – was from where the sermon was given. In our days, most of the service was taken from level 2. On only very rare and special occasions was the top pulpit used. But it was lovely when it was.

I always found this impressive. Usually, before the sermon, the Bidding Prayer was used. This was a particularly personal Bidding Prayer, which included a reference to all the members of the family. This filled one with a certain amount of embarrassment and some quite undesirable, undeserved and misplaced pride. Having prayed for the King and Queen and other members of the Royal Family, it went on to invoke the prayers of those in the congregation 'for the Nobility and Commonality of this land, and especially for the Rt. Hon. The Earl Ferrers, The Countess Ferrers, The Viscount Tamworth and all the members of their family'. The wording of the prayer was quite beautiful. It made one's spine stand upright, but I think that the Bidding Prayer is not used too much nowadays. It ran as follows:

Let us pray for Christ's Holy Catholic Church. Especially for that pure and Apostolic branch of it established in these Kingdoms, and herein for our most excellent Sovereign Lady, Elizabeth, by the grace of God, of the United Kingdom of Great Britain and Northern Ireland, and of her Realms and Territories, Queen, Head of the Commonwealth, Defender of the Faith, over all persons and in all causes, ecclesiastical and civil, within these dominions, supreme; for our gracious Queen Elizabeth, the Queen Mother, Philip, Duke of Edinburgh, Charles, Prince of Wales, and all the

Royal Family; for the Lords and others of Her Majesty's most honourable Privy Council; for the nobility, and especially for the right honourable the Earl Ferrers, the Countess Ferrers, the Viscount Tamworth and the family; for the gentry and the Commonality of this land; for the magistrates and others who are in authority, that all in their respective stations may labour to advance the glory of God and the present and future welfare of mankind, remembering that solemn account which they must one day give before the tribunal of God.

But for the sake of all, let us pray for the clergy, whether Bishops, Priests or Deacons, that they may shine like lights in the world and acclaim the doctrine of God our Savour in all things.

Finally, let us bless God for all His servants departed this life in His faith and fear, more especially for Robert Shirley, baronet, founder of this church, beseeching God to give us grace so to follow their good examples that, this life ended, we may dwell with them in life everlasting, through Jesus Christ our Lord, in whose most perfect form of prayer we conclude our address to the Throne of grace saying:

Our Father, which art in Heaven, Hallowed be thy Name. Thy kingdom come. Thy will be done in earth, As it is in heaven. Give us this day our daily bread. And forgive us our trespasses, As we forgive them that trespass against us. And lead us not into temptation; But deliver us from evil: For thine is the kingdom, The power and the glory, for ever and ever Amen.

Chapter 3

Life at Staunton Harold

CAMFER DIED IN 1937. Apparently – although I cannot remember this myself – aged seven, I bought five cigarettes out of my own pocket money to give to my father to help him over his grief. My father liked it.

We all moved from London to take up residence in this huge building of seventy-two rooms. A year or so before we went, my father had not been well and the doctor had said to my mother, 'Get him out away from London to get some fresh sea air.' So, they went down to Brighton for the day.

It was November. It was a miserable, cold, rainy day and there was hardly anyone about. My parents went on to the pier and saw the booth of a Fortune Teller. My father was a reluctant participant in this kind of futuristic prediction and, in a somewhat ungallant manner like a shy young boy shoving his sister forward, he told my mother to go and have a shot and see what the Fortune Teller would tell her.

The Fortune Teller told her two things of note. My mother had lost a silver teaspoon to which she was greatly attached. 35 Victoria Road had been searched up and down, but no, it could not be found. The Fortune Teller said 'Don't worry. The teaspoon will appear and probably when you will least expect it to do so.' My mother forgot all about that until, some time later, my sisters, Betty and Neppy, were playing around in the nursery and bumped into a piece of furniture. Out fell the silver teaspoon.

The other memorable thing which the Fortune Teller said was 'I see a large house with a lake in front of it. You will move there after the second full moon of next year. But just check that the property is properly insured because you will be burgled within a year'.

My grandfather died in February of the following year, 1937 – after the second full moon. When we moved to the 'large house with a lake in front of it' – Staunton Harold – my father studied the insurance policies with infinite care. He found that the House was insured for everything except … burglary. He had it insured. The House was burgled in November.

I never understand how these things work or what credence, or authority or respect, should be accorded to fortune tellers, clairvoyants and the like. One tends to dismiss them all as irrelevant rubbish and all part of a con trick. But is that so? Or is it because one does not like to get too close to them for fear of what they might say? I think that there is something in some of them somewhere but, on the whole, I prefer to stand at a distance – in happy ignorance of how they perform and of what they might divulge.

My father went down to Brighton some time later and went on to the pier to thank the Fortune Teller. But she had gone.

Life at Staunton before the war, certainly to us as children, was idyllic. A huge house – far too huge, but that was the way that the dice had fallen – an inside staff of some thirteen including Stone the Butler, and Mrs Stone the Cook, and an outside staff of about the same. As children, we knew nothing of the apprehensions which my father had of being left with an estate of 1,500 acres in pretty poor nick, a colossal house and a private church to run and to keep up, as well as a large mortgage on it all and huge debts bequeathed by Two Back. My father always said that the estate should have been sold when Two Back died. My grandfather thought the same, but he did not like to do so as soon as he had inherited it. Anyhow, he had two able sons, both of whom had been to Winchester, and maybe one or both of them might be able to make some money and find a way through.

Similarly, Daddy always said that he should have sold Staunton when he inherited it in 1937, but he did not like to do that just as soon as his father had died. That would have seemed peremptory and unseemly. But, of course, within two years the Second World War had started, and that put the lid on that idea – at least for the time being.

Neppy paid a short visit to hospital in 1938. This meant that she could not go back to school for a few terms. My parents, therefore, thought that they must get a governess to help both Neppy, whilst she could not return to school, and me before going off to prep school.

So into our lives walked Miss Mason – Margaret Mason, commonly known in later life by her friends as Margot. To us, though, and to all the staff at Staunton Harold, she was Miss Mason. She was twenty-one and had red hair. I was eight and shy. I was introduced to her by my mother. I was horrified. Red hair! When Mummy came to say good-night to me in my bed, I said to her, almost by way of admonition for having brought her into our life, 'But you know, Mummy, that I cannot stand red hair.'

Miss Mason was a lady, though, of exceptional talents. She taught us. She played the piano beautifully. She played tennis for Leicestershire. She was bright and able and ran everywhere. I have never seen – or heard – anyone run down a flight of stairs at the speed with which Miss Mason did. It sounded like a pack of dominoes collapsing.

She drove the car beautifully and loved doing so, to such an extent that, if anyone else were to drive whilst she was in the car she emanated an atmosphere of black fury – jealousy I suppose – but it was like having a joss stick in one's car, puffing out horrible vapours.

She came, though, to be an integral part of our family, staying with us for some twenty years. She became a hugely trusted, loyal friend and a real confidante. She became my father's secretary when Neppy and I went to school, and she helped to organise the estate – and everything and everyone else who came within her sights.

One day before the war, my mother and I were gardening, doing some weeding in one of the borders. Miss Mason was with us. A few weeks earlier we had been to see the film *Snow White and the Seven Dwarfs*. That evening, the Toxin rang at 7.30 to warn us of dinner at 8 p.m. So we gathered up our belongings and went off home in a line, with our hoes and rakes over our shoulders, just like the Seven Dwarfs, singing 'Heigh ho! Heigh ho! It's home from work we go.' My mother was in the front. I was in the middle and Miss Mason was at the rear. We gave ourselves the names of some of the dwarfs and, Miss Mason, inevitably being at the back, was called Dopey. Dopey she was from that day forward to the end of her life.

***

When the war came in 1939, the first thing which happened was that thousands of children were evacuated from Coventry which was likely to be, and which turned out to be, a prime target for German bombers. Some of the British children were sent abroad to places like Canada where they did not see their parents for years. Others were disseminated into the country.

My mother did the round of the houses on the estate and the nearby village of Lount to find out how many evacuees could be taken in by each house. Some said that they could take one, some two, some three. Those who said that they could all came to the Village Hall, which was known as the Recreation Room, in order to meet their new lodgers-to-be when they arrived. Several bus loads of them came, and my mother, rather like Lady Bountiful, sat at a desk distributing these poor bewildered children and their mothers to their new families.

When this was completed, rather like the five barley loaves and two small fishes, there were some fifteen evacuees left over. 'We will have them at Staunton,' said my mother, and off they went to this huge house, the like of which these children from Coventry had never seen before. They were terrified. They were put into bedrooms in the attics. The rooms there used to be the servants' quarters, and there were many rooms next door to each other along a long passage. There were two rooms on the ground floor near the back door into which my mother had put some chairs and tables, so that it would be nice and welcoming for them.

My mother went down to see them that night to make sure that they were all happy and content. She had come from dinner in her evening dress. People always changed for dinner in those days even at the beginning of the war. But there was no one in the two downstairs rooms. 'Oh well. They must have gone to bed.' So my mother went up to the attics. She went into the first room. No one there. The beds were empty. She went into the second room. No one there either. The beds were empty. And so it went on until she came to the end of the passage, and there they were. All fifteen children and mothers. They had got themselves into two rooms. A little mother with a white face said, 'Do come in.' They were scared stiff!

Not surprising when you come to think of it. They had come from Coventry. Their particular part of that town was like a village. Everyone knew everyone. They met their friends in the streets, in the shops, in the cinema and in the pub. No one travelled. It was quite a social life in its own way.

Now, what on earth had they come to? They had travelled from Coventry to the middle of the country. A terrifyingly huge house. No water. No electricity. No heaters. Only lamps and candles. 'Is there a pub?' 'Oh yes, down the drive – about a mile. Across the field on the left, but look out for the cows because they may chase you.'

They were terrified – and miserable. In those days, the men went out to work and earned the money. The wives stayed at home and cooked and looked after the house and children. When the husbands of these evacuees came to Staunton at the weekends to meet up with their families, the wives and children were thrilled.

'How are you getting on alone in Coventry?'

'Fine. Fine.'

'Who is looking after you?'

'A nice kind lady drops in and helps.'

'Oh she does, does she?'

You can see all the anxieties, tensions and miseries. The wives soon found themselves some transport and went home with their children to see what on earth was going on and to try and bring a bit of order and discipline back into the marital homes again. None stayed long at Staunton.

I hope that they enjoyed their introduction into country life, even though it may have taken some time to adjust. It was all totally new to them. They did not know what happened in the country. They did not know what baths were for. Some of their parents used them for storing coal. I remember one young boy, of eight years of age I suppose, Donald Bamber, being amazed to see a cow being milked and seeing the cowman squirt the milk out of the cow's teat into his face. He always thought that milk came out of bottles.

After a while the military came and requisitioned Staunton Harold. Two officers came to see my father in his Den at Staunton. 'How can I help you?' Daddy said. 'We want your house.' 'When?' 'Next week.' So it was.

I am not sure, and never have been, as to what is the difference between being requisitioned and being commandeered. I think that the language of commandeering is 'We are having this,' whereas the language of requisitioning is 'I hope that you do not mind if we have this.' The net effect seemed to be the same. The military takes over your property. And they took over Staunton Harold.

We stayed on at Staunton in a part of the house for a year or so before moving out and going to live in the Parsonage. The Parsonage was a horrible little house really. There were no two windows in it which were the same and they mostly faced north. The only room to face south was the larder. But we kept three big rooms at Staunton – the Hall, the Dining Room, and Daddy's study – for generally keeping things or for any parties.

When the military took over Staunton, life became very different. There were guards and road blocks everywhere, the drives were lined with half-moon corrugated huts containing ammunition. On Sunday, the chapel was full because there was a Church Parade to which all those who could not find a better excuse were obliged to attend. I remember thinking how smart it was to see some four soldiers collect the offerings on a plate and march up with them to the altar, halt, give them to the priest and about-turn. It was very disciplined and very effective. In some funny way it gave one a feeling of confidence – in them, in the military, and the way in which things were done. But that is one of the advantages of discipline, which is nowadays so frequently despised and ridiculed and, too often, rejected.

On some Sundays my father used to take the salute standing on the steps outside the front door as the soldiers all smart marched past after church. I sometimes used to stand by him. I felt very smart, but I think that others must have thought that I was horribly precocious.

The soldiers at Staunton were a good group of people, who were kind and understanding to us. I think that some of the officers could not believe their luck in finding a red-haired, twenty-year-old Dopey on the scene – beautiful, fresh, vibrant, confident and young – and I think that Dopey could not believe her luck in finding an endless array of young officers taking an interest in her. Boy! What has happened? She was like the cat who has been given a bowl of cream. I did not understand about that kind of thing then, but I do now! It was, though, all very proper and above board – at least I think that it was.

Oddly enough, the Other Ranks looked after their part of the house beautifully, but the Officers left theirs in a shocking state. My mother had left one or two nice things for them, like curtains and a carpet and the odd chair, in order to make the Officers' Mess look and feel more homely. They were ruined.

After the English soldiers, Italian prisoners of war and Germans came to Staunton. Although one hates to say it, they were far better custodians of the house than were our own English soldiers. They, particularly the Germans, looked after the house immaculately, and many of the Italians made lovely pieces of metal work, like cigarette cases and lighters which they engraved. They were beautiful works of art and they reflected the great skill of their makers. We loved these hand-made pieces, and I used to ask them whether they would make some for me, which they did.

The Italians used to walk home in the evening after a day's work on the farm. It was lovely to hear them, with their magnificent Italian voices, singing arias and operettas as they went down the Ashby drive, and to hear the music filter across the countryside.

One day, Dopey went down to Staunton and was horrified by what she saw. She went back to the Parsonage, where we were then living, and said to my father that he really ought to come down to the Hall.

He did. There were stacks of young girls with plunging necklines and skin-tight short skirts all over the place. It was crawling with them. They had come from heaven-knows-where by bicycle. My father sent for the Commanding Officer and gave him a monumental dressing down. He then went back home and rang up Northern Command and told them what was happening and said that it had to stop. When he rang off, he sat back in his chair and wept, 'Look what they have done to my lovely home. They have turned it into an unlicensed brothel.'

Staunton was built on an E-shape but without the middle bit, so the windows of one part of the house faced the windows of the other part, albeit at a considerable distance.

At the beginning of the war, when the military had only taken part of the House, we still lived in the other. One evening, part of the domestic staff, who were mostly girls of eighteen-to-twenty and who were living in one part of the 'E', were getting undressed. The rooms were lit by candle-light and the curtains were not closed.

The soldiers on the other side of the 'E' could not believe their eyes – a free strip-tease show! Before anyone knew where they were, the windows on the soldiers' side had soldiers practically dropping out of them, like the participants of a Punch and Judy Show.

The girls quite liked the attention they were receiving, and they improved their efforts. Neppy, though, sneaked on them and rushed along to my mother and said, 'You had better come and see what is going on down here.' My mother stomped down the passage and told the girls, 'Put the candles out immediately and draw the curtains.' They did. That was the end of that bit of fun.

***

During all the time when we were at Staunton, my mother took a great interest in everything locally. She was a Justice of the Peace. She was on the governing body of Ashby Grammar School. She was a member of the Women's Institute. She was a member of the Mother's Union of which she subsequently became the Presiding Member, and she ran the local Sunday School in the Church at Staunton every Sunday.

Each child would have a book into which you stuck the appropriate coloured stamp to show that you had attended Sunday School that week. A prize was given if, at the end of the year, you had a full book with no cards missing. It was rather like collecting cigarette cards.

I remember the school mistress's boy, Michel Rathbone – a clever but precocious child of about ten – telephoning on Sunday afternoon and asking whether, as he was ill and therefore unable to come to Sunday School, he would nevertheless be able to have the stamp for that week. My reply, at the mature age of fifteen, was 'You don't come to Sunday School to get a stamp. You come to learn about religion.' I do not think that he liked that.

My mother always ran a Nativity Play every Christmas Eve in the Church. She used to write it and 'direct' it and help, together with others, in the making of the costumes. The cast was all the Sunday School children from the estate and the nearby villages, aged from six to about sixteen.

There were always amusing anecdotes some of which one can never get out of one's mind. One young girl, Joyce Cave, playing Herod found it difficult to say 'Go and search diligently for the young child.' She used to say 'Go and search deliciously for the young child.' Even to this day I cannot hear that piece read without being taken back instantly, and with amusement, to that young girl's difficulty with Herod. She must be eighty, now.

Another was one Herbert Hurst. My mother said that he was too young to take part in the Nativity Play. He was about four. She told Neppy, who was then aged about fifteen, to teach him a carol. Neppy remembered Herbert Hurst sitting in one of the box pews of the Chapel swinging his legs. He could not say, 'In the bleak mid winter.' He could only say, 'In the blinking winter.' That became an expression in our family. If something was going to happen in the winter, Daddy always said that it would happen 'in the blinking winter'.

Again, it is surprising the effect which these episodes have on one's life – forever. It was only the other day that I had a letter from a man who lives in Suffolk, not far from where we now live, to say how he was brought up at Staunton and how well he remembered my mother and the Nativity plays in which he used to take part at Christmas. It made a huge impression on him.

When my mother died Neppy had several letters from people who had been children at Staunton in the early part of the war. They wrote and said what a tremendous amount Mummy had done for them in teaching them about religion in the Sunday school classes and the Nativity plays. They, in their turn, had become pillars of their church and so had their children.

One young child had walked all the way up the lanes from Heath End to the Recreation Room, a matter of some two miles and back again, just to go to Sunday school. That was quite an effort. Would people do that nowadays? My mother would have been thrilled to know what effects her efforts had had. It is another example of how you never know the effects which you have on other people.

My father was, by nature, very low church. My mother was, by nature, high church. My father could not stand incense, Hunting Pink, candles and even vestments. He liked the simple stuff of church life. Not so my mother, who enjoyed injecting a bit of spice and pageantry into the life of the Church at Staunton Harold. It was, of course, entirely the choice of my parents what, if anything, was put on in the Chapel. It was, after all, not a parish church. It was a private chapel, run by and financed by my father. Others came to it, as it were, by invitation.

My father always held reservations about a midnight service on Christmas Eve, preceded by a Nativity Play. He always felt that a midnight service, which was not in those days a very common occurrence, had too much of a flavour of popery about it, particularly when the parson wore, at Mummy's suggestion, some modest white vestments. And anyhow, Daddy did not like the idea of the children running around the Chapel and, in particular, around the chancel, turning it into a stage and making the whole place resemble a theatre. He did not find that in any way to be a soothing preparation for a Christmas service.

I always thought that that was a bit of an extreme position, although everyone is entitled to their own views. But Daddy came to the Nativity Play and to the Midnight Service. He tolerated them and, in the end, he liked them. He always, though, admired my mother for what she did, how she had galvanised people together to make a Nativity Play and how she had inculcated into these children, and indeed into their parents, who came to watch and thereafter to participate in the Midnight service, something much more than just the ability to act in a play.

In the early days of our time at Staunton, before the outbreak of war, my father had the advantage of a chauffeur, Lovatt. Cars, in these days, had no heating. No one had yet thought of – or if they had, they had not yet succeeded in devising – a system of heating a car with the excess heat from the engine. So whenever my mother went out in the car in winter she had a rug with a metal ring attached to it, which she would snap around her waist, and hot water bottles were produced to keep her and the passengers in the back warm.

Antifreeze had not been thought of by then. At night-time in the winter, a small oil lamp with a wick in it used to be placed on top of the engine and underneath the bonnet of the car, so that it would keep the water in the engine from freezing. Otherwise, you had to drain the water from the engine or risk having a cracked cylinder block. Woe betide anyone who drove the car out in the morning having forgotten to remove the lamp!

One employee at Staunton was found to have been pilfering and he was told to find another job. His future employer asked my father for a reference. Daddy said, 'Although the Doctor has said that he must not lift heavy things, he is pretty good at lifting light ones.'

The kitchen garden of some four and half acres was turned into a commercial nursery garden for the duration of the war. It was called Staunton Harold Nurseries, and many of the flowers and vegetables which were grown were sold on Fridays and Saturdays at a special stall which we had at Derby market. Derby Market was a pretty rough place, but Dopey, who by this time had joined the Women's Land Army and dressed up in the uniform of brown corduroy jodhpurs, beige shirt and green sweater, used to go there and do the selling. She also made sure that we had the best-looking stall on the market.

Nothing is ever easy in the growing and disposing of grown goods. Arum lilies were fine, beautiful, robust flowers, perfect for Easter. In time for the Easter market, they were very valuable at 5/– per bloom (a lot of money in those days). The week after Easter they were virtually valueless.

In 1942, my sister Neppy shocked the family, her friends, her school, the World, and anyone else who was in a shockable frame of mind, by announcing (very discreetly) that, at the age of sixteen, she wanted to get married. The man of her dreams was Maurice Robson. He was in the Army – an army chaplain – who had been at Staunton and who had seen, admired, got to know and love Neppy. He was thirty-two, twice Neppy's age. That did not half capsize the tranquillity of our happy family life. My father said that Maurice 'has pinched my best bud'. My mother said that, like Lot's wife, she had been struck dumb for three days and could not speak.

But, like most things in life, the initial shock was overcome and they got married and 'lived happily ever after'. They were married in 1944 in the Chapel at Staunton Harold, when Neppy was eighteen. Very few people came to the wedding because it had to be held at short notice when Maurice had a few days army leave. And, because Staunton was not a parish church which was licensed for the taking of weddings, a special licence had to be requested from, and was provided by, the Archbishop of Canterbury – in three days.

Maurice prepared me for my confirmation in 1942, when I was thirteen and, in the company of two other young boys, I was duly confirmed by the Bishop of Derby in Staunton Chapel on St George's Day, Saturday 23 April 1942.

The evening after the confirmation, and the day before I was going to receive Holy Communion for the first time which Maurice was going to take in the Chapel, we were having a family supper at home, and I repeated a stupid story which I remember one of my masters, Mr Ledgard, at West Downs telling me. It was about a man who got on a barrel at Hyde Park Corner. He was haranguing the multitudes and telling them to repent. In support of his case, he quoted Our Lord who had said 'In a little while you will see me, and in a little while you will see me not.' At which moment the top of the barrel gave way and, to the horror of the spectators, the speaker disappeared inside the barrel. A little voice from within it said 'Ha, Ha. But I can see through the Bunghole.'

All my family were kind enough to laugh at this with considerable gusto. What none of us realised was that the next Sunday – the next day – was the Third Sunday after Easter and this story in all its glory formed the entire gospel. It kept on repeating 'In a little time you will see me, and in a little time you will see me not.' In church, anything seems ten times funnier than it does outside, and this was no exception. Here was I, at my first sombre Holy Communion service, yet all doubled up with laughter – trying hopelessly to keep a straight face. But it was not possible. Nor could anyone else. The poor unfortunate Maurice had to read through the Gospel, with its constant repetition of the essence of the story, with a composed face. He managed to do so – but only just – which promptly made it far more funny for the rest of us. The Third Sunday after Easter has become known in our family, rather irreverently, as 'Bunghole Sunday'.

At the end of the war, Daddy said that Staunton would have to be sold. Everything had been sacrificed on the altar of Staunton. It cost a fortune to run and that left nothing for anything, or anyone, else. He added to me, very poignantly, 'I do not want you to have the worry that I have had!' Daddy wrote to me in August 1954, two months both before the sale and before he died. 'I do very sincerely feel if I had not taken this decision, you would have been forced to do so under far less favourable conditions.'

This threat had been hanging around the place for years. I loved Staunton. Mummy loved Staunton. We all loved Staunton. But then Daddy died late the night before the auction.

'Do you want to put the sale off?' I was asked by the auctioneer and the solicitors. Of course I did, but how could we overturn my father's conviction of the last seven years within twenty-four hours of his dying? It would look as if there had been a terrible family row and, anyhow, there would still be Death Duties to pay.

So the sale went ahead. I sat behind the Auctioneer on the stage at the Auction Rooms in Derby and I saw the lovely Staunton Harold Hall sold for £10,000 – to demolition contractors.

Some four months later, Group Captain Leonard Cheshire, VC, agreed to buy the house from the demolition contractors for £16,000. Fifty per cent increase in four months – highway robbery. Cheshire had no money. People gave him bits of money, shillings, pennies, £5, £10. But he was miles off the new asking price. Then, when he was right up against the buffers and had to pay the balance within a couple of days, someone advanced him an interest-free loan of £10,000. He got on to a train and rushed up to the solicitors.

So Staunton Harold now belonged to the Cheshire Foundation Homes for the Sick. People came from everywhere – miners, folk from Derby, from Leicester, from the National Coal Board – to give their time and effort in order to make Staunton once again a home, albeit this time a home for people who had been afflicted in life.

For some twenty years Staunton Harold gave astonishing happiness to those who lived there, remaining a gem in the countryside. It was then sold to John Blunt, the son of our old butcher. He and his wife Jacqueline have brilliantly and sensitively turned it back into the lovely family home that it always was, and have always been astonishingly kind to the previous owners.

***

Meanwhile, before the sale of Staunton in 1954, Daddy said that we – or Mummy and he because I was married by then – were going to live at Shirley. 'Our family has been at Staunton for only 500 years. But we have been at Shirley for 1,000 years.'

Chapter 4

West Downs

AT THE AGE of eight, in January of 1937, I was sent to my preparatory school at West Downs in Winchester. My father had been there when it was run by Lionel Helbert. He loved it and he admired Helbert greatly, as I think most people did. It was now run by Kenneth Tindall – who was also known as K.T. His wife, Theodora, was a sweet person but regrettably short and dumpy. I say 'regrettably' because her initials were TMT and she gained the unfortunate, and not very respectful, nickname of Tumpty.

I loathed West Downs – especially the first few days. So much so that I asked the Headmaster for some writing paper and an envelope. I wanted to tell my parents how miserable I was. He offered me a postcard, but I declined that by saying that the postman could read it all. So I was given an envelope and some paper.

I begged my mother to come and collect me on the first train on Monday – and such was my trust in her that I 'knew' that she would. As a postscript, I added that I would return to my parents the tip of two shillings which I had been given. My mother told me, later, that my postscript had completely unbuttoned her and made her burst into tears. I still have that letter. The Headmaster fortunately warned my mother in advance that a pretty miserable letter was on its way. He advised her not to take too much notice as I would soon settle down.

Little boys can be pretty odious and most new boys come at the beginning of the school year in September. There were only two of us who came in January 1938. One was Giles Allan – although, of course, I didn't know then that he was Giles. One did not know that kind of thing then. He was just Allan. The other was me, who was then Tamworth. We were the most junior. Allan and Tamworth were always at the bottom of every school list. Our peculiar isolation, as we were the only two new boys of the term, imposed upon us an instant friendship. When anything went wrong there was always a chorus of 'Oh, Allan and Tamworth'.

I had not met Allan since West Downs days when he was a squitty little boy and I wondered what had become of him. I met him in 2002 or thereabouts at an Old West Downs reunion dinner. Here was this huge, jolly, larger-than-life character, perpetually laughing. I asked him what he had done in life. 'I was the Regimental Lieutenant Colonel of the Irish Guards!' – alias Colonel Giles Allan, OBE. Help! Help!

West Downs was a school deeply conscious about health. Twice a day – once in bed in the morning and once standing together after prayers in the evening – the two sisters used to take everyone's temperatures with a thermometer which, together with about thirty others, was kept in a jar of methylated spirits. You were woken by a jab of glass being put into your mouth, which sometimes, because of your half dozy state, you would break and get glass and mercury into your mouth. You were left totally convinced that if you did not die from the one you would die from the other. If the glass did not break, which was of course the usual occurrence, you would be obliged to suck in methylated spirits. Charming.

Onions used to hang on the walls in the dormitories near the windows in bundles of about ten. The theory was that onions helped to avoid colds. I never thought that the theory proved very successful.

Then there was that remarkable institution of Sanitary Prep – from 8.40 a.m. to 9.10 a.m. – when you went after breakfast to your classroom to do some prep. It was also the opportunity for each boy to open his bowels. This was overseen by a sister who was on parade with a stick to ascertain the results. If there was no success, then the boy would be made to have another shot at 11 a.m. If that was not successful, then you were for the High Jump – syrup of figs at night.

Allan and I always used to take as long as possible over breakfast so as not to get to the classroom before our mistress, Miss Hills – or Miss Quilly, as she used to be known – arrived. There was good reason for this.

One little boy with red hair, Bucknall Minor I think he was, who had been in the school for all of one, or possibly even two, terms demanded somewhat aggressively 'Have you had a new boy's squishing yet?' You didn't have to have a lot going on in the Intelligence Department to gather what this was likely to be like and to realise that it was probably pretty disagreeable. It consisted of getting the poor newcomer on to the floor and the rest of the form all sitting on top of him. All pretty harmless in itself, but daunting to a frightened, lonely, isolated eight-year-old.

Table manners were drilled into one, as there was a master at each table to ensure proper behaviour. Anyone who fell foul of the standard was made to stand up, and therefore not eat, for ten minutes, or even for the rest of the meal. Everyone would then turn round and look at the hapless boy who was standing like a lighthouse in a calm sea and say, 'There is Smith standing up. I wonder what he has done.' Like the stocks, Public Humiliation has its own salutary effect.

A really bad misdemeanour had the boy standing on his chair at his table so that the whole school could see and take note. In modern political parlance this would be called naming and shaming. A boy who had really gone beyond the pale with bad manners was made to go and sit at the Pig's Table – eat on his own at a table in the corner of the room facing the wall. No one liked that, and no one respected anyone who was sent there.

I always regarded Mr Ledgard as an old and rather frightening master – and he was both – but he was a stickler for rectitude. He had white hair – and that made him even more frightening. He had a gammy leg and I thought that he was eighty, but he was probably only sixty-seven. 'You must eat your pudding with a spoon and a fork.' If a boy ate his pudding with a spoon only, Mr Ledgard used to say, 'Only savages eat with a spoon only.' I have never forgotten that. If I am – or anyone else is – tempted to do without a fork for the pudding, even if it is rice pudding, his words immediately come to mind, and I remind my children of them. It is funny how things that people do or say when you are young stay with you for the rest of your life – but that is what bringing up children is all about.

I was quite keen on gardening when I was about ten. I read a book all about allotments. It referred to digging the allotment, not just one spit deep, but two. This was called 'Bastard Trenching'. I mentioned it to my mother who said, 'Never use that word bastard. If you do so at school, they will sack you.' Help. What is this terrible word? Typical of a boy who likes playing with fire, I asked one of the masters, David Howell Griffiths, in the most grown-up unfussed way about 'Bastard Trenching'. There – I had said the word. For the next three weeks I was then terrified that I would be sacked.

When you were about to leave West Downs, you were given what in typically schoolboy language was called a 'Leaver's Jaw'. It was a one-to-one, with the Headmaster telling you all about the Facts of Life. It was a good practice but, despite everyone wanting to know what the Leaver's Jaw was about, it never got out. I always found that remarkable. You were told not to talk about it, and you did not. Nobody did. Trust can be forthcoming even at an early age.

We were looked after, and were taught well, at West Downs but, as a boy, I thought that life there was austere. I never really liked it at the time, unlike Winchester, later, which I loved from the word go – and not just in retrospect.

Back to my constantly recurring philosophy that one never knows the effect which one has on others by what one says or does, this was exemplified for me (although I did not realise it at the time) by the Master's Play at West Downs. As its name implies, it was a play which was put on by the Masters for the benefit of the boys, who provided the audience, and it was put on during my first term. There was a particularly nice Master whom I liked, called Mr Stanton. During the play, he was sitting writing at his desk in the evening. A villain entered his room through the French windows, crept up behind him, with the floor boards creaking, (which they were not supposed to do) and slapped a chloroform mask over Mr Stanton's face putting him out and rendering him unconscious. It terrified me.

I cannot remember anything else about the play, what the story was about or what the ending was, but I do know that every night, when I was at home until I was about seventeen, I always looked under the bed and in the sliding cupboard and outside the bedroom door in order to make sure that there was no one there who might come in and chloroform me in my bed. The play left a lasting impression of fear on me – but, poor Masters, that was the last thing which they intended to do.

'Shakespeare' was a magnificent room with a polished parquet floor where the whole school could meet and play or listen to talks. It was here that I learnt the simple art of going up to a boy, who was standing with his legs fairly close together, and with the side of my own foot, pushing his feet together. Down he went. Every time. It was a riot – or so I thought – but you could not do it too often.

I am afraid to say that I even did it years later at our daughter Angela's wedding. We were getting Hedenham Hall all tickety-boo on the morning of the wedding and I was in the drawing room on its parquet floor with a long-handled brush. I used it on Andrew. It worked every time. I am afraid that I still find it very funny.

It was Shakespeare where we would go for half an hour after lunch before setting off on games. It was used for playing with your toys and, as a really special treat, for one of K.T.'s Magic Lantern shows. We thought that this was terribly modern. The Magic Lantern had three lenses through which pictures were projected on to a screen. They were lit by three pairs of carbide sticks which, when attached to the electricity, gave off a bright light. It was the height of modern technology and we regarded those lantern shows as being on a par with going to the cinema.

If you had misbehaved at school, you got 'slippered', K.T. removing one of his slippers and administering justice through your pyjamas. This was always done in one of the tiled bathrooms in the evening and the noise rang around the walls and down the passage with an eerie openness. We all knew that someone was being dealt with.

Really bad behaviour, though, resulted in action being taken and the boy dealt with by the Headmaster during the day. He had a cane in his study, which he kept above the bookcase. It had a brown knob on the end. Caning was done with your trousers on, and it hurt. Being slippered was looked on with a certain amount of bravado. Caning was regarded as awesome and somewhat shaming. Everyone was nervous when the Headmaster appeared at Prayers in the morning wearing his Old Wyke-hamist tie. For some reason, the origins of which were never clear, his

Old Wykehamist tie was known as his Whacking Tie, and his wearing of it was a portent that some poor blighter was going to be in for it before the day was over.

Nowadays, I suppose, this would be called 'abuse'. I have never been able to understand that. Apart from anything else, I always thought that that word meant something different. For all that, and for all the rubbish which is talked about corporal punishment, nowadays, it never did me any harm, and I never objected to it being administered. Nor do I think did it do many other people harm. Nor do I think that many people objected to it. Nor do I think that those who did administer it were sadists, as is so often made out. They were just administering justice for the betterment of the boy, the school and eventually society, in the context and within the parameters of the society of the day. But things change. So do practices. So do perceptions. And, I suppose, so must we. But I do not like doing so.

Two occasions stand out in my memory of West Downs. They are both trivial, but it is always the trivial which stand out.

On one occasion there was an appalling flu epidemic and many of the Masters had succumbed. K.T. therefore arranged for my mathematics class to be taught by one of the cleverest boys in the school. So it was that I got taught by Jeremy Morse, aged twelve, a fact about which I have never ceased to remind him. He later became Sir Jeremy Morse. We were the same age, although our academic propensities were light years apart – and here was he teaching me.

Jeremy and I had been at Wagner's together. We were at West Downs together. We were at Winchester together. And, later, we were to be Fellows of Winchester together, of which he was then Warden. Jeremy claims that, at each of those incarnations, I masqueraded under a different name – this is not quite true, but is near enough for after-dinner talk. In fact, I was Shirley at Wagners, Tamworth at West Downs and Winchester, and Ferrers as a Fellow of Winchester. All pretty confusing if one is not dead on the ball.

Jeremy achieved Tindall's greatest ambition by coming top of Election to Winchester – heading the list of those awarded scholarships. Tindall was so thrilled that he gave the school a day off.

When he was at Winchester, Jeremy was picked, at the age of seventeen, to go to the bankers Glyn Mills, which later became Child & Co. He had a glittering financial career which included being Governor of the International Monetary Fund and Chairman of Lloyds Bank and then subsequently Fellow of, and Warden of, Winchester College.

Jeremy is, of course, brilliant. He has an acute mind miles up the Richter scale from most of us. He is married to his lovely wife Belinda. Some years ago they asked Annabel and me to dinner and, when we went back into the drawing room after dinner, I saw a fat book sitting on the table called *The Theory of Numbers*. I looked in it and about died. It was full of the most impossible and incomprehensible equations of inordinate length and complexity. I said to Jeremy 'Is this your bedtime reading?' He said 'As a matter of fact it is – and I found a mistake in it the other day in one of the calculations.' I asked what he had done. He had written to the editor, who was deeply grateful to him. The editor agreed that there was an error, and he published a Corrigendum to go with all future copies of the book. Not many people could do that.

The other unusual matter which I have never forgotten is that I first met insurrection at West Downs. There was to be a new Head Boy. 'We' all thought it would be Thornton. 'We' all wanted Thornton, but the Headmaster decided that it should be Hitchens. For all his life afterwards, Mark Hitchens has been a wonderful upholder and promoter of West Downs. He seems to know everyone past and present and now, at the age of eighty-four, has written two books about the school.

But at the age of twelve, for some reason, doubtless of little importance, Hitchens did not have the support of the boys.

A campaign was started, by whom I do not remember, probably of doubtful worthiness and of even less delicacy, of trying to get the situation reversed. This was to be achieved with nothing more sophisticated than the slogan 'Up with Thornton. Down with Hitchens.' At the slender age of ten, I thought that this was dicing with death and would invite a reaction of gargantuan proportions. Little slips of paper were dropped all over the place, ensuring that the idea got well publicised at the same time as ensuring the anonymity of the perpetrators.

This was brought to a head when Tindall was to take our form for

Latin and this offensive slogan had been written on the blackboard. Just before the Headmaster entered the classroom, and in order to ensure that there was, as it were, a double whammy, a similar slogan was written on a piece of paper and put on the Headmaster's desk. That did it. The school was brought together in Shakespeare, but the eruption was not as seismic as I had expected. We were just told to stop being foolish. Hitchens had been chosen to be Head Boy, and Head Boy he would be. And that was that. Hitchens was Head Boy. And the school reverted to normality.

Because England was likely to be invaded, and the invasion was likely to be on the south coast, Tindall elected to move the whole school to Glenapp Castle near Ballantrae in Ayrshire. Can one imagine moving a whole school, desks, beds, kitchens, goal posts, everything – let alone boys and masters, cooks and wives – from Winchester to Scotland in the middle of a war? It must have been a hideously formidable task, but it was achieved – and without apparent fuss.

We did not go back for the Christmas Term until November, and so my father made sure that I had some outside teaching from the Parson's brother, appropriately known as Mr Parsons, and that I learnt two things. One was Rudyard Kipling's 'If'. 'If you can keep your head when all about you are losing theirs and blaming it on you.' Wonderful poetry. The other was 1 Corinthians XIII – 'Faith, Hope and Charity.' Both of these were superb choices, and they have had treasured spaces in my limited mind ever since.

Glenapp Castle was, we thought, a huge place. Our dormitories had chandeliers hanging from the ceilings which tinkled as they got regularly hit by sock-balls. It was wartime and there was Double Summer Time so that the best could be made by farmers of the hours of daylight. As we were in Scotland, where anyhow it remained lighter for far longer than it did in England, it used to remain light until midnight in the summer. We thought that that was very exciting, but it made going to sleep at normal times difficult. Sometimes we would watch Tindall with his dinner guests wandering around the garden at midnight, and it was still light.

After about a year at Glenapp Castle, West Downs moved to Blair Atholl in Perthshire, which was the home of the Duke of Atholl. Another huge move. That was an even vaster house because it contained a school for backward children in one of its wings. For whatever reason we never came into contact with them.

The Duke of Atholl died when we were there. He is the only person in the United Kingdom, who is allowed to have his own Private Army, the Atholl Highlanders, who turned out for his funeral.

The janitor at Blair Atholl was a man called Mungo. He used to stoke the boilers, clean the shoes and ensured that everything which should function did function. He was a huge, great, beefy, scruffy Scotsman with a face like a monkey, of whom we were all slightly in awe. He came into the classroom on the day of the funeral to show himself off in his uniform of the Atholl Highlanders. He was transformed. A different man. An upright man. And a proud man. So it was that the Duke was taken to his final resting place on a farm cart.

The walls of the hall in Blair Atholl were bedecked with guns and pistols and spears and daggers – a formal and glorious sight which was somewhat lost on the budding youths who were then to stay there. As the school was in Scotland it took a greater number of Scots boys as pupils than it did when it was in England. There was one young boy, whose surname was Douglas. He periodically lost his temper – and in a big way.

A 'Douglas Bait' was punctuated by crying, screaming, kicking and biting – anything, everything, preferably people – so we all learnt to get out of the light. But this was not very successful because, when a person is in this state, he wants to be the centre of attention and, if everyone has vanished, there is no one left to be at the receiving end of his fury. He accordingly tore around the rooms trying to find groups of people, who were doing their best not to be found, and on whom he could discharge some of his venom.

Those were usually disagreeable and somewhat frightening experiences. The worst came one day when there was a yell of 'Douglas Bait' and Douglas, in a fit of total apoplexy, had torn down one of the spears, all of twelve-foot long, from the wall and was charging down the long straight passage like a Zulu warrior with the spear parallel to the ground, in pursuit of some poor miserable boy – *any* poor miserable boy – whom he could find in his path. As one of the more senior boys – I was thirteen by now – and one of the bigger ones I was told to go and 'catch Douglas'.

I did not relish this order – nor the experience. I could see big and uncomfortable trouble ahead. We – myself, another boy and a rather small master – approached him as if he were a rampaging lion, from the rear. We managed to get hold of him and, as I stood behind him holding onto his arms, he was relieved of his weaponry. But the crying and screaming and kicking was still going on – and was getting worse.

Then we had to watch out for the biting, which was getting more savage. You really did have to watch out. Fortunately, it all seemed to resolve itself in the end. I am sure that now, at the age of about seventy-nine, he is a staunch pillar of society.

Common Entrance was the dread and fear of everyone – to pass an exam to get into your public school. My father and uncle and grandfather were all at Winchester and it was to Winchester that I was destined to go. But Winchester did not have any truck with Common Entrance. It had its own Winchester Entrance. That was much more alarming and it carried with it its own reverential aura. I was terrified of doing it.

There was a mystique about the Winchester Entrance. It was supposed to be more clever, more brainy, more this and more that than Common Entrance. It never occurred to me that I might fail it. I was terrified of taking the exam but I always expected, not in a self-satisfied way but more in a sort of fait accompli kind of way, that I would pass it. Such confidence was far from shared by my parents, who were pretty sure, I think, that I would not pass it. Nor was it shared by my Headmaster. But they all had the good grace not to share their doubts with me – ever. I *did* pass it. I got into Winchester in the house – Kenny's, D house, Culver House, Fearon's, or whatever people like to call it – where my father and where my grandfather had been. Uncle Andrew, my father's brother, was far more impressive. He was a scholar and so he had gone to College.

Chapter 5

Winchester

I LOVED MY time at Winchester from the very moment that I arrived there. We were lucky. We had a wonderful Housemaster in Freddie Goddard. He knew everything about the House and he knew everything about everyone who was in it. But he never let on and he never interfered. It was by no means common to all the other houses. It just goes to show that so much is up to the Housemaster – who he is, the way in which he conducts himself, the way in which he runs the House and whom he chooses for his House.

Nowadays, there is so much 'hype' about passing exams, with the person who gets more marks having more of a 'right' to go to a certain school or to a certain house. But a school – and its influence in the moulding effect which that school has on a child – is made up of three things. Its history – and that should never be eschewed – the teachers and the pupils. If, in a fictitious example, all the pupils are terrible, it would not matter how good the teacher was, the children would still remain terrible because they would all be affected, and infected, by their peers.

Equally, if all the pupils were wonderful and all the masters rotten, the pupils would not get anywhere. So, the ability of the Housemaster to select 'good' or 'right' or 'suitable' children – whatever you care to call it – has a great effect on the other children in the school, on the ability of the school to perform its proper task and on the standing of the school in the eyes of others.

So much, nowadays, goes on numbers. The person who gets 8 out of 10 for history is better than the person who gets 7 out of 10. A person who gets a first-class degree is better than a person who gets a second-class degree. Why? Because they have been evaluated by numbers. What is the point, though, in employing a person who has a first-class degree if, by his arrogance, he upsets all the people with whom he works? It may be better to employ someone who is less academically brilliant but who is able to get on with others. This is only a trifling example and is not a reflection on academic ability.

I was always surprised that people did not notice more about Diana, Princess of Wales. She did not have any O levels, or any A levels, but she took the world by storm. People loved her. She loved others and she cared for them. On her death, mountains of flowers were left at churches and cathedrals everywhere throughout the country. It showed to me that the true purpose of education is not just physical or academic achievement, important though they both are, but the drawing out, the encouraging and the nurturing of the whole person.

My father used to say that the qualities which he valued most in life were Truth, Beauty and Goodness. I, in turn, marvelled at his choice of qualities, because none of them can be subject to numerical evaluation. They are there or they are not there. They are in the eye of the Beholder and of the Almighty. They are not subject to statistical computerised analysis.

Anyone who goes to Winchester – it does not matter who pays, parent or State – enjoys a huge privilege. It is a wonderful place. It has magnificent buildings and the playing fields are a sight of beauty. To see acres of beautifully mown grass in the summer surrounded by tall, forever ancient green trees, with young men in white shirts and white trousers, is a sight never to be forgotten. One American looked in amazement at these beautifully mown grounds and said to the groundsman 'Say, Buddy, how do you get those grounds like this?' The groundsman replied, 'It is quite simple really. You just mow them and roll them. For 600 years.'

I chugged slowly up the school. I was never at the top of any form, sometimes nearer to, but fortunately not completely at, the bottom. There was this terrible sword of Damocles which hung over us, not wholly fictitious, that, if you did not get a remove once a year to a higher form, you got sacked. Whether that did happen or not, it did not half concentrate the mind.

'School' is a magnificent Wren Building which, in our day, housed most of the school for important lectures and other such occasions. There is displayed on one of the walls a notably large painting which warns in censorious terms and with graphic description: *Aut disce. Aut discede. Manet sors tertia caede.* 'Either learn. Or go away. But there is a third alternative. Be beaten.' Not many schools would dare to subscribe to such a philosophy nowadays, but in the fifteenth, sixteenth and seventeenth century that was par for the course – as it was in the eighteenth, nineteenth and twentieth centuries. And I doubt if it did many people much harm. Despite our present softy approach to many things, the picture and the words still stand in glory on one of the walls of School.

In the last two years of my time at Winchester music meant everything to me. I had been taught the piano ever since I first went to West Downs, but I was extraordinarily incompetent at it. I used to try to learn pieces – and where to put your fingers – by heart. As for sight reading… that was like another language. Singing, though, and music had always been in my system.

One day when my parents came to take me out from Winchester, we went to Chapel. My father was so impressed by the choir that he said afterwards that, if you went through Europe, he doubted if you would find a better choir anywhere. That might have been an exaggeration but I can see the look on his face as he said it. He found it very impressive.

I thought that I would, therefore, try for the choir, and that Daddy would be so pleased if I made it, but I did not expect to. I was given an audition at the beginning of the term, along with a number of others, with Dr Sydney Watson who was in charge of all music. No one ever told you that you had been accepted to join the choir. The only way in which you knew was that you had not been allocated a seat in Chapel with the rest of your form. I had not. I was therefore in the choir – as a tenor.

So started my instruction in, and love of, music and church music. Sydney Watson was a great enthusiast, a great teacher and a wonderful organist. He used to say that on Sunday we will have 'Dyson in C' or sometimes 'Me in E', meaning the work which he himself had composed.

A friend of mine who was in the choir, Ted Bonner Maurice, said that I ought to come to Glee Club, which was a club of singers from the town and the school. 'We are doing the *Messiah*.' My everlastingly shameful question was, 'What is that?' It was an unforgettable response. We did the *Messiah* and I have loved every bit of it ever since.

Religious inculcation was part of the ethos of Winchester. This was not surprising as it was a Bishop, William of Wykeham, who started the school in 1382. We had to go to Chapel every day. Twice on Saturdays and twice on Sundays. It was rather like cleaning your teeth. You just did it.

The most memorable service was on Saturday evening which was always started by the choir, dressed in scarlet cassocks and white surpluses, processing up the aisle to the 122nd Psalm – 'I was glad whey they said unto me, we will go into the House of the Lord,' sung to the Beethoven style chant. It was a magical experience, the memory of which all Old Wykehamists hold dear. They have now, of course, stopped it. Typical.

Many years later, when I was a Minister in the Home Office, the new Common European Union format passports were introduced. As the Home Office was responsible for passports, I was asked if I would like to have one of the low numbers. I said 'Yes please, 007.' I was told that I could not have that as it had already been bagged by the Foreign Secretary. The Prime Minister had snitched 001 – the lowest number.

So I said that I would like to have 122 to remind me of the 122nd Psalm which we had every Saturday at Winchester and which we all loved.

The sad part is that no Wykehamist in the future, were he asked the same question as I was, would reply '122' because he would not know the Psalm because he had not had the experience of having it drilled into him regularly every Saturday. Which all goes to show that part of the educational process rests, not upon what people are taught, but on what they absorb – almost by a process of osmosis, and osmosis, if my inadequate scientific memory remembers correctly, is when one fluid is separated from another by a permeable membrane, yet the elements of one of the fluids can find themselves passing through the membrane and being absorbed into the other fluid.

For me Winchester was a hugely happy place. Lots of friends, lots of exercise, lots of work at which I was not proficient, but it was all part of the general struggle of life – and, of course, at that age, it felt as if one's time at Winchester would go on forever. Five years was an eternity.

The War was in full flow. We watched the endless stream of aircraft with their special markings fly over Winchester on D-Day. We had had the odd bomb drop on Winchester which we all found brought reality a bit too close by half. We had seen some of the older prefects leave only to return nine months later dressed up as Commissioned Officers. We thought that they were really grown up then, and indeed they were. Some of them did not return.

The school was treated periodically to special lectures by some very distinguished people. During one term alone, we were addressed by no lesser figures than General Sir Bernard Montgomery (later Field Marshal Viscount Montgomery of Alamein and Hindhead), Lord Louis Mountbatten, who was exceedingly amusing and kept his audiences in stitches with laughter, and Field Marshall Lord Wavell, himself an old Wykehamist, clever and erudite, but whose lecture was remarkably dry and uninspiring.

If we were lucky, an important visitor would say that he had asked the Headmaster if the school could be given an extra 'Half Remedy' which is Winchester-speak for half holiday. This was, of course, hugely popular to the men in the school.

Montgomery's son, David, was in the school and his father used to come down and lecture to us once a year and tell us how the war was going. I shall never forget the awe and the wonderment with which we listened to this remarkable soldier, who had just come back from the front line where he was running the military campaign and was conducting, and winning, the battle against Germany. Here was this hugely high-profile person, immersed in all the drama and anxiety of war, standing up and talking to all of us. He used to ask the Headmaster for a *Whole* Remedy – a whole day off – and we loved it. Monty could not bear people to make noises whilst he was talking, and so, halfway through his lecture, he would say 'And now we will have a break for five minutes for coughing and sneezing and blowing your noses'. Everyone coughed and sneezed and blew their noses as if there was no tomorrow – even if they did not need to.

Engraved in my memory for ever is the occasion when Montgomery uttered these unforgettable words to us: 'By no possible, conceivable chance can Germany win the war and by no possible, conceivable chance can we lose the war.' That was from the Front Line. From the Top. From the Boss Guy. It instilled into us a mixture of wonder, excitement, relief and pride.

The V1 rockets, or doodle-bugs as they were called, used to fly over Winchester on their way to London. At that stage in the war, they gave a hideous twist to the advancement of military capability. They were, literally, unmanned flying bombs. They were put on a certain course of direction on the Continent and the engine was pre-directed to stop at a certain time and down the bomb came. They emitted a certain droning noise specific to them. When you heard the engine stop, you knew that the bomb was coming down. People became a little blasé and said that you were alright if you heard the engine stop because the bomb would continue down a flight path and land several miles beyond you. The time to worry was when you did not hear the engine stop.

On one occasion, when we were in the dormitory about to go to sleep, we heard a doodle-bug's engine stop, and one man, Giles Myrtle, later a great friend of mine, a tremendous games player – cricket, fives, racquets, the lot – suddenly uttered a crie de coeur to the prefect in the dormitory, 'Bertie, Bertie, shall we get under the bed?' Bertie was the nickname given to the one who was later to be Sir Michael Butler, a very distinguished diplomat who became the United Kingdom's Ambassador and Permanent United Kingdom Representative to the European Communities in Brussels.

A young boy, Martin Nourse, aged thirteen, came to my House, Kenny's. He was two years younger than me, but he was a clever-guts. I was always getting stuck with my Latin and I used to go across the room to Martin to ask his help. He always gave it willingly – and easily.

He was a delightful person and still is. We became great friends. His elder brother, Christopher, was also in Kenny's, and his father, Harry Nourse, was a doctor in Cambridge. When Annabel and I were married some years later and lived in Cambridge, Harry Nourse became our GP and he saw most of our children into the world.

Martin, meanwhile, became a barrister and a very successful one too, ending up as being, as Sir Martin Nourse, an Appeal Court Judge.

Martin and Lavinia now live near Newmarket. They used to come and stay with us sometimes to shoot. I remember, one cold November day – I suppose that we were fifty-five or some such age then – I was walking Martin across some heavy plough to take him to his peg. We had mused over how everyone always complains about 'the Establishment', and Martin said, 'Of course, we are the Establishment now.' I found that a little unnerving. I had always thought of myself as being on the bottom rung of whatever ladder it is that we were trying to climb.

Martin and I both became Fellows of Winchester and, as he lived near Newmarket and I lived near Bungay, I frequently used to offer him a drive home in my car after the Governing Body meetings. I loved it. We talked and gossiped about all we that we had discussed at the Governing Body meeting earlier that day and had great fun assassinating everyone's characters – or at least dissecting them.

It was a huge privilege to be a Fellow of Winchester, a Member of the Governing Body which, later in life, I did for fifteen years. You either finished at the age of seventy-five or after you had done fifteen years, and then you were obliged to tip over the edge of the weir and go. When I think of all the clever people, the able people, the scholars, the men who had got to the top of the school or, in later life, the top of their businesses, and yet it was me, not them, who was asked to join the Governing Body, I feel immersed in gratitude and total humility. It really was a privilege.

I later became Sub-Warden under George Younger and, when he became ill, terminally ill with cancer, I stood in for him as Acting Warden. This would normally have been great fun but, as happens periodically with all organisations, a row blew up and the Dons' Common Room, and everyone else, seemed to be in total turmoil. It was unpleasant and it was sad, for it resulted in the Headmaster, Nicholas Tate, leaving. I was sorry for him. He was a nice man, a good man and an intellectual, but the dice were loaded against him.

When George Younger died, my position of Acting Warden came to an end and Andrew Large became Warden. Tommy Cookson returned to Winchester, where he had been a Don before, to become the Headmaster. A breath of fresh air blew through the school. It all – thank Heavens – settled down again.

***

During my last year at Winchester, I discovered a technique which I have used constantly throughout my life and which has enabled me to appreciate, and to *enjoy*, life all the way through. I was never any good at history and, one night, when everyone else had gone to bed, I remained at my desk working away at the eight pages of history which I had been set, and trying to remember it for tomorrow's lesson. I suddenly thought 'Here am I, working away like mad into the middle of the night, worrying about whether I am going to get 7 or 8 out of 10 for history tomorrow. And I am not enjoying this lovely place, Winchester. In ten years' time, when I am twenty-seven, with all the cares of the world on my shoulders I will look back and say "I wish that I had enjoyed Winchester more instead of worrying about such a pathetic thing as whether I was going to get 7 or 8 out of 10 for history."' So I shut my book and went to bed. The priorities were right.

I have applied that same principle all the way through life with children running around all over the place and with the fervour of trying to make ends meet and I would then say 'Just imagine yourself ten years older at thirty-seven looking back and you will say "Here I am with the children all growing up getting to the really difficult stage with school fees to pay, you were so lucky ten years ago. I wish I was ten years younger. But I *am* ten years younger, because I am now only twenty-seven."' So enjoy not having the worries which you will have in ten years' time.

The practice can be used with vastly increasing effect as life goes by. When you are sixty and you feel that you have passed, as the mechanics would say, Top Dead Centre, and you are getting old, imagine yourself ten years older at seventy looking back and saying 'Oh you were so lucky when you were sixty, bright, able, full of go and not hobbling about with arthritis which you now are.' But you *are* only sixty. So enjoy it.

When you become seventy, hobbling around with arthritis and you feel that you have really had it, imagine yourself being ten years older at eighty, possibly in a wheelchair and having had a heart attack, and you will say 'Oh I was so lucky when I was seventy.' And so one goes on. It is a very good technique for enabling you to enjoy life and to realise how lucky you are – at any one moment or, indeed, at all moments.

The great thing in life, wherever one is, whoever one is, whatever one is doing, is to remember how lucky one is. It is too easy to let all the things which you feel have gone wrong or which irk you sit up like hob-goblins in front of you saying 'Isn't life awful?' and one feels that, if only these could be overcome, life really would be fine. Yet one takes for granted all those things which have gone right as if they would have gone right anyhow. But, they might well not have done.

A happy home, a wonderful wife, lovely children, an interesting job, if any of those have gone right, one is hugely lucky. They might not have gone right and, in many people's cases, they have not gone right. So let us rejoice – and give endless thanks, always – for all the things which have gone right and for how lucky we have all been in our own different ways. My father used to say to me 'Just remember, when all things seem to be going wrong for you and when you feel why has this got to happen to me and to no one else, there is always someone saying "Gosh! He is a lucky chap. I wish that I was he."'

***

I learnt to play the bugle in the corps at Winchester. At five minutes to 12 on Wednesdays, I was excused the last five minutes of the lesson, in order to sound the reveille to encourage everyone to come and play soldiers in the Corps.

From the bugle, I transferred to the trombone. I usually cracked the notes and was not very versatile on it but it was a lovely impressive instrument. I enjoyed extending its pipe to the maximum and seeing some wretched violinist in front of me being taken aback by this golden stalk appearing momentarily over his shoulder – and then disappearing again. There were not too many parts for trombones, so it was suggested that I changed to the trumpet. That was lovely. It is a fine instrument – but a very anti-social one. To rehearse at home the walls and floors are covered with carpets which dull the sound, but, as part of an orchestra and in a big hall, it is a magnificent instrument. I loved the Trumpet

Voluntary – George Eskdail, in those days, was my idea of the perfect trumpeter, and he played that piece of music, accompanied by the organ, quite beautifully.

I once played the trumpet in the Derby Philharmonic Orchestra when I left school. That sounds very smart, but it was not really. I was a very poor player and I succeeded in playing a whole piece by César Franck a semitone flat. No one noticed. I had tuned my trumpet to be an A trumpet but it should have been a B-flat trumpet. With César Franck, and with tremendous crashing noises and discords all over the place, that may have been possible. With Handel it would have been disastrous.

My sister, Neppy, got married at very short notice because Maurice did not know when he was going to get any leave as it was 1944 and the war was in full flood. I was at Winchester at the time. I was allowed off for three days and went home. The wedding was taken by the Bishop of Derby, who dressed like a proper Bishop should dress with gaiters and a homburg-like hat with ribbons, which went down to the rim. All very impressive – and rather awe-inspiring.

The fairly small reception – again because it was wartime and, with such short notice, it was difficult to tell a lot of people – was in the Hall, Staunton Harold Hall.

The Headmaster of Winchester, Walter Oakeshott, had a young daughter, Rosie, who was still at home aged about six. As his wife, Noel Oakeshott, was a cousin of ours, Noel asked my sister Betty if she would like to come and help look after Rosie at Winchester just after Betty had been demobbed from the WRNS. Betty agreed. It was quite fun having an older sister there when I was a more senior member of the school and a prefect.

Betty used to say, when I was going to meet her, 'Just put your head through the door [of the Headmaster's House] and shout for me.' Can one imagine a boy at school opening the door of the Headmaster's House and shouting?

The Headmaster had a secretary, Jennifer Hill. She was about eighteen and was drop-dead gorgeous. Everyone thought so, but I had the advantage that she worked near Betty and therefore I had an entrée, as it were, to her. She used to bicycle to work, which itself was a glamorous sight and, if you received a smile from Jennifer Hill, you were like putty for the next two hours, and your day was made.

The prefects in Kenny's, of which I was one, wanted to ask Jennifer Hill to tea on Sunday. How were we to achieve that? We'll ask Betty, which I could easily do, and ask Betty to ask Jennifer. Betty saw through that like looking through a pane of glass, but it all worked, Betty realising that she was a complete gooseberry, but it was all good fun.

I never played much cricket when I was at Winchester, other than at the beginning when we all did. I always thought that I was rather a good cricketer, having been in the first XI at West Downs, but 'they' thought otherwise at Winchester and I spent most of my time rowing.

I was going through the long lanky process which was going to take me to a height of 6ft 6 inches. I remember one of Freddy Goddard's end-of-term Housemaster's reports 'Poor Robin. Rowing is doing him good.' It said bundles. I always thought that it was an extraordinary sport, where you practically crucified yourself in pain and agony and exertion for eight minutes only to say 'Hoorah we won' or 'That's not fair, we lost'. But, like all things, there are many more plus sides to indulging in a sport other than just winning or losing.

I always thought that Winchester did very well in its rowing, considering the circumstances under which it took place. The river was very narrow. You could only race one behind the other and the cox had to have his wits about him or else the oars – or the boat – would hit the bank. The coach did too. The towpath is exceedingly narrow and one of the Dons, Sponge Walker, was bicycling down the towpath yelling instructions to the crew only to cycle straight into the river. The crew loved it!

Only fours or sculls or double sculls could be rowed at Winchester, 'Down River' as it was called. When training for Henley Regatta and rowing in eights took place, we had to go to Southampton Water. It was considered good for one's training if we bicycled there and bicycled back. It was about twelve miles in each direction. On the way back we sometimes treated ourselves to a ginger beer shandy at a pub. Having that on a warm summer's evening after a lot of physical exercise was like tasting nectar. It also had the added pleasure in enabling one to feel that one was

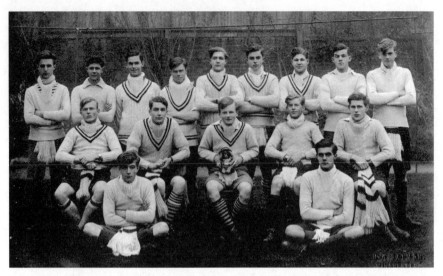

Winchester College Football Commoner XV 1946. F. bottom right.

momentarily escaping from the authority of the school. Whenever I have a ginger beer shandy now, it always takes me back to those days.

I was chosen for the 1st VIII and I was President of Boat Club – for one term. It was not a huge attainment for my five years at Winchester but it was, at least, something. We were all devastated because we could not go to the Henley Royal Regatta. Some boy had contracted polio and as it was considered to be very infectious, the whole school was in quarantine and our visit to Henley was cancelled. I think that it put my father into a flap, a flap which he did not pass on to me. He himself had contracted polio when he was fifteen at Winchester. He had about eighteen months away from school and suffered from a lame leg for the rest of his life from which he never recovered. To make up for the disappointment of missing Henley, we went to Henley Town Regatta and Maidenhead Regatta in the holidays instead. They had nothing, of course, of the prestige value of Henley, but they were still fun. All of us went to stay at the home of David Rutherford, who was in the VIII, and who became President of Boat Club after me. His mother was so welcoming to us. To have nine young men of eighteen to stay in your house for a week, when they all ate like savages, was quite an undertaking. I remember, after one race, drinking twenty-two cups of tea. Mrs Rutherford could not believe her eyes – and she never forgot it. We all enjoyed the regattas and it made up for the disappointment of the Summer term.

The time came when I had to leave Winchester. I was miserable. I had loved it all so much. It was one of those emotional days – the term ending, friends leaving, the umbilical cord attaching the boy to the school, his life for the last five years, being irrevocably severed, and the traditional hymn for the last day of term 'O God our help in ages past' being sung and dissolving everyone into tears.

I found myself walking up and down Meads, that beautiful playing field near Chapel, with Canon James Mansell. He was one of the chaplains, who used to be my Div Don, in the early days at Winchester. He put his arms around me to comfort my crying. I suppose that nowadays some silly ass would say that that was assault or abuse and should not be done. It makes one wonder how insensitive and imbecilic our law makers can be and, worse than them, the officials who think up the interpretation of the statutes and the wording of the regulations which catch people when they should not and when they make it a criminal offence for a teacher to touch a pupil.

Later, James Mansell became one of the Canons of the Chapel Royal and was attached to Buckingham Palace. I used to meet him from time to time when I was in government. He never forgot me crying on my last day at Winchester. He used to remind Annabel and me of it every time that we met until he died aged about eighty. He used to say – and one waited for it. – 'I shall never forget walking up and down Meads with Robin who was in floods of tears at leaving Winchester.' I have always thought that it was lovely and wonderful that a place can have so endeared itself to a person that it should have that effect on him.

That night, the last night of the term, we went to bed. We woke up to be told that 'the school has burned down!' As it was 1 April, everyone said 'Ha, Ha. April Fool.' But it was not. There had been a fire and a major part of the school's premises by the Headmaster's house had been burned down.

Some of the older boys had been doing some play-reading in a disused part of the Headmaster's house, sitting around in comfortable chairs after dinner. It had become a little cold, and so an electric fire was brought up and turned on. After a while there was a smell – of burning. They discovered that the electric fire had burned a small hole in one of the comfortable chairs and some of the stuffing was smouldering.

Immediate first aid was provided. Water was thrown on to the affected part and the potential fire was extinguished. One of the senior boys wrote a very apologetic letter to the Headmaster, telling him what had happened and how they had extinguished any potential trouble in the chair. He offered to pay for any damage which had been done.

They went to bed. In the middle of the night the wind got up and fanned the latent flames in the stuffing of the chair and it all caught fire. The damage was about two million pounds. The boy's letter was put in the School Archives. He was not held to his offer 'to pay for the damage'.

That morning we all got up early and I went to the station to catch the 7.37 train to London which arrived at 9.11. The times of that train are embedded in my memory for ever to the exclusion of other much more valuable information – and, anyhow, the train times are miles out of date. But the memory does not always release that which would be convenient if it were released, but it seems to give away with abandon that which would make life easier if it were retained.

You could tell on the platform who was leaving because, as was the custom, those who were leaving had just become Old Wykehamists and therefore they were wearing for the first time, with a mixture of pride and nostalgia, their 'Old Wykehamist' tie.

Winchester was full of its own curious practices and even language, known as 'Notions'. New Boys used to have a Notions Examination after the first two weeks of being at school to see if they knew enough. This was not a very formal affair. It was conducted by one of the prefects sitting on a bed in a dormitory, when everyone was in their pyjamas, and waving a cane – which was periodically brought into action if the poor miscreant had been unusually hopeless.

One of the notions was 'To toll round Fizz Caps and sport me a hairy bastion.' What does that mean? 'To run round to the school shop and buy a penny cream bun.' How, or why, it could mean that remains a complete mystery, but that didn't matter, you had to learn it.

One of the many other notions was that when the school song,

'Domum', was sung you all had to stand on your chairs. I shall never forget the total amazement of Annabel seeing the then Chancellor of the Exchequer, Geoffrey Howe (afterwards Lord Home of Aberavon), standing on a chair in the middle of Meads (a field) to sing 'Domum' during the 600th year anniversary celebrations. She thought that everyone had gone mad!

There ended for me a happy, glorious and formative part of my life. I was just so lucky. I loved it and, from whatever angle one likes to look at it, it was a great privilege.

***

Many years later, some sixty in fact, the current Headmaster of Winchester, Dr Ralph Townsend, wrote a charismatic piece about why Winchester College is a special place. He concluded with these words, referring to what a boy would remember:

> He will know that our aim was not merely to get him a good passport to a good university, but to inspire in him a deep and lifelong love of learning and beauty; that while he lived among some of the most beautiful buildings of any school in the world, what really mattered was the quality of Winchester's teaching and the friendships that flow from it; that what William of Wykeham's motto means when it says *manners makyth man*, is the cultivation of an unselfconscious and natural courtesy, respect and modesty in all he does, so that while he will be deeply grateful to what his parents did for him in sending him here, he will not be arrogant or boastful, and he will respond to the opportunities life affords him with confidence, imagination and sensitivity. If everything works as it should, he will be a force for good in the world!

What remarkable words. But Dr Townsend is a remarkable man. Erudite, scholarly, a deep thinker, with the ability to communicate his thoughts. What a rarity. What a gift. Winchester is indeed truly fortunate in having a person of that calibre to be Headmaster.

Chapter 6

Dukie

My cousin Dukie, with whom I passed those childhood summers at Littlehampton, turned into a fine person. He became Managing Director of *The Times* and then Chairman of the BBC, which exalted position he held for ten years. On his retirement he became a Peer, as Lord Hussey of North Bradley. The BBC was like a can of worms. Dukie told me that he did not trust anyone in the BBC whom he had not appointed himself.

Before that he went to Rugby where he excelled in athletics. Then he went into the Grenadier Guards. At one point during his training Dukie was sent off to a very tough outward-bound training camp. As soon as they got off the train the Sergeant said, 'The camp is up there. Run.' And they ran everywhere for the whole of the next week. It was exhausting. The only time when you could rest was in your bed at night.

One of the operations included being loaded up with kit on your back, and having a rifle with you and doing a long cross-country run with an assault course at the end and being told to go harder and harder all the time. There was a sewage pond at the bottom of a dip through which you had to go before swimming across a river as a nice finale. You lay down on your back on the slope with your feet forwards and your rifle tucked in alongside you with the butt nearest to your feet, and then slid down into the sewage pond.

Dukie arrived at the top of this slope, exhausted. He rested whilst the previous fellow went down the slope. Dukie said that the only thing which kept him going was watching this wretched man go down before him. His rifle butt hit a stone and twizzled him around so that he went in all the sewage head first. The language was such that would make even a Sergeant's Mess quiver. Dukie just roared with laughter.

With his training over, Dukie was sent to Anzio in Italy where there was severe fighting with the Germans. Within three days, he was badly wounded. Dukie always felt that all that training, which he had undergone, had been wasted for him to be wounded before he had time to do anything, and that it was slightly unfair that his contribution to the war effort lasted for only three days.

The day before he went to Anzio, he said to a friend, who was later killed, 'I don't really mind if I am killed, apart from its effect on my family and everything. What I do not want is to be badly maimed.' Poor Dukie. The dreaded scenario came to pass, and he was to be badly maimed.

Dukie was taken, with his platoon, up to a hill at Anzio under mortar fire. They were lucky. They had no casualties. Large numbers of Germans came to within 200 yards of their position. There was a lot of firing. Dukie and two others jumped into a six-foot deep ditch which was thick with brambles. It was dark. A German came up to the side of the ditch and said, 'We know that some of you are down there. Unless you come out and surrender, we will throw grenades into the ditch and fire a machine gun down it.' Dukie was beginning to think of calling it a day. But Norman Johnson, one of the others who was with him, said, 'Oh no no. We will stick this one out.' Dukie winced. The German counted to three and Dukie, Norman and the two guardsmen buried themselves as deep as they could into the bottom of the ditch.

The Germans dropped in the grenade and the machine gun opened up. Terrifying. But, because of the brambles, quite extraordinarily, none of them was touched.

They eventually had to get out of this hellhole and back to the battalion. They worked their way through the German line, when it was still dark. When challenged at one place, Dukie replied: 'Officier. Gute Nacht.' He said that he could have put his hand on the head of the Spandau guns as he walked through them.

It was becoming light and they decided to run for it and vault a machine gun. Dukie, having been a substantial hurdler at school, got over the machine gun successfully but, because he was tired, he slipped. He was then in the disagreeable position of being two yards away from a trenchful of Germans. Dukie thought that there was nothing to do other than to run for it. Then he received a burst of gunfire – one bullet through his hand, several in his leg and one in his spine. No more running. Dukie always said that he was very lucky, as the machine gunner must have been the worst shot in the German army. He should have killed him stone dead. That brought Dukie's fighting war to an end.

He was taken to a barn by the Germans where he met up with Norman Johnson who had also been hit by a burst of machine gun fire in the thigh, but not too seriously. They spent two nights and two days there. Because they were being shelled and mortared by the Allies the whole time, the Germans could remove neither them nor even their own wounded. Indeed, the Irish Guards, in their counter attack, got so near to the barn that, whilst there were four Germans and a Spandau firing from the door of the barn, inside the Germans were surrendering to Norman and Dukie. Norman was even telling them where to stack their rifles when … stony silence. The Irish Guards retreated. One of the ironies of battle, Dukie recalled, was that the moment of victory and the moment of defeat are separated by only a few seconds.

The Germans were very kind and offered Dukie cigarettes, but he did not smoke. His leg was very painful as it had been broken in several places. He was later taken off by ambulance to a Casualty Clearance Station where he laid on the floor for the best part of a day. He was then taken to the operating theatre, and the German, who spoke only a little English, said that he was to going to amputate his right leg. Dukie, not unsurprisingly, asked if that was necessary. 'Yes,' he replied. 'You have the poison.' Pointing to his lower half of his leg, he said, 'At the moment, it is here. By tomorrow morning, pointing to his thigh, 'It will be here and by tomorrow night, you will be dead.' 'In that case, you had better go ahead,' said Dukie.

Apart from one charming German who kicked him hard in the ribs whilst waiting for the operation, he was treated with great kindness. Later, he was taken to a major hospital in Rome. There were 120 Germans. Dukie was the only Englishman. Understandably, he felt a little lonely. He had not realised how serious it all was until they changed the dressing. They had just cut the trouser off at the thigh and guillotined the leg. He then had an operation to remove the bullet in his back, but that did not work. It was to give him years of discomfort and uncertainty.

After five days in Rome, Dukie with some others were put on a train to the Italian border. It was terrible. They were down to half a tumbler of liquid a day and virtually no food but the Germans were still very kind to him, and he was driven to a convent-run hospital in the Alps.

Dukie was given some hot soup, the first hot food he had had since he had been wounded. He felt sleepy, very sleepy. He was out of pain and it was very contenting. Dukie suddenly realised that he was very close to death and that, if he went to sleep, he would never wake up again. So, he deliberately moved himself about so that his wounds hurt and inflicted pain on him. That way, he could not go to sleep. Eventually, he did go to sleep and he did wake up. But it somehow gave him an inner determination to win this battle.

He was then sent to another hospital, Stalag 9B in Bad Soden, where he was to spend the next seven months. It was a Quaker-run eye hospital and all the surgical treatment was done by a German Colonel.

A young Quaker non-combatant, Robert Smith, was working in the hospital and was helping with an operation in the eye theatre. He had much to do with Dukie and he recalled his experiences vividly.

'I was helping with an operation in theatre when out of the corner of my eye I saw a cart with a stretcher on it, and a German guard, wending its way from the railway station a mile or so away. Major Charters, who was in charge of the operation, said to me "Smith, go down and see what is happening."

'I had to take all my operating clothes off and wash and tidy up. By the time that I got to the front door, the cortège had arrived and was standing outside at the barbed wire. It was Duke Hussey on the stretcher, but I didn't know who he was then or anything about him.

'He did not have anything wrong with his eyes. We had no idea why he had been sent to an eye hospital. We were totally unequipped to cope with anybody with major wounds.

'I was, of course, kept inside the barbed wire whilst his fate was discussed – whether he should be sent on to a major Prisoner of War hospital about four hours away by train, or whether he should be admitted here.

'The German doctor and the guards who brought him were standing there arguing about this when from nowhere out popped one of the sisters – Sister Egberta was her name to the best of my recollection.

'She was very young and very pretty and in a sense quite pro-British. She went round to the back of the cart that Duke Hussey was on, gave him a quick looking over, then turned to the German doctor and said, "You will have to admit this patient to this hospital because there is no way that he is going to stand another four hours' journey. If you do send him on, the chances are that he will die on the way. There will then be an inquiry about his cause of death, an investigation will be carried out by higher authorities, and you will have to explain why you did not admit him in accordance with the orders which you had received from the guard, and why you sent him on. And if he dies, and if you don't have a good explanation for that, then I reckon you are going to get sent to the Russian front."

'At that point there was a silence. The German doctor then said, "Well, I think in all the circumstances, we shall have to admit him."

'We got him inside the hospital and into a room. I was put in charge of him along with another of the medical orderlies, Tom Hooper, who took over when I was off duty.

'Duke Hussey was in a dreadful mess, really dreadful. His uniform was still all plastered with mud and his leg had been amputated, very badly amputated at the knee, and he had other injuries – a serious one to his back. And indeed, I think the Sister's assessment was quite right. I don't think that he would have made it if he had not been admitted.

'We immediately cleaned him up a bit and did a blood test. I couldn't believe my eyes. His blood was so poor that I got one of the other better-trained orderlies to have a look at it under the microscope. He said to me, "This man ought to be dead." I said, "Well, he's not. He's upstairs in bed and we've got to do something about it." And the other fellow said, "Well, it means a blood transfusion as soon as possible."

'Because he was in a very septic condition, I was deputed to have no more to do with eye patients but to be effectively in charge of Duke Hussey.

'I asked the Germans if they'd got any blood available. "Oh no," they said. "It's all in use on the Russian front." So I checked the records for patients' blood groups and our own groups as well, the staff and everybody. We had them all recorded. And I found that there were about four patients who were suitable for a transfusion. I had never done a blood transfusion before. Frankly I was terrified. One of the other orderlies took the necessary blood from one of the other patients and then it was up to me to try and get it into Duke Hussey. I was very lucky that one of the others, quite contrary to the rules, came along and gave me a hand and we got the blood running properly. His blood deteriorated quite rapidly as the weeks went by and about every three weeks we had to give him another transfusion.

'The other thing was the dressing of his wounds, and that fell to me. Being an eye hospital, we weren't equipped to deal with a raw amputation across the leg. We didn't have any antibiotics, of course, in those days and he was really suffering from septicaemia. We were left with having to do what we could.

'When the German doctor had finally agreed to admit him he said, "He will be dead within fourteen days." I didn't think so. He had a glint in his eye and I was always impressed with his will to live and his humour. It must have been an extremely painful business for him but he never complained.

'He was with us for about six months. I would say we not only held our own with him, but he got slightly better. All the time he was with us he had one-to-one treatment.

'There is one aside which I should perhaps mention because it shows the attitude of the sisters. When he arrived his uniform was all messy from, I suppose, having fallen in the mud, so we got it off him and put it outside the door. About a week later it turned up all spruce and clean.

'I eventually found out that it was the sister who had come to the gate on his arrival who had taken the uniform away and had done her best to make it wearable again. She was the junior sister in that place.

'It reminds me a bit of the Sound of Music with Julie Andrews. She had rather that attitude to the situation. I am quite sure that the Mother Superior would never have allowed any of this if she had been asked, but she wasn't asked.

'I think the German sister did as much as I did by her interventions in one way or another.'

Dukie had endless blood transfusions. Everyone in the hospital had offered to give his blood for Dukie. Of course, only some were of the right group, but they all offered. He was very ill when he was there. When Dukie was being repatriated, a Texan pointed to him and said, 'They dug his grave when I was there. He is lucky to be with us.'

Dukie was repatriated on his 21st birthday – 29 August 1944. He was carried out on a stretcher. The whole camp was there. The nuns were there. The German Colonel was there. The German Colonel called out the guard to salute, and the Prisoner of War band played, 'Happy Birthday to you'. It was very moving.

Dukie returned to England and was sent to the military hospital at Chester. He was there for three or four months before being moved to Roehampton. Dukie had a number of operations on his spine trying to get the bullet out, but they could not get it. As a result, the wound suppurated for years and needed treating twice a day. Eventually, the surgeon said that they could have another go. But it was very risky. It might not work. And if it does not, you will die. Dukie said, 'I cannot go on like this. Let's do it.' They did it. It did work. He did not die. He lived for another sixty years.

He had lived a dicey life, in and out of hospital during that time. My godfather, Neville Ford, told me that he had gone to say 'goodbye' to him on five occasions, but still Dukie defeated them all and continued to live.

He was always kind and generous. For one who had gone through that terrible experience he said afterwards:

You would expect care and comfort from your own countrymen, par-ticularly if you were wounded, and to be a wounded officer in 1948 and 1949 was to be a rather glamorous figure. But from the moment I was wounded, right through to the end, in October 1949, I was treated marvellously well. From the soldiers in the barn, who offered us cigarettes, to the Germans who nursed me in Rome and the Italian girl who came to see me, the Lutheran priest who wrote the letters, the nuns who nursed me so devotedly and used their black-market skills to get me extra food, and the German colonel who called out the guard for me – all those people were so kind to me.

Some forty years later, Dukie went back to the hospital with his wife, Sue. He recorded,

When we arrived, we were given a huge tea while they were looking up the records. They produced a little old nun who couldn't have been more than 5ft tall and was in her eighties. She bent down and lifted up my trouser leg and said, 'I remember now. So ill.' It was Sister Egberta. She took my hand and burst into tears, and the Mother Superior burst into tears. Sue burst into tears. And I burst into tears. We all burst into tears.

But the most moving moment of all was when they took us into the Chapel, where they had recorded the names of all the people who had died in the hospital. My name was there because they didn't think that I could possibly live. They showed it to Sue and me, and then the Mother Superior pulled out her pencil, put a cross through it and wrote: 'Married, with two children'.

Dukie's war record was a remarkable example of courage, humility and determination. He never talked much about it, but he did give one interview to the *Daily Telegraph* of 8 May 1998. I am so glad that he did because the details of some of his experiences would otherwise have been lost, and it is from that that many of my own inaccurate memories and stories have been rectified and for which I am indebted.

When the German Ambassador in London read Dukie's account of his war in the *Daily Telegraph* and the full-hearted praise which he gave to those who had been his captors, the Ambassador was deeply touched – both by what Dukie had said which would help to recreate friendship between our two countries, and by Dukie himself. As a result, he offered Dukie a dinner at the German Embassy, at which Dukie could suggest the guests. That was an act of glorious diplomatic generosity to thank Dukie for his own generosity.

It is no wonder that Dukie became such a family icon and how everyone, not only in his family but outside it, held him in huge awe and admiration. Dukie would not have liked to admit that, because he was a man of great humility and love, but it is so. He was a great man. But he was then only twenty-six.

Dukie later went to a hospital in Oxford. It was when Annabel was at Cuffy's, a Finishing School. Cuffy had fairly strict rules, which you would have to have if you were responsible for ten pretty eighteen-year-old girls in Oxford, but she had a soft spot for Dukie whom she admired enormously, and she greatly encouraged the girls under her charge to visit 'this poor young man'. Because he was a wounded soldier, he was also a fairly glamorous young man. They often used to go and see him and to take him some tit-bits.

As would happen with this kind of situation, it got abused. Any girl who happened to want to go out with any disreputable young man of whom Cuffy did not approve merely asked for permission to go and see Dukie, and she was let out like a greyhound out of a trap.

After all these major dramas were over, Dukie wanted to go into the questionable career of newspapers. He became in charge of the advertisement department of the *Daily Mail*. One day Kellogg's gave him two advertisements, one to be inserted during January, and the other to be inserted during February. Dukie got the two muddled up and inserted the one destined for February into January's slot. There was a fearful row. Some big-wig in Kellogg's rang up in a furious temper. Dukie said that he was horrified that the *Daily Mail* should have made such an error. 'I am afraid that it is a new man who is responsible. I shall see him myself and will not half tear a strip off him.' That worked. The character cooled down immediately. 'Oh that is very kind of you. As long as you have it under control, I am very grateful.' Of course there was no other person. It was Dukie himself but, as usual, he had charmed himself out of a difficult situation.

Dukie had a scintillating career in Fleet Street, including being Managing Director of *The Times*, at the time when they were trying to incorporate computers into the running of their business, and at a time of vigorous union opposition. It was not an easy period.

The culmination of Dukie's career was when he did two stints of five years each as Chairman of the BBC. No one had been chairman for ten years before. When he retired, the Prime Minister, John Major, gave him a magnificent dinner at No. 10. I suppose that there must have been eighty people there or thereabouts. Annabel and I were asked, too. I was a Minister of State in the Home Office at the time.

John Major was amazing. He had just returned from a G8 meeting in Italy and must have been pretty exhausted, but he was all bright and perky at the dinner. He made a speech thanking Dukie for what he had done and said how Dukie had said of the time when he had been wounded, 'When you are lying awake at night in the cold under the stars, you realise that each day is a bonus for you.' The Prime Minister then turned and said, 'And every day, Dukie, that you have been with us has been a bonus for us.' It was very moving. I turned to the girl on my right and said, 'Wasn't that a wonderful speech?', but the poor girl was crying. She was Jane Fellowes, Princess Diana's sister.

Dukie then got up and gave a very good speech. At the end he said, in relation to being Chairman of the BBC, 'Sometimes in life one is given a seemingly impossible task in an area with which one may not be wholly familiar, and one just does the best that one can. You, Prime Minister, took on the most daunting of tasks at a difficult time and you have done it with great success. If I might say so, Prime Minister, every day that you have been with us has been a bonus for us, too.' Again, it was very moving and everyone clapped with feeling. I turned round to the girl on my right and said, 'Wasn't that a wonderful speech, too?' But she was crying – again!

I do not say that with any criticism. Far the reverse. Words can touch people and move them, and it is good when they do. Good speeches do that. They move people. Both speeches did that on that occasion and they made it a night to remember. Both the leading characters that evening had created emotion by what they had said in relation to what each had done. Simple words – but they said volumes.

Chapter 7

National Service

AFTER WINCHESTER, WE were now out in the big, wide world. In fact, one had moved from one institution to another – from school to the Army. The guardians and the mentors might have changed, but guardians and mentors the Army had too.

I went down to Caterham on 8 April 1948. Michael Thornton, my old friend from Winchester days, joined up with me in the Coldstream Guards. We were part of the Brigade Squad, a squad of young men who were supposed to become officers if they passed all the tests.

I remember my father telling me, when I was seventeen, that one would retain hardly any friends, possibly one, from one's prep school days, and only about three friends from one's public school days. The majority of one's lifelong friends, he said, would be from the friendships which one made at university – and with that can be included National Service. He was right. I found this to be almost unbelievable at the time and bound to be wrong in my case, as I had so many friends at Winchester, but my father was right.

Many of my friends from Caterham days were old Etonians. I commented upon the fact years later to one of them, Tony Lloyd, who subsequently ended up with the distinction of becoming a Law Lord, saying that however one used to complain about Eton, it did in fact produce wonderful people. He replied with modesty 'Yes, but remember the old Etonians whom you met at Caterham were the very best. They are not all like that.' It corresponds with what my father used to say, 'Eton produces the very best and the very worst. Winchester produces consistently a very

Ensign in the Coldstream Guards

high level. It will never produce the very best. But it will never produce the very worst either.'

Michael Thornton and I did not know many others – but we soon did. Many of them became my best friends all the way through life. Tony Lloyd, Jock Lane, Jan Collins, Hugh Currie, Patrick Mitchell, Jack Stewart-Clark, David Nixon to name just a few. They all enjoyed different careers after the Army and many were successful and made a public impact on the life of the nation. It was fun.

We have always had a reunion every ten years since we left Caterham reminding us of the date on which we all went there. About twelve of us were involved. After thirty years one was a Dean (Patrick Mitchell, of Wells) one was a judge (Tony Lloyd) and one was an Archbishop (Nicky Bowen, Roman Catholic Archbishop of Southwark).

Caterham was three months of being drilled and being made ship-shape (if that is not too much of a naval expression in an army context). We had a superb Sergeant in charge of us, Sergeant O'Brien of the Irish Guards. He was just so unbelievably smart that one could only try to emulate him – not very successfully. Although he could be tough, he was also kind and understanding.

I shall never forget his riposte one day, after our squad had been inspected by Alan Pemberton, then a Captain and later the Adjutant of the 2nd Battalion in Malaya and afterwards a Lieutenant Colonel. Alan Pemberton must have had a bad night because he found fault with all of us – every one – when he inspected us. He then told Sergeant O'Brien in front of the squad that the squad was very badly turned out and that Sergeant O'Brien should feel ashamed. When Alan Pemberton had left, Sergeant O'Brien turned to us and just said, 'Thank you.' It is funny how a few words can speak volumes. They did, and we all felt so ashamed both of ourselves and for him.

The person who was directly responsible for our squad was Guardsman Curley. Although he was only a guardsman, at Caterham his superiority was conveyed to him by him being called Trained Soldier. It was 'Yes, Trained Soldier,' 'No, Trained Soldier,' and he was referred to as Trained Soldier Curley. He was also in the Irish Guards.

He was bog Irish, a rough character who had had the raw edges worn off him by the military discipline of the Brigade of Guards. His language was pretty basic, with every description – and almost every word – being pre-empted by the adjective f…

On one occasion, when we were all sitting on our beds in the evening cleaning our kit – this went on for four hours every evening – Trained Soldier Curley entered the barrack room and, in order to convey the fact that something had gone wrong, or merely just to shock the poor little molly-coddled boys, he stood still in the middle of the barrack room which he had just entered and, with considerable emphasis, spat out the expletive 'f…'. In order to emphasise the real horror of the matter which was worrying him, as if his expression had not adequately conveyed its enormity, he added 'Double f…'. It is odd how that further emphasis was supposed either to have sorted out his frustration or to have resolved his problem.

There were many stories told of how fiercely 'regimental' some of the Non-Commissioned Officers were. One was walking around Caterham Camp on a Saturday afternoon with his wife and daughter. An officer came walking towards them in the opposite direction. As they passed, he was reputed to have given the order 'Wife and Child, eyes right.'

Another Sergeant in charge of the Guard Room answered the telephone to find that there was an officer on the other end. He promptly saluted the telephone and gave the order 'Guard Room shun.'

On one occasion, Michael Thornton, Stan Howard and I were walking back from the NAAFI with a supply of cakes and biscuits in our hands. An officer and a Sergeant appeared from around a corner and we all saluted. Stan, though, had too many biscuits in his right hand and so he saluted with his left hand, hoping to get away with it. The two passed us, but there was obviously something wrong, and the Sergeant eventually fluffed to what it was. He turned round and bellowed 'Come 'ere, you'. Michael and I waited in silent contentment as a torrent of abuse was passed on to the wretched Stan.

In August of 1948, after three months of being drilled – in all ways, mentally, emotionally and physically – to become reasonable military representatives of our various regiments, we left and went to the OCTU (Officer Cadet Training Unit) at Eaton Hall outside Chester.

It was a colossal house owned by the Duke of Westminster and not a very pretty one either. It has since been pulled down, too, and replaced by another – which I gather is even less pretty, even though it may be more convenient. I gather that that has now been pulled down and replaced by yet another. The main attraction, which we did not realise at the time, was that there was a huge picture hanging in the hall, which used to be the recipient of fairly harmless paper darts and other missiles which were thrown at it by young officer cadets.

The picture was subsequently sold for the then colossal price of £250,000. It was the *Adoration of the Magi* by Rubens, now worth millions of pounds and hanging under intricate protection beyond the altar at the east end of King's College Chapel in Cambridge. It is horrifying, in retrospect, to find how little that we or 'they' knew about this magnificent painting and that this masterpiece should have been subjected to such cavalier treatment.

When we were at Eaton Hall, we sometimes would ask one of our colleagues if he would do our guard duty for us over the weekend if we wished to go away when we had been drafted for guard duty. The going rate was ten shillings for the weekend. One of our number, Patrick Mitchell, was wonderfully tall, lanky, most unmilitary, but an excruciatingly funny person both in himself and as a mimic. He reckoned that he was going to go into the Church. Whether it was that or his genuinely generous character (and I fancy that it was that) he used to do your guard duty for nothing. He subsequently became Dean of Wells and, later, Dean of Windsor.

I am sure that there were several cinemas in Chester, but the only one worth going to was the Tatler. It used to have, if not pretty, certainly very sexy, usherettes who would, if you were lucky, come and sit next to you and chat you up provided that you had a seat near the aisle at the back. This was considered, and was, quite exciting. One always sat at the back and near the aisle!

Towards the end of one's time at OCTU we had to go to Devon to a battle camp when live ammunition was used. This was the apex of one's time at OCTU. We arrived at Okehampton by train one evening in November. It was foggy – deeply foggy. We all got into three-ton trucks to be driven to the camp. So great was the incline that I do not think that our vehicle moved out of second gear for the whole of the journey. When we woke up next morning, we could not see beyond ten yards. It was thick, thick fog.

Using live ammunition for the first time was quite an excitement and, when you were lying down giving covering fire, one tended to aim at something just to see if you could hit it. A concrete pill box, which happened to be near at hand, was a nice easy target, big and robust, and it was much more sport to hear the bullet ricochet off it in a typical whiney whistle. This was fun. We did it again and again, until the officer in charge said, in a remarkably la-di-da accent, 'Don't fire at the stones.' A minute later there was another whistling scream and the old Sergeant next to me said 'Cor. That f...er hit a stone!'

At the end of each day at Okehampton, after we had been out on the moors doing exercises with live ammunition – bullets, mortars, hand grenades and so forth – we were inspected and had to hand in any unexploded live ammunition left over.

One of the drills was to Port Arms – which meant that, whilst standing up, you threw your rifle against your chest with the muzzle pointing up in the air, and pulled the bolt back and forth six times in order to remove any unused bullets from the rifle and the magazine. You then pulled the trigger. This became an automatic and somewhat boring rigmarole until, on one occasion, some dozy character had not done it properly. He had not ensured that the rifle was properly empty, and pulled the trigger. Well, there was the most appalling bang, and the poor fellow who was standing in the line next to the dozy character found a bullet whistling past his nose at great speed and a very short distance away from him. They were both quietly shaken but, fortunately, no damage was done. As usual, the rest of us found it very funny.

One day, for some remarkable reason, when we were being inspected on our return from the moors, one smoke bomb had escaped the vigilant eye of the inspecting Sergeant. David Tate, who was one of our officer cadets, was in the Irish Guards – impish, jolly, with an infectious laugh but totally and charmingly irresponsible – got hold of this smoke bomb and went through our Nissen Hut knocking it on the head against the end of each bed as he passed by. This seemed to me to be a completely crazy thing to do and I was glad when he had completed the ceremony at the end of my bed and had passed on to the next one. Having hyped us all up to wonder what on earth was going to happen next, David said 'What are we going to do with the smoke bomb now? We cannot keep it. Let's throw it in to the next door Nissen Hut and smoke them all out of it! That will be good fun,' and roared with laughter. He reacted neither to persuasion nor to reason. Common sense did not even enter the frame.

The next thing that we knew was that the inside of the next door Nissen Hut was thick – thick – with smoke. It seemed like an impenetrable fog. Grey, huddled figures were seen rushing around like shadows trying to escape. We all thought that this was excruciatingly funny, until it transpired that the particular Nissen Hut into which the bomb had been thrown did not contain our friends, but it housed the Headquarter Company – all the old soldiers who were supposed to be teaching us and looking after us. They found nothing whatsoever funny about this. They all rushed into our hut to see us all, like little angels, polishing our boots.

They were furious. After combing the barrack room and questioning everyone, David Tate was duly found to be the perpetrator and was put under Close Arrest.

When he came up in front of the Company Commander for punishment the next day, I was one of the two 'Escorts to the Prisoner'. Michael Thornton was the other. David had to be hatless between Michael and me and we were marched in and out of the Guard Room and company office at a rate of knots – as if we were in the Rifle Brigade. We two escorts felt slightly smug, because we had enjoyed all the fun, yet there we were being totally responsible, 'guarding the prisoner', and watching poor David get what was coming to him. I cannot remember what the sentence was, but it was nothing too alarming.

When we left Eaton Hall, as young subalterns, Michael Thornton and I were due, with some others, to go to Malaya on, I think, 18 December. It was in a troopship called the *Dunera*, and it took four weeks to get to Singapore. Nowadays, it takes thirteen hours by aeroplane to go to Singapore and everyone says what a long journey it is.

But, before we went, a very important thing happened.

At home, we had got up a party to go to the Meynell Hunt Ball. It was always a very grand occasion with all the girls dressed up to the nines and all the older ladies looking very elegant. It was held that year at Kedelston Hall, the home of Lord Scarsdale.

My father and I went over to have lunch with Tony and Peter Lothian at Melbourne Hall, some three miles away from Staunton Harold. After lunch Tony said to me, 'Robin, will you be terribly kind? We have got up a party to go to the Meynell Hunt Ball too, and my sister, Annabel, is coming to stay for it. But everyone else is much older and I am frightened that Annabel will be bored stiff. Would you be terribly kind and dance with Annabel? ...' *Be kind and dance with Annabel?* To be *asked* to dance with her – this glorious girl aged eighteen. In my books, it was like being asked to dance with the Archangel Gabriel.

On our return home, my father said how delightful and charming Tony and Peter were. 'If there were only more people in the world like those two, what a lovely world it would be.' What a glorious thing to have said about one.

There, at the Hunt Ball, was this unbelievably beautiful girl, with a lovely, gentle, smiling face and a staggering figure, dressed in a bright red off-the-shoulder, flowing dress. And it was my 'duty' to dance with her. I just simply could not believe my luck! I made the best of every bit of it until Johnny Kerr, Peter's brother, came and broke it up by saying that Tony had got an attack of asthma so they were all going home. I minded that greatly. I did not realise, until years later, that Annabel minded that greatly too. And neither of us realised, or could have thought, or could have ever expected, that, within three years, we would be married.

When Annabel used to come to stay with Tony and Peter at Melbourne and I was at Staunton, we used to meet, either prearranged or by lunching. There were no mobile telephones or texting. They wouldn't have been any good because I don't understand them anyhow. Annabel used to say that she was 'going out for a walk'. I used to take a gun and say that I was going to try and find a rabbit. This thrilled my father no end as he was always conscious that I tended to hang around in the afternoons and do nothing. What are you going to do? Cut some trees down? Have a bonfire? Go for a walk? Do some gardening? *Anything*. And here was I going out to shoot a rabbit without being pressurised from anyone. Whatever next?

Little did he – or anyone else – realise that I was going to walk quite a distance – I hated walking – to Spring Wood, and meet Annabel who had walked over from Melbourne.

We sat on logs and wandered through the woods and talked and had a lovely time. We really loved it. It was dead romantic. No one seemed particularly surprised when I returned without any rabbits.

Chapter 8

Malaya

I WOULD NOT have missed my spell in Malaya for anything, although I did not enjoy it much at the time. I was not much good at it. I was always getting lost with my platoon in the jungle. I hated those long marches, with one's feet preferably in a stream to keep cool, and I was always terrified of meeting a bandit which, after all, was the main purpose of being there. I was always rather frightened, too, by one's brother officers in the Mess. They all seemed so confident and so knowledgeable and so efficient, and to this long, lanky, inexperienced young subaltern it all seemed a bit daunting. But the year there did me a power of good, as it did most other young national servicemen.

You were made to grow up, and one of the huge advantages of those National Service days compared to the 'gap' year which children nowadays have between leaving school and going to university, is that you had a job to do. You were paid for it. You were responsible *for* others and you were responsible *to* others, and others were responsible both *for* you and *to* you. Too often nowadays the attitude is, 'there is a lump sum of money, go off and enjoy yourself wherever you may wish to go, and come back in nine months' time.' I think that that is bad, on principle. It is rather like saying, 'you have had a tough time at school and now you deserve a rest. Go and have a holiday – and get lost for a while.'

Whilst the reasons for all this are very understandable and well-meaning, there is an aura of selfishness about it – *my* holiday, *my* break, *my* gap year, what shall *I* do? With National Service, you weren't given too many choices. You were told what to do and where to go and, to get on with it. Your conduct and performance were watched and scrutinised. The services also had that perfunctory ability of making people do what they did not want to do.

I always thought that one of the best examples of that was in a war film about the Welsh guards called *They died with their boots clean*. All the soldiers were piling on to the beach at Dunkirk hoping to be rescued by that remarkable flotilla of boats from England when some German fighter aircraft appeared and strafed the beaches randomly, killing the waiting soldiers all over the place. One young soldier, understandably terrified, bleated out, 'I don't want to die. I don't want to die,' to which the Sergeant replied, 'Well you might bloody well have to.'

Whether that was true or apocryphal is irrelevant. I merely remember it in the film not just as a typical old-soldier remark, but also because it encapsulated so much of the peculiarities and, in some way the advantages, of service life – you bloody well had to do things which you often did not want to do. Fortunately, that was not always being shot at or dying.

You see it so often when people plan their lives too well. First, we will live together. Then we will get a mortgage. Then we may get married if we find that we get on alright. Wife – or girlfriend – meanwhile goes on the pill so that she can earn more money and get stuck into her career. Then they decide to have a baby. Then, later a boat or another house and then another baby. Somehow, it seems all too structured and self-orientated. It frequently does people a great deal of good when a proverbial RSJ gets thrown into the wheels of the bicycle and the machine comes to a grinding halt. Then you have, unwittingly and unwillingly, to go on a course dictated by events or by others as opposed to one of your own making.

In December 1948 we were all set to go to Malaya. When we were concluding our time at Eaton Hall, we had to say which battalion of our regiment we would like to join. Michael Thornton and I said the Second Battalion of the Coldstream Guards because they were going to Jamaica and we thought that that sounded fun. In fact, the plans were changed. The Second Battalion never went to Jamaica but was sent off to Malaya instead to help to fight the war against the bandits – the

Ensign in the Coldstream Guards in Malaya 1949

Communist Terrorists – in the jungles in Malaya. That was a very different kettle of fish.

We left Southampton for Singapore and Malaya on 18 December on the troopship *Dunera*. It was an old wartime ship doing its last tour of duty before being scrapped. My immediate friends on the ship were Michael Thornton, Hugh Currie, Stan Howard, Paul Graham-Watson (who was in the Scots Guards and who was later shot in a tragic error by one of his own men in Malaya) and Pat Bunning, who later became a distinguished professor in Nigeria.

We arrived in Malta on Christmas Eve, and I shall never forget the magical sight of coming into Valetta harbour and seeing all the Christmas lights, and the lights of all the cars twinkling away, and hearing the sound of carols from the churches wafting across the water. It was quite an ethereal experience.

It took four weeks to get from England to Singapore. At Singapore, four of us had tea in Raffles – a must – and then we went by train to Tapah. It was a pretty rickety railway and the engines were fuelled by wood. As there had to be a sentry standing on the outside of the carriages, where one carriage joined another, one had to be careful to avoid the lighted sparks from the engine landing on one's clothes and burning a hole in them – which, of course, they did.

There was a bullet-hole in the window of my carriage, just to remind us that this was not a holiday jaunt. I remember Captain Dagger, who had come from Tapah to be in charge of us, saying 'If anything happens and the enemy starts to interfere with us, give them everything you have got.' It put the wind up me.

On our arrival at Tapah Road where the station was, we were taken to Tapah, a small village about forty miles north of Kuala Lumpur. That is where our battalion was situated – on a site outside the village. We were all under canvas. There were only about three wooden buildings, the Officers' Mess, the Sergeants' Mess and the cookhouse, in the whole camp. There was, of course, no air conditioning, only fans going round in the ceiling like propellers. The weather was always thunderously hot and humid – but this was Malaya.

I shared a tent with Hugh Currie, another vast young officer. He was about 6ft 4in compared with my 6ft 6in. He was the most convivial of tent-sharers. On one occasion he was trying to get ready for dinner, black tie order without jackets. His shoelaces had got tied in a knot, and such was the heat and the humidity that the poor man was sitting on the edge of his bed in a total muck-sweat trying to get the laces untied and then properly tied.

I admired him enormously for many reasons, but especially for one. He did not like alcohol, so he did not drink any. To have gone through twelve months in Malaya in the Officers' Messes and in the Sergeants' Messes saying, 'Orange squash please,' showed huge strength of character. The inevitable happened on Christmas Eve when we were in the Sergeants' Mess and, after six orange squashes, and a lot of persuading, Hugh gave in and had a glass of beer. Some Sergeant then charmingly laced it with a couple of double whiskies. Hell, that fixed him! When he got back to the tent and lay on his bed he was completely garrulous, which went on and on. I went to sleep, but Hugh was still at it!

When we used to talk of girls, which was a perfectly natural thing to do, I remember telling Hugh that, if the Almighty were to come down and carve a statue of the most beautiful girl in the world, the result would be Annabel Carr.

Tapah was otherwise best known as being the bottom end of the road to the Cameron Highlands, a lovely hill station where the weather was cooler and you had fires at night. The road to the Cameron Highlands, though, was very dangerous. It was thirty miles long, narrow and very windy, and, of course, it was uphill (unless you were coming down, when, of course, it was downhill!). The bandits would fell a tree so that it would fall across the road. An unsuspecting car would come round the corner, find that it had to stop and then all hell was let loose. The bandits would open fire and kill everyone.

The army's answer to this was to have a convoy in both directions– at 11.00 in the morning and 3.00 in the afternoon. One convoy started at Tapah and went to the Cameron Highlands. The other started at the Cameron Highlands and came down to Tapah. Anyone – private car, lorry or businessman – could join this, with the military in the front and at the rear to give protection. It worked well. The road has been much improved since then. It is much wider and less twisty, and not dangerous.

My company was sent on detachment to the Cameron Highlands under Maggie Gibbs, a Major who was our Company Commander. He was a kind, quiet person, with a gift for things artistic, and he did not seem to me to be at all a natural soldier, although he was certainly a very popular one. He was a delight and he had a goose which he insisted should be properly attired and should wear a Coldstream Star which the poor animal had to have attached around its neck. It looked very smart.

John Riley was the swash-buckling second-in-command, whom one would be prepared to follow anywhere. He later left the Army and went back to his native Jersey where he became a Big Cheese running, amongst other things, the television company.

Peter Stewart-Richardson, who was always called Scrubber and now lives not far from us in Norfolk, was a Captain and I found him quite terrifying. It was my first day in the Cameron Highlands and I was being

driven by Corporal Bodell in a jeep up the drive to Buckit Lowick, the
Officers' Mess, when Scrubber, whom I had not met before, was standing in the drive swinging his pistol around and ordering us to stop. He
looked at me. 'Get out. Get into the back.' End of conversation. I did
what I was told. No conversation.

I sat next to him at dinner. Whilst laughing and joking with the other
officers, he said nothing to me, the new boy. No conversation. Three
quarters of the way through dinner, he turned to me. 'When are you
leaving?' – not the most welcoming of questions to a person who had
only just arrived. In fact, so miserable did Scrubber make me feel that I
had to confide my disquiet to the Regimental Padre, Beverley Coleman,
who was there too. He told me not to worry. 'It is just Scrubber. He is
like that.' I subsequently got to know and to like him – but I always
watched my Ps and Qs in his presence.

It was in the Cameron Highlands that we were visited by Brigadier
Erskine. He happened to be a friend of my Uncle Andrew's. I thought
that he was very senior and very old – but I suppose that he was probably
only forty-four. He was later killed when an aircraft in which he was
flying crashed into the jungle. I was detailed by Maggie Gibbs to be in
charge of the drinks before lunch.

'What would you like to drink, sir?' I asked the Brigadier. The dreaded
answer came: 'Pink Gin please.' I did not know how to make a pink
gin. I had never done it before. I put the gin in the glass. That was easy
enough, but I could not get the pink out of the bottle of angostura
bitters. It would only come in drops. After endlessly shaking the bottle,
I removed the cork and poured the stuff in. There must have been a
half inch layer on the top of the gin. I gave it to the Brigadier. He said
nothing. But he did not drink it.

The main haunt of the Cameron Highlands was the Smoke House
Inn. It was a lovely old English type of inn run by Margaret and Frank
Walker, who were interned by the Japanese during the War. Their friend,
an old lady called Hutch, was always there too. They were real relicts
of the old colonial days – charming and fun. It was always good to go
down to the Smoke House Inn to have a drink in the evening. There
was usually a jolly company of people, usually Coldstream officers, but

others, too. If you stayed to dinner the food was always quite excellent. But I dreaded the monthly bills. It was not cheap.

When we were in the Army in Malaya, operations in the jungle were usually for the day but, as time went on, they were extended for two or three days and occasionally for a week. But then there would have to be air-drops to supply the soldiers with more food and sometimes clothes. This was always an excitement as a clearing had to be made in the jungle, an 'X' laid out and this information relayed back in the hope that the aeroplane would find the dropping zones.

There were hardly any helicopters in those days in Malaya and the air-drops were usually done by Dakotas. The dropping was not all that accurate. Dakotas – DC3s – were a relic of the war. They were very slow and they climbed very slowly too. This meant that the pilot had to be quite sure that he could get himself out of any valley or low place into which he had got himself. They usually did.

There is hardly any jungle left in Malaysia now but, in those days, most of the map was white – uncharted. There were two roads, one which went up on the west coast of Malaya and one which went up on the east coast. Outside these areas, you were on your own. The rivers were usually well mapped and, on patrol in the jungle, one relied on the rivers – not just for accuracy of mapping but also for keeping cool. Walking with a rifle and all your kit on your back in the steamy heat of the jungle made you perspire profusely but keeping one's feet in the water acted like the radiator of a car. The blood in the feet cooled down. The cold blood circulated through the body. And the body remained cool. The fact that you were walking about with soaking wet boots and socks on did not seem to matter at all.

My memories of Malaya in those days were a country covered in jungle. It was always hot and always steamy. The sun would shine in a beautiful clear blue sky which, in England, would be the omen for a perfect day. But between 2 p.m. and 4 p.m. the heavens would open and the unwary got soaked to the skin.

There was still the post-colonial atmosphere – lots of British expatriots, rubber planters, tin miners, representatives of large companies like Shell, soldiers and Malayan Police Officers. They made their own entertainment of cocktail parties and dinners, where 'stingers' (whisky and soda) played a prominent part. Most reasonable-sized towns had a Honki-Tonk which is where you could go and dance. You would buy a book of tickets and dance with the girl of your fancy in exchange for a ticket.

The girls would sit in a row on either side of the room waiting for someone to ask them to dance and give them a ticket. It seemed to work quite well. It was said that the girls on one side 'did' and the girls on the other side 'didn't' – but no one seemed to know whether that was true and, if it was, no one seemed to know which side did what and when, and whether the other side did or did not do that which the other did or did not do. We never found out! It was good clean fun – at least I think that it was. Certainly it was a way to brighten up a dull evening.

Malaya was expensive, and I was always sailing very close to the wind with my bank account, even though I did not spend very much. I thought that the only thing which I could do was to write to my father and ask him if he would be kind enough to help me out a bit.

The Commanding Officer was Lt Col Victor Fitz-George Balfour – an upright and imposing man, whom I held in great respect. He said, 'I had a letter from your father this morning,' – Help – I didn't think that that would happen – 'saying that you were feeling pushed for cash. I think that he wanted to know that you were not behaving frivolously. I shall have to reply to him. I promise that I will not cart you.' It was a lovely expression. I thought that that was such a kind and understanding thing to say.

Some twenty-five years later, I met Lt Colonel Victor, who by then was General Sir Victor Fitz-George Balfour and who was twice as frightening, on a bus in London. He said, 'Come and sit down here, Robin, and tell me what you are doing.' I said that we were moving our house in the country and our flat in London within six weeks of each other. He replied in the most devastating way, 'Robin, have you forgotten the elementary military principle – always keep one foot on the ground at any one time?'

I have never forgotten that. He was just so right. We thought that we were being crisp, decisive and tidy. Actually we were making a great big mistake.

— TO —

Lt. Col. R.G.V. Fitz-George-Balfour,
COMMANDER OF THE BRITISH EMPIRE, MILITARY CROSS

and Officers and Other Ranks
of the 2nd Battalion Coldstream Guards.

GENTLEMEN,

WE, the Chinese community of Batang Padang, Tapah, beg leave to tender you our sincere thanks for protecting us from the terrorists and to express our regret at your impending departure.

Though we have known you for only two years we have learnt to admire your courage, exemplary conduct and, not the least, your true sense of sportsmanship on and off the playing field.

You have upheld the highest traditions of your famed three-hundred-year-old Regiment in the manner you have fought this "Anti-Bandit War" for us. We, as members of the civilian population, owe you all a debt of gratitude for coming all the way from your homeland in your effort to restore peace and prosperity to Malaya.

We wish you Godspeed.

Yours very sincerely,

LIM CHENG CHUAN,
FOR AND ON BEHALF OF
THE CHINESE COMMUNITY, BATANG PADANG.

Tapah, 23rd July, 1950.

Letter from the Chinese community thanking the Coldstream Guards
for their work in Malaya

One evening, out in the jungle on patrol with my platoon, we were going through a swamp. It went on and on, and it was getting dark. We could find no dry land. So I said that we would have to stop there and sleep in the swamp. My wonderful platoon Sergeant, Sergeant Barber, came up to me and said that the men did not feel too happy about going to sleep in the swamp. I was not surprised. Nor did I. But I said that I could not see how we could get out of it. 'I think that if we go this way, we may be able to find some dry ground,' he said. So we moved on. And we did. The relief! We spent the night in a Chinese hut – a basha. We had sentries posted to look out for any bandits coming in the long grass, or lallang as it was called.

I went to sleep, like everyone else exhausted, and I was woken up by a sentry to be told that there were noises in the lallang and that people were approaching. Everyone was woken and we 'stood to' looking for who was where. It was a very dim light. In the middle of the night, in a dim light with the noises of the jungle round about you, your imagination goes into overdrive and your eyes play tricks upon you – and not very nice ones, either. We went forward in a line to try and flush out the person. I could swear that I saw someone in the lallang, but there was no one there. I found that spooky.

Years later, a new doorkeeper in the House of Lords was helping me on with my overcoat. He said, 'When you have a bit of time, can I brew up a cup of tea?' I looked at him in the face, now bereft of a fiercely intimidating bushy moustache, and it was Sergeant Barber. I was so pleased to see him. One day he said to me, 'You remember that time when we all stood to because of the bandits when we were sleeping in the Chinese hut?' 'Yes,' I replied, 'I remember it well.' 'Well, it wasn't a man. It was a pig.' To this day I still think it was a person. Sergeant Barber would have none of it.

Sergeant Barber was always a particular friend in the House of Lords. It is funny how these experiences which you share when you are young – I was nineteen, he must have been twenty-five (but to me he felt like forty) – bring you together forever. He came to Hedenham to help with Angela's wedding, together with another Coldstream doorkeeper, Kirk, and Red Coat. Red Coat is the name of the doorkeeper who stands outside the Peers' Entrance with, as his name implies, a red coat on and a very smart top-hat with gold band. They were all dressed in their House of Lords uniform and they looked magnificent. They certainly added stature, and even grandeur, to the occasion.

On one occasion we had some people to dinner in our flat at 65 Warwick Square. I spilled the gravy on my shoe. It completely took the shine off it. Nothing that I did would get it back (I cannot think what it did to our stomachs). The shoes were virtually useless, as one cannot wear a pair of shoes with one toe-cap shiny and the other one dull. When in the House of Lords, I asked Mr Barber what to do. 'Bring the shoes here and give them to me.' I did.

Some ten days later I saw Mr Barber walking down the corridor in the House of Lords looking very odd with an awkward lilt from side to side like a duck, his hand behind his back and his tail coat sticking out. 'You are walking in a very funny way, Mr Barber. What is the matter?' I asked. He withdrew his hand from behind his tail coat and there was my shoe, with its toe-cap shining brightly. 'Your shoes, my Lord.'

The doorkeepers in the House of Lords are a magnificent breed of people. They are usually ex-Warrant Officers from the services. They have a wonderfully disciplined and courteous approach to life having spent years of their life in positions of authority bossing people about, yet being bossed about too. They have an instinctive knowledge of what is right and what is wrong and how to behave. They bring lustre, methodology and distinction to the House of Lords with their smart tailcoats and the gold badge hanging on a chain.

The doorkeepers come under Black Rod, whose proper title is Gentleman Usher of the Black Rod and whose assistant is the Yeoman Usher of the Black Rod. They are always senior retired officers from the services – Generals, Admirals, Air Marshals. The services used to take it in turns to provide the next Black Rod, but it has become a little less regular of late.

Chapter 9

London

I was in Malaya for twelve months and returned to England in January 1950.

When I had left Winchester, I applied to go to New College, Oxford. New College was built on the lines of Winchester College and various members of my family had been there, so it seemed a natural and consequential move. A lot of Wykehamists also went to New College. I went up for an interview, but I was turned down. That was quite a blow, but I was never a great intellectual and so I suppose that it was understandable.

I therefore applied to go to Magdalene College, Cambridge because my uncle – my mother's brother, Marmaduke Morley, who had been killed in the First War – had been there. The idea of going to Cambridge, when one had always been 'pro' Oxford, took a bit of readjustment but, amongst the pile of letters waiting for me at home on my return from Malaya in January 1950, was one Magdalene offering me a place in the autumn. Things sometimes happened like that in those days. I had never been for an interview. I had never taken an exam, but I was invited to be an undergraduate. It was a great excitement and a great privilege.

My father thought that, before going to Cambridge to read Agriculture, I ought to brush up on my science by going to Loughborough College in the intervening months. I was not too keen on that.

On my return from Malaya, my parents decided to have a welcome home house party in Staunton Harold. We had been living in the parsonage since 1940, when the military took over Staunton Harold, but my father retained three rooms at Staunton: the Hall, the Dining Room and his study. Some of the locals were asked to the party including Tony and Peter Lothian. Tony telephoned to say that she had her sister, Annabel, staying and could she bring her, too.

So, the glorious Annabel was to come to the party? She did, aged nineteen. She looked wonderful. I was overwhelmed by her – her gloriousness and her modesty. I even plucked up courage and asked if she would like to come to the theatre with me in London. I had never asked a girl to come to the theatre before – and so this really was growing up. I had never seen *Oklahoma*, which had hit the high-spots in London, and I knew that Annabel would have seen it. But, no, she had not. She said that she would love to come with me, but she would have to ask Tony first who was her half-sister and her sort of mentor. Fortunately, Tony said yes.

We went to see *Oklahoma* and I had booked a table at the only reasonable restaurant that I had heard of. I did not know any restaurants in London. I had never been to one and I certainly had never taken a girl to one, but Michael Thornton was my guide. 'Go to the Caprice. It is behind the Ritz and sometimes it has actors and actresses there. It is quite smart, and it is quite expensive!' I had no other choice. So the Caprice it was. I did not realise that it was enormously smart. Nenella, Annabel's mother, was in Norfolk at the time and she wrote a letter to Annabel and very touchingly said, 'Don't let Robin spend too much money on you. I don't that think that he has very much.' That was such a kind thought.

So started a wonderful romance which has continued for the rest of our lives. As Annabel was going to spend a second season in London, I wanted to be in London, too. Dopey – the ex Miss Mason – who was now my father's secretary suggested, first to me and then to my father, that, instead of going to Loughborough College I might go to work in my father's old firm of stockbrokers in London, George Henderson. Wonderful idea. Daddy thought that that was a brilliant idea, too. So off I went to London to get a taste of City Life and a taste of Social Life. Annabel and I spent three idyllic months in London. It was enormous fun, and I never regret a minute of it. I had a bed-sitter at 9, Clivedon

Place, just off Sloane Square. Aneurin Bevan lived opposite, not that that made much difference, other than curiosity.

One day Annabel and I arranged to meet at the Grandstand in Hyde Park. 'Open your diary,' she said. 'I have got you asked to this dance on Tuesday, that cocktail party on Thursday, that dance on Monday' – and so it went on. White tie and tails every night and the girls in beautiful long evening dresses. Annabel had the most beautiful dresses of all, and was by far the prettiest girl of them all. She was just stunning. I fortunately managed to see off any prospective predators who were hovering around like bees around a honeypot. I think that they realised that they had not got much of a chance of a look in.

A dance was not a proper dance without Tommy Kinsman. He played everywhere – the Hyde Park Hotel, Claridges, 6 Stanhope Gate, 23 Knightsbridge, Londonderry House. He had a wonderful drummer, and his pianist, Jack Barker, played without ever seeming to look at the music. Unfortunately, Jack Barker then set up on his own, and this ended a happy and musically perfect arrangement with Tommy Kinsman. With either band, when Annabel and I went onto the dance floor, they always changed the music to the Harry Lime theme, which was our favourite tune and for which we had always asked. But they still played it even on the occasion when we hadn't put in a special request.

We really saw the last of the great days. A mother of a debutante, whom one probably did not even know personally, would ask one to a dinner party of twelve or so, usually in their own house, and then we went on to the dance. It was a must – an invariable must – to dance with the girl who had sat next to you at dinner on your right, the girl on your left and the hostess. Thereafter you could dance with whom you liked.

It used to end up with me doing my 'duty' dances and then spending the rest of the evening dancing with Annabel. It was a good system. Everyone got a look-in and no one was left high and dry – anyhow to start with. Now no such courtesies seem to apply. Annabel and I had a dinner party before a dance many years later after we were married and when we were living at Hedenham Hall, and I asked a friend of mine who had been at Winchester with me to come to the dinner. He sat next to Annabel during dinner, but he did not dance with her or with the other girls next to whom he sat, or with any other girl in the party. I thought that that was downright rude.

At the Debs' dance you used to see about seventy per cent of the same people each evening. But that was fun. Many of them became great friends. Some remained acquaintances. Some people rather snootily said that it was a marriage market. It was not, really. It was a lot of young people coming together from all different parts of the country, meeting and getting to know others, and making friends which they would never otherwise have been able to make. It was also done in very convivial circumstances.

Of course, some people got married. But that was not the prime purpose of it. It was to widen your circle of friends. All I know is that we both enjoyed it, and all the many friends which we made, enormously. It was a lovely and happy time and we felt so privileged to have been able to do it and to have been part of it.

I often feel that subsequent generations have missed out by not having 'the season' as part of their life. In those days, there was very little sexual licence amongst those who took part. There was no pill and the girls were understandably scared stiff of getting pregnant, the consequences of which, should it happen, were dire and the disgrace catastrophic. You could count on the fingers of one hand those who 'did' and they were not respected. The result was that most of the girls were virgins. They often got married young – in their early twenties – and had their babies when they were young. Annabel has always said that the right time for child-bearing is in your twenties. It is natural. You are young. You have energy. You are young with your children – and, if you are lucky – with your grandchildren, too.

Nowadays, people are obsessed with work and with the income from it. They have few opportunities to meet others. The pill is rampant, so you can get what you want without being married. There is not the slur of bedding – or being bedded – before marriage. Rather the reverse, when you lose your virginity, whether a boy or a girl, it seems to be a matter of pride and of interest about which you happily talk about to others. No shame. People often live together before being married, which makes the act of marriage and a white dress seem slightly out of context. The age of marriage has become higher. Babies are born to older mothers, increasing the difficulties of child-bearing and increasing the difficulties which age makes of looking after them.

The fertility rate lowers when you are in your thirties, making people resort more to *in vitro* fertilisation, and to all the pressures and complexities which that brings.

It is not surprising, therefore – if pathetic – that nowadays people of both sexes resort to putting advertisements in the paper for someone with whom they might wish to spend the rest of their life – even a man seeking a man or a woman seeking a woman. It is just unbelievable, and I cannot believe that people are happier with the society this has produced. We were just so much luckier. The pressures were there, but they were different. They were not nearly so great or so beastly.

Chapter 10
Magdalene College

I WENT UP to Magdalene College, Cambridge in October 1950. My father took me up to 'see me in'. I was to be in digs in 29 Thompson's Lane, which was run by a formidable but kind lady, Mrs Wortley. She gave us wonderful cooked breakfasts in our rooms. Her husband was also kind but rather pathetic – 'I am going to go on until I die'. As we entered Thompson's Lane, there was a huge billowing of blue smoke halfway down the street. As the smoke subsided, out emerged an old-fashioned bright yellow Mercedes Benz with cowling on the outside and a young man, Michael Parker, standing by it, all smiles – 'Just starting it up!' It came, as I found out later, and as did all Michael's motorised experiences, equipped with the statutory Blonde Girl.

I read Agriculture. It was fun, but hard work. In those days, Agriculture was important. It was after the war, and some food was still rationed. It was vital to increase the output of our home agriculture and to save on imports. It was an exciting time. Make the fields bigger. Drain them. Increase their yields. Mechanise. Increase the size of dairy herds. Agriculture as an industry was respected. So were the people who worked in it.

By comparison with today's prices, wages were very low. When we started to farm three years later in 1953, the agricultural wage was £5-13s-0d per week with overtime two shillings and ten pence per hour, and three shillings and two pence at the weekend (16p in today's money). Overtime at the weekend was so expensive that I did most of it myself. But a brand new Ferguson tractor could be bought for £500. Nowadays, the Agricultural wage is something like £300 per week.

To read Agriculture was, therefore, to do something useful and to prepare oneself for a vital industry. For some extraordinary reason, I had always wanted to farm. And there was Staunton, that 1,400 acre estate which had been in my family for 500 years, which I thought that I ought – and indeed should – try to look after. How different it all is now, when agriculture is despised and run down, and where the only thing that matters are the bees and the butterflies and 'wildlife', and everything has to be 'environmentally friendly'.

In the old days, when you had a delivery of lime for a field, you were sent a lime subsidy form which you completed. The subsidy came about three weeks later. Years later we moved to the Single Farm Payments Scheme where the forms are unbelievably complicated and they have to be accompanied by Digital Maps which are checked by a satellite. A friend of mine, in 2005, had a visit from two men from the 'Rural Payments Agency' (a really dreadful name). They spent four days checking the measurements of the hedges and ditches on the maps – and then gave him a sixty-page document to complete. That is after the government decided to install a wildly expensive computer, which was so badly designed that farmers were not paid.

The point is that in 'the old days' it all worked. Now it does not – and the expense and the bureaucracy behind it all is terrible and debilitating.

Agriculture at Cambridge was an important subject. It was taught within the impressive precincts of the School of Agriculture. There were about 120 of us in my year and some – the rather more intelligent and sensible – went on to read Estate Management, and it was all backed up, practically, by the University Farm.

But, in concert with the times, nowadays the Agriculture course no longer exists. Nor does Estate Management. And the University Farm has been sold. They have all been replaced by Rural Studies or some such bland name.

The great highlight for those of us doing Agriculture was in the middle of our first term. It was the Agriculture Ball, held in the dance room of G. P. Hawkins, above the Dot Café. Annabel and I went to it. It was that night – 17 November 1950, the night of the Agriculture Ball – that Annabel and I became unofficially engaged, in my room at 29 Thompson's Lane.

We would probably have to wait until I had left Cambridge, another two and a half years, before getting married, but we had 'an understanding'. That was the main thing. The next day we went to Boots and bought two small china dogs. They cost one shilling each. Annabel gave me one, and I gave her one. The idea was that they would sit on our respective mantelpieces and, one day, they would end up on the same mantelpiece together. They did. That was to be not two and a half years later, but nine months later.

My parents were slightly shell-shocked for the second time by their children – this time, by the idea of their son, a 21-year-old undergraduate, getting married. My mother, a deeply kind, caring and loving person, understood the passions and longings of love. My father was more practical. How can you get married when you have no job, no qualifications and no income? 'You have not even earned your boots and spurs yet' (a reference to my degree). If one had said, 'what's more, Dad, in six years' time we will have four children!' The mathematics just would have stacked up. I think that he would have collapsed. It is surprising, though, how, when presented with things in life, somehow one muddles through, and we did.

On top of it all, Annabel was a Roman Catholic. That just about put the boot in. My father and my mother loved Annabel. To start with, she was stunningly beautiful – my father once said 'Poor old Bob. I don't blame him. She is a proper little Madonna.' She was kind. She was gentle. And she was one of those people whom you can see just by looking was a lovely, 'good' person. But she was a Roman Catholic – and that presented problems.

Daddy had always said, in a manner which did not reflect his natural generosity, that he had three pet aversions in life: Nannies, Horsey people and Roman Catholics. As Annabel was a Roman Catholic and her father rode in the Olympic Games, she did not score too high in that league table.

Our family had always been Anglican – until, as Annabel once pointed out, before the Reformation when they were all Catholics. But what about the Chapel at Staunton, built by Sir Robert Shirley to the glory of the Church of England, only one of three to be built during the time of the Commonwealth? My mother was always a fairly high Anglican, my father a low one. He did not like incense, vestments and, as he called it, Hunting Pink. This all caused terrible unseen problems for us young things, like the rumbling of an earthquake.

It was my father's younger brother Andrew Shirley who, unbeknown to us, really saved the day. He had married someone, whom he did not love, 'out of duty' because a baby was on the way and later he was not able to divorce her. His life was made miserable. Bust-up marriages did not go down well in Society in those days and that brilliant scholar at Winchester ended up by selling books on the shop floor in Harrods. Uncle Andrew said to my father, 'Look what happened to me when I was unable to marry the person I wanted to. If they love each other, let them get married.'

So we did. Three cheers for Uncle Andrew.

It was Saturday 21 July 1951. Annabel looked unbelievably lovely. We were married in the Catholic Church in Bungay, which does not hold many people. A mixed marriage, in those days, was frowned upon by the Catholic Church – no flowers, no hymns, no music. But the old priest in Bungay, Father Chatterton, was a wonderful man. 'Oh, that is alright,' he said, 'have your flowers and have your music.' And we did, and that magnificent organist, Dr Sydney Watson, who was in charge of music at Winchester and who had, unknown to himself, inculcated in me my love of music and who was then at Eton, came and played the organ. We both felt so proud.

The Reception was at Annabel's parents' house at Ditchingham Hall. It was lovely, overlooking the lake. There was a large marquee on the lawn to contain not only those who came to the service, but the many people locally who, because of the size of the church, were asked to the Reception only.

My father had been unwell and was unable to come. My mother came on her own, and she and I spent the night before the wedding with the Turners. They were three unmarried brothers who had been in the services. One, Colonel Vic, was in the Rifle Brigade and had been awarded the Victoria Cross. Another, Brigadier Mark, was in the Royal Artillery and had been awarded the Military Cross. The third was Captain Cecil who had been in the Navy. He had no decorations so, in his family, he was nicknamed 'The Coward'. There was a fourth brother who was killed. He was also awarded the Victoria Cross – posthumously. The brothers lived together with their sister, Mil, unmarried. So, of the four brothers, two had Victoria Crosses, and one had a Military Cross. A pretty amazing record for a family.

They were great friends of Annabel's parents and they lived across the road from Ditchingham Hall at Ditchingham Cottage. They were in charge of what nowadays would be called the 'logistics' of the wedding – how many people were coming, how many cars and where to put them. In true military fashion, they even measured the seats in the church and calculated that each person would require so many 'bottom inches' of seat upon which to sit. They were also in charge of the champagne at the Reception. At one moment, Mark came up to Bill and said, 'They are drinking the champagne at a bottle a minute, and there are only thirty minutes of champagne left.' Annabel was peremptorily – and, not knowing the reasons, I thought rather early – sent off to change!

Annabel and I, then went off to the Wentworth Hotel in Aldeburgh, a lovely quiet, country hotel overlooking the sea in that magical doll-like seaside village. The head waiter, who had been there, and was to be there, for many years said, in what I thought was rather a blasé fashion, 'We have plenty of champagne of different types for you, all cold in the fridge.' I thought he was trying to foist this upon us. I also thought it was quite expensive. So we had white wine. Can you imagine anything so stupid – to say no to champagne on one's wedding day? I still bitterly regret that. We have always had champagne on every wedding anniversary since then – and it does not matter what it costs – just to make up for such unbelievable stupidity.

The next day, Sunday, we went to church in Aldeburgh – Annabel to the Catholic church, me to the Church of England church. That seems a pretty funny thing to have done, too, but we did it.

We went to France for our honeymoon. Mrs Phipps lent us her house at Croix-Valmer, near Nantes, for ten days. There was a lovely couple who looked after it, Germaine and Emile. I remember Germaine showing us around the garden and pointing out a particularly secluded spot on a rise in the ground overlooking the Seine and saying in a knowing way 'Personne ne vous voit.'

Then we went to the Ile d'Oleron, where we met an actor, Hugh Sinclair, and his wife, Rosalie, who were staying in the same hotel. He oozed charm from every pore and was a delightful person. We got to know them well and I subsequently became godfather to their son, Nicholas.

Our honeymoon lasted for six weeks. Everyone said 'What on earth are you going to do with yourselves for six weeks?' We said that it was the Long Vac in the summer and that it would be the last holiday that we would have for years and so we were jolly well going to make the best of it.

We were very avant-garde because I had bought a special kettle which could be run off the electrics of the car. I persuaded the mechanic, who serviced Daddy's Standard and which Daddy had very kindly said that we could take on our honeymoon, to absorb the cost of fitting the plug for the kettle in the car with checking the brakes. I did not tell Daddy. We were travelling through France with the kettle all coming to the boil feeling that this is really the high-life when suddenly smoke started to billow from everywhere around the passenger seat on which Annabel was sitting and there was a fearful smell of burning rubber. Annabel gently screamed. I jammed on the brakes and we quickly evacuated the car. What had happened was that the kettle had quietly moved backwards until it had made contact with the metal of the passenger seat and had shorted everything. No more boiling kettles on the move. It was only done when stationary.

The country's financial stringencies at the time allowed one to take abroad only £100 each and £25 for the car. So, with £225, we were able to spend six weeks in France – *and* buy a whole set of Limoges china. We lived pretty frugally. Sometimes we camped in a tent. We used to go and ask permission from whoever appeared to be the landlord. The scruffiness or grandeur of the house would determine whether or not Annabel wore her engagement ring as well as her wedding ring. One night, when we were in our tent, it rained so much that we bailed out and spent the rest of the night in the car. It might have been cosy but it was not very comfortable.

We stayed in a scruffy little fishing town above a café in the port. Every evening we came in and had the same dinner. Meat was in short supply in England and, when we went to pay the bill at the kiosk in the centre of the café, the woman always said 'Alors. Deux coverts Deux entrecotes. Deux legumes... Une bouteille de Vin de Pesceurs.' This was fisherman's wine, which we always called Peacher's Wine. It was the cheapest there was, but we liked it.

We used to buy a picnic for lunch and eat it on the beach. We had a lovely wedding present from Fanny Argenti, which was a bright red picnic box. We used to have our lunch a little later than the others on the beach. We found that people had by then left the beach to go and have their own lunch and it was quieter. Afterwards, we used to put what was left over, such as butter, cheese and wine, into Fanny's picnic box and put the box underneath the car to keep it in the shade. The inevitable happened one day. We drove off and forgot the box. No more lovely wedding present.

On our return home, we stopped at Limoges and went into a beautiful china shop. We bought a whole set of Limoges china – twelve soup plates, twelve meat plates, twelve pudding plates, twelve side plates, serving dishes and a magnificent Legumière. I think that the total cost was £75.

When we returned home, my father said that, as we only had a tiny flat in Cambridge, we could store all our Limoges china in Staunton Harold. When we came to collect it some two years later, I picked up the first box and it felt light. I looked inside. No china. It had been filled with books. The second box the same. In the third, there were some plates left and these we still use. They are so pretty – but the lovely Legumière went. When, some ten years later, we were visiting France, we called in at Limoges again and found the same shop. The plates were still there, but they were so expensive that we could not afford to buy them! Such is life.

We rented a tiny flat in Cambridge – but we loved it. It was ours. It was our home. It had three rooms – the drawing room, the bedroom and the kitchen. The lavatory was up the garden path. We had a bath on Mondays, upstairs in the landlady's flat. The bathroom was used as a kitchen for the rest of the week and it had to be tidied up before we had our bath. Mrs Day was an old lady (or so we thought) about eighty. She reminded us of Granma in a Giles cartoon. She never went out much but she used to have to know what was going on.

We used to see her grey head behind the lace curtains watching what was happening. This was infuriating, so we used to try and creep into the house as quietly as possible in an endeavour to outflank her curiosity. I think that she never opened her windows with the result that the air was heavy and stank of old fried onions. Whenever Mrs Day or her daughter went out from their flat, they had to come down the stairs, open the door at the bottom and walk through our passage to the front door. They were then followed by this appalling smell of stale air which cascaded down the stairs and which required the front and the back doors to be opened for about ten minutes in order to remove it – whatever the weather.

Our flat was very small. You could touch any part of any of the walls in the bedroom from the bed. There was no refrigerator nor deep freeze (there were no such things in those days), no central heating and no telephone. If we wanted to make a telephone call, we had to find the money, then go and find a telephone call box and watch the money disappear into the cavernous beast, coin by coin. We did not make many telephone calls.

We kept a strict watch on every penny which we spent – butcher, baker, grocer, greengrocer – and I did the accounts every Saturday. We always had fish on Fridays. It used to cost about 11d – less than one shilling, or less than five pence in new money. There was one week when the fishmonger's bill was three pence in old money – three herrings, one for Annabel, two for me, and they were one penny each. The irony was that, twenty years later, you could not buy herrings at all. They had all been fished out.

There had been so many arguments and discussions about us getting married. Annabel was going to be twenty-one. One of them was that if we got married, I would not do any work at all, as we would be spending all our time holding hands and, carrying on, I would not pass any exams. That did not prove to be quite true. My first year at Cambridge, when we were not married, I got a Third. Then, we were married and the following year I got a Second. My father wrote and congratulated Annabel. I was deeply, deeply touched – and I still am. It was such a kind, generous, understanding thing to do.

I loved Cambridge. So did Annabel. We were hugely happy there in the first two years of our married life. Our main form of hospitality was to ask people to tea. We could only ask four people, space and furniture providing the limitations. One day a friend arrived, unexpectedly bringing Boz Ferranti. Boz asked if he could join us, too. To my eternal shame, I said no. I thought that we would not all fit in. Looking back on it, I could not see how anyone could be so disgracefully inhospitable to a friend, especially to the one who had found our flat for us.

Robert was born when we were still at Cambridge on 29 December 1952. Nenella, Annabel's mother, who was Italian and was always a frantically fussy person especially over babies, used to send us a chicken every week in order to ensure that Annabel was healthy enough to bear a child. Although we welcomed it, I found such fastidiousness to be wildly irritating.

As we knew that Nenella would fuss, Annabel had told her that the baby was due to be born on 6 January – a week later than it actually was due to be born – in order that she would not put us all into a tizzy by all her carrying on.

On 27 December Annabel thought that things were happening – so I rang Mrs Miles, who was going to look after her. She said that, as there was the most appalling pea-souper of a fog, Annabel had better come in that night. Fine. I would order a taxi. But no taxis were going out. The fog was too thick.

So I rang for an ambulance. It came. It parked outside the house, and put its bright lights on so that we could see the steps into the ambulance. I took Annabel into Mrs Miles, and I returned to the flat. Next morning, down comes Mrs Day with her white hair and irritating questioning manner, 'Everything alright? Everything alright?' The fog had been so thick that you could not see across the street. But she had managed to see the five minutes during which the lights of the ambulance were on and she thought that something must be afoot. She was, of course, right but, if you do not ever go out and having nothing to interest you, a baby being born in your house is, I suppose, a major event of unparalleled importance. She was a quizzy old lady.

I took Annabel into the nursing home on the Saturday night. On the

Sunday, I thought that I ought to let her parents know, even though they were not expecting the baby to be born for another week. I got hold of Bill, her father, and said that I had taken Annabel to the nursing home, but not to worry, everything is alright.

He said, 'That is fine. Nenella got up early this morning and is in church at the moment. Last night she said, 'Come on Bill, pack the bags. We are going to Cambridge tomorrow.' How do you account for that? She had no reason to believe that the baby would be born until a week later. We have always said that Nenella had some kind of extra-sensory perception, and she did.

Mrs Miles was another of God's wonderful creatures. She had been a maternity nurse, and then decided to turn her own small house into a nursing home looking after up to two mothers at a time. Mrs Miles did everything. She looked after the babies and the mothers. She did the cooking and the washing and welcomed the visitors. Her only help was a daily who did the housework.

When we first visited Mrs Miles I asked what the charge was for all this. If my memory serves me right, it was £35 per week 'and I charge £1 extra for doing the laundry'. I was an impecunious undergraduate, and so I said, 'I will take the laundry back and do it at home.'

Mrs Miles thought that that sounded pathetic and so, with great generosity, she said there would be no charge for the laundry.

Mrs Miles looked after four of our five children but by the time that Andrew was born, she had retired. We both admired her enormously and we all became great friends until her death when she was over ninety.

At the end of her life, she wrote a book – aged ninety! – called *The first ninety years of a Cambridge Girl*. She was a deeply religious person, and I venture to enclose a few extracts of her book in which she refers to some of the complex problems of life with such simplicity and candour.

I think to myself, How could Man have imagined the sky, the mountains, rivers, oceans, deserts, forests and fens and placed them so perfectly in relation to each other? Who could make them work together – the tides, the seasons, night following day, the sun moon and stars lighting up the sky which is full of flying creatures with perfect plumage, who have their own language?

Who could have imagined the process of plants, crops and trees developing from tiny seeds, not forgetting our own babies and young of every species? Then there are the animals and fish. Not one detail has been forgotten in their various coats, scales and shells and every living creature is equipped to do its own thing.

To me God the Father is the supreme inventor, engineer, architect, planner, electrician, artist and operator.

I see the Creator in every flower, leaf, in every living creature and, of course, in all the people I know, but especially in those who think they have no faith. Theology, the Bible, History, Sermons and Teaching, all have their vital place. But, if in doubt I suggest we plant our feet firmly on the ground in our garden, a meadow, beside a stream or stand at the window and look at what is around, above and below us. It's not a bad idea to start with the things we know touch and see. If we start at the bottom we can only stay there or move up, even if only a step at a time.

What a remarkable lady, and what a wonderful but simple perception of the Almighty.

***

Magdalene played a central part in our lives, principally because it was there, when I was an undergraduate, that Annabel and I were married. I always love, therefore, any occasion to return to Cambridge, and especially to Magdalene. It is always happy and always nostalgic.

The last occasion I went back for a dinner, just the other day, every conceivable form of self-induced calamity took place. I had a great welcome from one of the Porters, who used to be in the Fire Service. He remembered me from when I was in the Home Office, coming to inspect the Fire Service in Huntingdon, where he had served. That made a happy start.

He then gave me the 'key' to my room. It was not what one normally thinks of as a key, but rather a flat piece of tin which you poked up the door handle. Quite simple really. But, when I tried it, it was far from simple. I shoved it in this way, that way, the other way round, upside down, all ways. It did not matter what one did. It just would not work. The handle would not turn. So, standing outside the building in which was my allocated room, I had had to find out the telephone number of the College and ring the Porter. 'I cannot get in,' I said. The Porter was kindness itself – he would come and let me in. He came. He pushed the piece of metal up. The handle turned as if it was in oil. Magic. Nothing wrong. I felt such a fool and apologised profusely.

I settled in to my room and began to change. My doorbell rang. It pealed. I went to see what was up. Another 'diner' was trying to get in to the building without success. I gave him a knowing smile and proudly let him in. He apologised profusely. 'I tried. I could not open the door. I am so sorry to be so foolish.' I was relieved that there was now more than one of us in that category. But that was not the end.

I returned to my room. The door had closed itself. My key was inside. I could not get into my room. My new friend's key, like mine, would unlock the door to the building but it would not unlock the door to my room. The Porter was called again. He cheerfully arrived and let me in. I felt an idiot for the second time.

The dinner was fun.

The next day, however, I managed to pull my packed case onto the floor via my foot, onto which it landed after scraping my shin all the way down. Stiff upper lip and all that. Don't worry. Forget that the last time you did that to your shin it took six months to recover.

I went to Chapel and had a typically huge College breakfast. Before leaving, I decided that it would be prudent to visit the loo. So I chose the lavatories next to the Junior Common Room. I surveyed them with a certain amount of apprehension and distrust. They were modern, like cubicles, and made out of plastic panels – all slidey. No hooks. Nothing to hang on to. The seats looked low. Nevertheless, I decided to give it a whirl. When later I tried to stand up, I could not do so. I could not get up. I opened the door and tried to hang on to that. No good. After eight exhausting shots, I thought that I would try getting on my hands and knees to see if that would be easier.

These cubicles had all the width of a sow's farrowing crate. They were not constructed with these forms of gymnastics in mind. It was not easy to turn over. But it was achieved. Now to stand up. No more success this way. After another ten tries, in which every muscle was exerted to its extremity, I gave up and remained kneeling on my knees, which were now beginning to feel very painful. I was stuck there for an hour.

Eventually, someone entered the lavatory. I shouted, 'I am stuck. Can you help me?' He came over. 'I can't open the door. Move your legs', he said. The farrowing crate was not designed for this kind of manoeuvre from an octogenarian. Eventually, though, it was achieved. One look and he said, 'I had better get a Porter.'

Two Porters came. I was hauled out. My knees were like jelly. I was taken back to the Porters' Lodge, passing a door, would you believe it, which said 'Disabled Toilet'. It was just next to where I had spent the last disagreeable hour. I was given a mug full of hot, sweet tea. A traditional remedy but very effective.

'Perhaps we ought to get a Paramedic to see you' suggested the Porter.

'What on earth do you want to do that for? I only got stuck in the loo. A Paramedic will scoot me off to hospital.'

'Yes, he probably will.'

'Then forget it.'

I eventually got in to my car and went home. The next day my legs felt as if they were made of solid concrete. I could hardly move.

The Porters were wonderful. They always are. They are a breed of their own – to be admired, cherished and loved.

This litany of misfortunes, which characterised what was supposed to be a happy twenty-four hours, made me wonder, believe it or not, *Whatever Next?*

Then I realised that colleges are built for young people in their twenties and not for old men in their eighties.

That, though, was all part of the rich tapestry of life. One is just so lucky to have been there and one is so lucky to be able to go back there.

Chapter 11

Farming

WHEN WE LEFT Cambridge, in June of 1953, we went to start our life in agriculture, and to live at Hill House Farm, Hedenham. It was a farm of 150 acres, and on this we were supposed to live and bring up our family, which at present already numbered one. We must have been mad. It was not great land either – some was light and very stony, which dried out in the summer. The other was really heavy clay which, when it was wet, attached itself to your boots as if it were a heavy clay plate and, when it dried, it became like concrete.

A year or so later we took on the Brickyard Farm of 100 acres, making us 250 acres – an improvement, but it was still mad. The enthusiasm of youth, though, is important.

We had twenty-three cows. Not twenty, not twenty-four, but twenty-three – a pathetic little herd in today's light. Bill very generously gave the farm to Annabel and set us up with the cows. We milked them three times a day, the last milking being at 8 p.m. One does crazy things when one is young, especially when you are trying to make money. They were good pedigree Friesians and this was supposed to make them produce more milk and make them more valuable. We had a very good cowman – twenty-eight, I suppose, when I was twenty-four – Ronald Woodhouse. Bill had employed him and passed him on to us to look after the cows.

I remember Bill saying, 'My worry is that I do not think that you can afford Woodhouse. He is very expensive.' His salary, which included milking the cows three times a day, Saturdays, Sundays, Christmas Day, Boxing Day, Good Friday, Easter Day, the lot, with a half-day off each

week and his annual holidays, was a total payment, inclusive of all overtime work, of £9 per week. But then the Agricultural wage for the other
farm workers, of whom there were four, was £5-13-0 per week.

We started pigs, and Annabel and I went off to see a lovely pig breeder,
Mr Rushton, of Chatteris in Cambridgeshire. He had a fine herd and
an excellent pig man. We looked at the pigs for about half an hour.
There were two young gilts at £45 each. I asked Mr Rushton if he could
let us have them for less, as I thought that you were always supposed
to bargain. He replied so gently and courteously. 'I do not bargain,'
he said, 'but there is something rather touching about you two young
people starting up a new herd, so I will let you have them for £42.' It
was so kind of him. I shall never forget it – firm, but understanding,
kind and infinitely courteous. Regrettably, he died a few years later, far,
far too young.

One of the first things which we did on getting to the farm was to get
a puppy, a yellow Labrador, whom we called Shandy. She was the first of
a number of Labradors which we had, mostly yellow. The names were all
called derivatives of Shandy – Candy, Brandy, Sandy. The black one was
called Sambo. I suppose that we would be locked up for calling him that
now. Shandy was a lovely little puppy. We bought her from an ex-Naval
Commander who lived on a converted motor torpedo boat permanently
moored on the river at Trowse on the outskirts of Norwich. Space was
pretty tight in the boat but it had all mod cons including a landline
telephone. I remember that his son had an electric train set which, due
to the need to economise in space, went all the way around his bedroom,
at bed height, so that he could play with his train in bed. Exotic!

We had a broken night when we first had Shandy home. We took
her up to our bedroom, so that she would not be lonely, and we put
her in a box beside the bed. As soon as the light went out, she started
to whimper. I put a hand in the box to comfort her. That worked. But,
whenever I removed my hand, the whimpering started again. In the end,
I had to leave my hand in the box. Not dog, not wife, not I got much
sleep that night.

So, we started our working life on this 150-acre farm with a cowman
and four others. In a very avant-garde way, we did not have a horse and

cart. Bill thought that we would not be able to manage without one. I thought that horses and carts were old-fashioned, and we did manage without one. We had two paraffin Ferguson tractors.

Harvest was gathered with a binder, which cut the corn and tied it into sheaves which were then thrown on to the ground. The sheaves were then picked up by hand and put into stooks. When the sheaves were dry, they were carted to the farmyard and put into corn stacks, which then had to be thatched before the rain came. The corn was processed through a threshing machine in the winter, requiring a team of eight or nine people. It was fun to chat together after a day's work and I always brought a barrel of cider for the harvest. Every night during harvest, the men used to come to the back door and we would drink cider together and discuss the day.

In order to ensure that as little corn as possible was wasted in the harvest field George Utting, our dear wonderful loyal retainer, used to go round the fields, scything the corn down for the width of the tractor so that the wheels of the tractor would not flatten the corn on its first time round with the binder. Nowadays, corn seems to be flattened with abandon by machinery but, in those days, people were more frugal and more caring.

We used to grow twenty-three acres of sugar beet. They were lifted by squeezing two rows of beet into one with a 'sledge'. Then each beet was lifted, banged together with another sugar beet, to knock the soil off, and then topped. It took all from September to January to lift those twenty-three acres. Now, with a six-row harvester, the twenty-three acres is done in a day. Progress? I suppose so, but the cost of it all is out of this world.

The first self-propelled combine which I had, several years later in 1960 or thereabouts, was a Massey Ferguson six-foot cut. I was so proud of it. It was powered by an Austin A40 engine, and it cost about £600. A fully fledged 'proper' self-propelled combine was far too expensive. That was £1,750.

Several years later, I bought a new self-propelled New Holland Clayson combine. It cost £3,700. It was so expensive that I bought it on the Never Never system – Hire Purchase. The combine, which the contractors now use in 2010, costs in the region of £250,000. One wonders how this can be justified, where all the money comes from and who benefits. Is farming really better now than it was years ago? Are the people involved in it happier and more content than they were before? Are we really producing 'better value for money', that modern, hackneyed phrase which seems to have to be applied to everything nowadays suggesting that otherwise it is pointless doing it, buying it or using it. Or is it that we have jumped on to a carousel which is going faster and faster, and one longs to say 'Stop the World. I want to get off.'

Some years later, David Chance, a near neighbour and friend of ours, and I decided to 'pool our resources' and buy a bigger combine. It was a New Holland Clayson combine, bright yellow – £7,000. We decided to buy one together, as the cereals grown on our two farms together would justify a bigger machine.

The arrangement was quite simple. I would have the combine on Mondays and Fridays, and David, because he had a larger acreage, would have it for the rest of the week. Well! You would never believe it – every Monday and Friday the weather was fine. For the remainder of every week it poured with rain.

It was so embarrassing but it was a perfectly fair arrangement which we had made. Somehow – I cannot think how – our friendship managed to survive it all.

He was very kind. He asked me to shoot one day in November. One of the drives consisted of walking through a field of wheat. It was still standing, but it was soaked and rotten. All my harvest was safe inside. It was just so dreadful, but David was a real gentleman.

When we were doing our work on Agriculture at Cambridge we were always told that mangels and swedes were excellent for cattle. They were huge things and they contained 90 per cent water and only 10 per cent was dry matter. With the impetuousness and knowledge of youth, I said that I was not going to continue to grow mangels and swedes as it was easier to get water out of a tap. I, therefore, decided to grow fodder beet instead. This was a fairly new idea. Fodder beet had much more dry matter in them and only contained 75 per cent water. So I decided to grow these for the dairy cattle.

Again at Cambridge, we were told that, when you make changes to a cow's diet, you should make it gradually over three or four days and not do it all at once. So this is what I decided to do. I told the man who was feeding the cattle to give them 10 cwt of fodder beat. There were, of course, no scales and it was all a matter of guesswork. He must have put not 10 cwt but two tons into the trailer, which he emptied in the field for the cattle to eat *ad libitum*. They loved it. They wallowed in the luxury of it.

That night, at about 8 p.m., when the cattle were tied up in the cowshed being milked for the third time, Woodhouse, the cowman, came to me and said, 'I think that you had better come and see the cows.' 'Why?' I said. 'I can't get any milk out of them.' He was quite right.

The next day they all had the most appalling diarrhoea, with the stuff going with all the velocity and volume as if it were out of a hose-pipe. Instead of sending away twenty-eight gallons of milk the next day, we only sent six. The yield never did recover. Two cows died. It was all a horrible disaster, and the lesson from Cambridge was learnt the hard way. The news of all this went, as disasters usually do, through the community with all the excitement as if we had put a man on the moon.

Some six years after we had started our farm, we had to make a decision – either to get out of cows or to expand. We decided to expand – from twenty-four cows to twenty-seven. These are piffling figures compared with nowadays, but they were very big figures to us then.

Later, we started broilers. I asked Willer, the pig man, if he would like to look after some chickens as well as pigs, as I was thinking of expanding our meagre flock of 150 laying hens. He said, 'Yes. How many do you want me to look after?' '10,000', I replied. The poor man practically fell to the floor. Later, they were expanded to 56,000 which were grown four times a year, making an output of nearly a quarter of a million birds.

Broilers became very important to us. They were the largest single item on the farm. It enabled the output of a small farm – then only 250 acres – to be increased dramatically. But everything had to go right. These tiny chicks, 70,000 of them arrived and were put under 'hovers', large cylindrical metal objects which hung from the ceiling and created the heat under which sat the birds. It was a lovely sight to see them at night all lying down giving off a quietly contented cheeping noise.

There were hazards all the way along the ten-week period of their lives

– disease, draughts, too hot, too cold, wind and then what became the real fear: Fowl Pest. That was a National Notifiable Disease. If you suspected that your birds had it, you had to let the Ministry of Agriculture know. Their vets would come round and, if Fowl Pest was diagnosed, the birds would all be killed and the owner compensated.

It was a pretty unpleasant occurrence, but it became one of the hazards of poultry farming in the 1960s, especially in East Anglia.

My then farm manager, Frank Bainbridge, came to me one day and said that he had a very red eye which itched. I suggested that he went to see the doctor, which he did. He came back and told me that he had … Fowl Pest! I could not believe it. Rather unsympathetically, I roared with laughter, and suggested that he had better be slaughtered and that I should be duly compensated. He did not find that in any way funny.

The terrible time was when the birds were caught. We used to get up at 2 a.m. to catch the chickens – four in one hand and three in the other and then hand them into the crates in the lorry – until 8.30 a.m. And then do some more between 11 a.m. and 2 p.m. We went home exhausted, and stinking of chicken. And the next day we would do it again. The third day was free. The fourth day, we would do it again – at 2 a.m. It was the most horrible job, and we all felt totally knocked up by the end of it.

In 1969, the year in which my mother died, we bought another farm at Mundham of some 180 acres. We had been wanting another farm badly to expand our enterprise and I happened to sit next door to a man when we were having refreshments at a stand at the Norfolk Show. I asked him what he was doing. 'I am going to Canada – if I can find someone to buy my farm,' he said. 'Where do you live?' 'Mundham,' he replied. I could not believe my ears. Mundham was about three miles away from us. So we bought it.

I was on one of my weekly visits to my mother in Derbyshire when she was not too well and when she was coming towards the end of her life. She always took a huge and maternal and loving interest in our lives and particularly in our farming activities. The agent had told me that he hoped to know whether we had been successful in our bid at midday that day. I was with my mother in her bedroom. The time went by. The agent had not telephoned. My mother said, 'Go on. Ring him.' I rang him. We had been successful. I shall never forget my mother's expression of total happiness, as she sat in her bed with her arms wide apart in preparation for a huge embrace, which she gave me. She was a wonderful, caring mother.

So, there we were, now farming 450 acres, at the age of forty, with four children, later five, to bring up. It was still madness. People say that farming is fun. I have never found it that way. It was very hard work. It always seemed to me a bagatelle whether you made any money or not and, in either event, there was never any cash. Overdrafts always went up. However hard you tried, they never seemed to come down.

If the farm did make a profit, not only did we have to live, but there had always been some horrifying piece of equipment which had to be bought or drainage which had to be done as well. I am afraid that I always found it – and still do – an intense and constant worry. I shall never forget our first two years of farming. The first year we made £500. The second year we lost £500. So, we had worked for two years for nothing. And we still had to live. It was crazy. We so nearly gave it up. We should have done, but the reason why we were there was because I had always wanted to farm and we were supposed, eventually, to look after the estate at Ditchingham. To buzz off when you had only just started and because the going was a bit rough might look as if one had not got enough guts or determination to see it through. My father-in-law would be upset and, anyhow, what would we do and where would we go?

The answer is that we should have had enough guts to say, 'This is a stupid way to live and to try and earn money.' I constantly regret that I never did so. But, as Annabel has so often said when I have bored her with my recriminations, 'Yes, but it is a wonderful way in which to bring up children. They had the freedom of the farm and the fresh air and lots of friends in the countryside.' Darling Annabel always looked on the bright side. She was always the silver lining behind any cloud.

I remember my father saying to me, when I was starting to read Agriculture, that in the days after the war, if anyone was going to be responsible for land or to try and farm it, he had got to know all about it. You cannot just leave it to an agent to do.

That was so true then but, of course, it is all different now. It is much better to get someone to look after your land whilst you go into the City or elsewhere and make the money to enable you and your family to live there. Robert has been sensible enough to do that. I wish that I had. But times were different then, and I remain content that, despite the anxieties, I have just been in so many, and in so many different, respects a hugely lucky and a very fortunate person.

Despite our always dicey finances, we were lucky to be able to take our children for a seaside holiday each year to Devon. At Hedenham we were only 17 miles from the sea but, oh no, if we wanted to take the children to the sea, we had to go 330 miles to Devon.

Why? Annabel's parents had built a house – St Anthony – in North Devon. It is a most glorious place overlooking the sea and is loved by everyone who goes there. In the 1930s, when Annabel was about seven, her parents rented a house down a road which had five other houses along it. It was a miraculous location – the sea, the sand, the waves, the climate.

Nenella noticed that, beyond the last house, there was a plot of land for sale. 'Bill, we must buy that plot and build a house on it. Let us go straight away to the agents.' If Nenella got the bit into her mouth, she was unstoppable.

'We want to buy that plot.'

'You cannot.'

'Why not?'

'Because we sold it to a gentleman yesterday, and he has set sail for China. He has paid the deposit and he has three weeks in which to pay the balance. If he does not pay the balance in three weeks, then you can buy it.'

Nenella was a bundle of nerves. She wanted the house – badly. Then she was told that she could not have it. Then she was told that there was a chance that she could have it.

Most people would be deterred. Not so Nenella. She had great determination, and was a staunch Roman Catholic. What has that got to do with it? This. She decided to pray with great fervour to St Anthony and said, in effect, 'Please, please let me be able to buy this plot. And if you do, I will build a house on it and I will call it St Anthony.'

Three weeks later, the agent telephoned to say that the gentleman who had gone to China had not paid the balance and that she could buy the land. She did. And she built a house on it. And she called it St Anthony. I love the story.

Everyone loves St Anthony. Annabel does. I do. The children do. And all the grandchildren do. So do all the people who take it for a period during the summer. It is built halfway down a cliff. It is simple, but modern (in the 1930s style). Virtually every room faces the sea. It can accommodate eleven people. There are spectacular views of the sea, the surfs and the sunsets, and the beach between Putsborough and Woolacombe is full of the finest sand imaginable – two miles long and half a mile wide at low tide. Perfect for children.

One of the worst and most haunting nightmares I have is being in the next life and, as a penance for all the sins which one has committed in this life, being made to count the grains of sand on Woolacombe Beach. Dreadful. Quite awful. Simply unthinkable. Can one imagine – one million, two hundred and thirty thousand, three hundred and fifty one, and then one drops the handful and has to start again? And then, look at the size of the beach... Too terrible for words.

Meanwhile, for those of us who do not have such frantic debts to settle in the afterlife, it is a place of constant and continuing joy. How lucky we have all been.

In 1964, we moved into Hedenham Hall, having spent ten happy years at Hill House. Much had to be done to it – rewiring, redecoration, new Aga. It cost £6,000 – a huge sum then. A trivial sum now. We were there for twenty years. All our children were brought up there. Andrew was born when we were there. Angela was married from there. They were intensely happy times and Annabel has always loved Hedenham Hall. It caused her huge grief – and continuing grief – when it had to be sold.

When Bill Carr died we were left with the responsibility of two big houses – Hedenham Hall and Ditchingham Hall. One had to go. We could not really afford to live in either, but to sell both was out of the question.

Annabel adored Hedenham, but Ditchingham was the family house in the middle of the estate. It was the centrifuge around which the rest of the estate should spin. It spooked me that my father died leaving a large house with a lake in front of it and then, when Annabel's father died some thirty years later, he too left a large house with a lake in front of it. I minded, and have continued to mind terribly, that Staunton was sold, even though Daddy said – and I understand the reasoning – that it had to be. It does not fall to everyone, though, for the carousel to come round a second time. Having seen my family home sold and having minded that so much, I did not think that I could ever have lived with it to see Annabel's family house sold too, and to think that I should have been responsible for having to say that it must go.

Annabel agreed, with much sorrow, that it was Hedenham that should be sold and that we should go to live at Ditchingham – but Annabel did so love Hedenham. She had not been particularly happy as a young girl when she had lived at Ditchingham.

So, Hedenham was sold, and various other things too, and we took on the modernisation of Ditchingham. A wing was knocked down. The house was re-roofed – with lead. The plumbing and the electricity were renewed. Dry rot was removed. It was redecorated and we heated it all with a straw boiler. Everyone said that a straw boiler would not work – but it did, beautifully – and Ditchingham Hall became the warmest house in Norfolk. I felt very proud of that. All in all, it was a Magnum Opus, but Ditchingham was a beautiful house and it was in a beautiful setting – a Capability Brown setting. It needed to be put right and enjoyed. It was.

I loved my father-in-law and my mother-in-law greatly. They were enormously kind to me. They welcomed me to Ditchingham and all that went on there with remarkable kindness and huge generosity and love as if I was their son. Not many parents-in-law would have done that. It would have been too easy for them to think 'Here is this young pup. He thinks he knows everything and he behaves as if he thinks it is all his. Well, it isn't.'

Not Bill and Nenella. I have always been acutely conscious that Ditchingham – the Hall, the estate and everything which goes with it – was not mine and that it never would be. It belonged to others and I merely had the privilege – and a great privilege it was – of trying to steer it through the murky waters of life.

Chapter 12

The Chartley Cattle

I T IS ODD how funny things happen to you when you least expect it, but which then have a lasting effect upon your life.

I never forgot that stuffed Chartley Bull which used to be in the Hall at Staunton. He was a formidable beast and there were two comfortable armchairs, curiously placed on either side of him and each underneath a horn. In order to protect the 'sitter' from any cerebral damage, a cork was placed on the end of each horn. It looked most odd. This was in 1935 or thereabouts.

We were always told about the Chartley cattle as children. They were animals which roamed the forests at the time of William the Conqueror. One of the descendents of Baron Ferrers, who had come across with the Conqueror, was Baron Ferrers of Chartley Bouchier and Louvaine, and he was given permission, in 1248, to fence in part of the Needwood Forest in Staffordshire. The enclosure became known as Chartley Park and the wild cattle within it became known as the Chartley Cattle. The descendants of these cattle remained in Chartley Park until 1905, when they were sold by 'Two Back'.

They were very distinct cattle, white with black noses, black ears, black fetlocks and a black mascara-like line over the eyes, and they boasted those large horns. They were wild and, in those days, aggressive.

They were sold to the Duke of Bedford for 1,000 guineas in 1905 and were put on to railway wagons. Then followed a traumatic event which nearly extinguished the Chartley Cattle for ever. The straw on the railway wagons, in which the seven cattle were put to take them down to the Duke's home at Woburn, caught fire. Most of the animals were burned and some died. There was one bull left, but so terrifying was the fire that the bull panicked in the melee and knocked his horns off. The stubs became diseased and the bull died.

The Duke of Bedford decided to cross the remaining Chartley Cattle with his Longhorns in order both to infuse new blood into the herd and to keep the herd going, but the characteristics of the Chartley breed are so strong that the Chartleys of today are almost indistinguishable from the Chartleys of earlier times.

In 1968 there was a violent outbreak of foot and mouth disease throughout the country and the Chartleys were sent down to a separate part of the farm to keep them away from the special deer which they have at Woburn. If the Chartleys got Foot and Mouth, then the special deer would be slaughtered – and that would be disastrous.

So the Duke of Bedford decided to sell the Chartleys. I was told of his intention to do this and, on the basis of 'it would be fun, wouldn't it, to have just one or two animals for old times' sake', we went to Woburn, but we came back having bought the whole herd of twenty-four of them – delivered. 'Delivered' was important. They had huge horns and I thought that they would only get one on each lorry.

These things always happen at particularly inconvenient times. We had recently sold our dairy herd and we had turned the whole farm down into an arable farm. I explained that we could not take them immediately, February, as we would have to sow grass for them, but that we could have them in July. That was fine. It was one of the best deals that I had ever done. When I bought them in February there were twenty-four of them. When they were delivered in July, there were thirty-three of them!

One of the Dukes of Bedford had been President of Whipsnade Zoo, and he had put some of the Chartley Cattle there. Some two years after buying the cattle from Woburn, Whipsnade Zoo contacted me to say that they wanted to get rid of their Chartley herd and, if they could not sell them, they would 'shoot them and feed them to the lions'.

The thought of that was just too terrible. So I bought them as well. It was not that I was intent on empire building, but I took the view that, if opportunity knocks, you ought to open the door.

So it was that the Chartley herd was reunited with the Ferrers family in whose possession, bar those seventy years, it had been for 700 years.

There was an old superstition which said that if a black calf was born in the Chartley herd it meant that Lord Ferrers would die. One day I went up to the farm and saw a tiny black calf in the yard. I said to my farm manager, 'Help. What are we going to do?'

'I shouldn't worry', he said.

'But you know what the superstition says.'

'Yes, but we have had two black calves already. I did not tell you about them but sent them straight down to the knackers, and you are still here.' I thought that that was very kind.

Since then we have had lots – far too many – black calves and, mercifully, I am still here.

My father-in-law did not like the Chartleys. If he was out shooting and he dropped a bird into a field where the Chartleys were, Bill would send his Labrador after the bird. The Chartleys hate the dogs and the dogs were scared stiff of the Chartleys. The Chartleys would chase the dogs all over the place. The dog did not like that. Nor did Bill. He said that it was like starting up a zoo and that it would cost fortunes. 'No more than the cost of keeping your hunting horses,' I rather impertinently said.

I took one of the young bulls to a sale and sold it for a thousand guineas – a lot of money in those days. Bill found out from my farm manager for how much the bull had been sold. The next time that he saw me he said, 'I hear you have sold your bull well. Blast you!' It was a delightful way of saying 'Well done.'

These animals give us all great pleasure, especially in the spring when they have lost their winter coats and they look sleek and beautiful with their tiny calves with them, all white with little black noses and bright eyes, and skipping around in the lush green pasture.

Their wild manner of living over all the centuries has built into them a strong maternal instinct. The mothers look after their calves with so much care. They lick them and love them, and protect them, and the little calves copy their mothers.

I often think that we could benefit in taking time off from this absolutely hectic life just to watch these wild animals of nature. We would learn a lot about motherhood. Now they are in the perfect place – in the park overlooking the lake at Ditchingham Hall.

Chapter 13

Government

I FIRST WAS made a member of the government in 1962. I was thirty-three. I was made a Lord-in-Waiting in Harold Macmillan's government. The salary was £2,000 per annum on which one was expected, I suppose, to live, to keep a wife, to bring up one's children and to have somewhere in London in which to live. It was not much, but Annabel said, 'Now that you are earning a salary, for goodness sake go and buy yourself an overcoat.' I did. Annabel was wonderful. She always remembered the basics of any situation. It was made for me by my wonderful tailor, Mr Thornton of Denman & Goddard. It had a velvet collar and a deep red silk lining. It cost £40. It was a superb overcoat. I still wear it now. Even if the buttons are called upon to do a little more than their originally intended work, it is still a lovely coat.

My mother had a carer, who was looking after her at Shirley. I shall never forget her saying to my mother, 'Poor Lord Ferrers. He chose the two worst paid professions in which to be involved – agriculture and politics.' How right she was.

At that time when I was first a Lord-in-Waiting in 1962, No. 10 Downing Street was being renovated. In answer to a Parliamentary Question in the Commons as to why so much money was being spent on No. 10, the Prime Minister replied with words to the effect of 'Because it is in very bad order. That only refers to the structure of the building. There is nothing wrong with the occupants.'

The Prime Minister had, therefore, transferred not only himself but all the functioning of No. 10 to Admiralty House at the top of Whitehall whilst the work on No. 10 was being carried out. Harold Macmillan asked all of the government front bench in the Lords to dinner – as a good PR exercise and also, I suspect, so that he could try and get to know some of them better.

I shall never forget a framed photograph of Jack Kennedy, the President of the United States, sitting on the black grand piano. On the photograph were written the simple but prophetic words 'To Prime Minister Macmillan, who has so often pointed the way.' It said stacks. Short sentences often do.

The duties of a Lord-in-Waiting were not, in those days, very onerous. The curious point was – and still is – that it is a political appointment. You are a government Whip in the House of Lords and yet, every six weeks or so, you would have a week on duty where you represented the Queen, meeting people at airports, saying farewell to others, calling on retiring Ambassadors and thanking them on behalf of the Monarch and attending Memorial Services on her behalf. It is curious that the Queen is always distanced from politics and, correctly, remains aloof from them, but yet three of her personal representatives are straightforward political appointments.

It was a fascinating task. As Lord Longford once said, it is the lowest form of political life and yet, when you represented the Queen, you blossomed out as Pooh-Bah. You took precedence over everyone, even the Prime Minister. You were met in a huge Rolls Royce with a crown on it. The proper dress was black jacket, striped trousers, bowler hat and umbrella. The chauffeurs were seasoned servants of the Royal Family and knew the drill backwards. You must never arrive early. That throws everyone into the most appalling tizzy.

I once went to a Memorial Service in 1971 for Viscount Malvern who, as Sir Godfrey Huggins, was Prime Minister of Southern Rhodesia. It was in St Martin-in-the-Fields. We arrived early and so went around the block. And then, would you believe it, we got stuck in a traffic jam. Fortunately, in the end we were only minutes late. I was met at the west door by the Rector and taken up to my place at the front of the congregation on the left-hand side. The congregation stood. They sat when I sat down. I looked round, very gingerly, and saw behind me the Prime

Minister, the Foreign Secretary, an ex-Foreign Secretary, current and ex-Cabinet Ministers, the lot. And there was I, the most junior member of the government, sitting above them all. It was quite alarming.

There was another occasion when I went to welcome the President of the Cameroons at Victoria Station. He spoke no English. I rehearsed my welcome in French and, as was the protocol, I was the first to greet him in front of Harold Macmillan, the Prime Minister, and Lord Home, the Foreign Secretary, both in morning suits. It was quite awe-inspiring for me. After all, I was only thirty-four, and here were the two major people in the government – the Prime Minister and the Foreign Secretary – and I was standing in front of them both.

President Tito of Yugoslavia paid a state visit. I went to welcome him at Heathrow. The aeroplane was late, and I was waiting with Ted Heath, the then Prime Minister, in the VIP lounge – not a very easy or relaxed occasion. They never were with him. Then they announced that the aeroplane was going to land right at the other end of the airport in two minutes' time. We had to rush over to the new place. Ted Heath said, 'Can I come in your car?' – a surprising question from a Prime Minister.

When we arrived at the other side of the airport, we got out to walk to the aircraft. I think that every Yugoslav in London had found his way to the airport and to the right place and was there, so the police put up crash barriers which appeared from nowhere. The Prime Minister and I, as luck would have it, were the wrong side of the crash barriers. We were stuck. It was just so embarrassing. The Yugoslavs were not going to give an inch. This was their President and they were there – so. Eventually, we got through and there was the aeroplane sitting on the tarmac. We had to climb up the steps. 'Go on. You go first,' the Prime Minister said as he shoved me forwards, and we tore up the steps. It was pretty undignified. When the Prime Minister got home he was furious! He rang up Diana Makegill, the Head of Protocol at the Foreign Office after midnight and gave her a resounding rocket for putting him in such an embarrassing position.

At the general election of 1974, no one thought that Ted Heath would win. The party were wholly against him and everyone said that it was a foregone conclusion – Ted Heath had had it. There was, though, one person who always thought that he would win. Ted Heath. And win he did. Annabel always held him up as an example to me. 'It just goes to show. If you think that you are right, whatever anyone else says, have the confidence to stick to your guns. Ted Heath did, and he won.'

I once went to bid farewell on behalf of the Queen to a retiring Ambassador, who had a reputation of being a rather suave individual. He was Sir Christopher Berkeley. He very graciously offered me champagne at 11 a.m. in the morning which went down well. In the Foreign Office his nickname was Through-a-glass-darkly-Berkeley!

After these escapades one was taken back to one's flat in this glorious Rolls-Royce, changed and settled down to bacon and eggs. It was all pretty heady wine, and it was important not to get too influenced by this temporary transformation into non-reality.

The political side of being a Lord-in-Waiting was that you were a Whip and your business was to ensure that you got the government's business through the House of Lords. There were usually six of you – the Chief Whip or Captain of the Gentlemen-at-Arms, the Deputy Chief Whip or Captain of the Queen's Bodyguard and then about four Lords-in-Waiting.

Macmillan once said that the difference between a Whip in the Commons and a Whip in the Lords was that, in the Commons, you had to get the people in to vote but in the Lords you had to encourage them not to come in – otherwise they might listen to the argument and vote the wrong way. That was, of course, a reference to the difference between the strength of the Whips, and the way in which they operated, in the Commons and in the Lords. There were also about three departments with which a Lord-in-Waiting was supposed to assist with taking Bills through the House or with answering questions, always a frightening experience.

When Macmillan became ill and resigned, the problem was who was to take over. Rab Butler was the obvious and natural successor. He had been No. 2 and he was expected to be – and he expected to be – No. 1. But his personality did not endear him to everyone and he was considered to be a bit of a cold fish.

Annabel and I went to the Conservative Party Conference at Brighton.

The place was alive with rumours and speculation. Macmillan was in King Edward VII's hospital with a prostate problem, and the Queen had gone to see him in hospital – which itself was quite an unusual thing for the Monarch to do. It was then that Macmillan said to her that he would have to stand down. Viscount Hailsham, the Leader of the House of Lords, went to see Macmillan in hospital, too, and Macmillan told Hailsham that it was he whom Macmillan wished to see succeed him.

By some peculiar chance, which had never occurred before, there was a brief chance for a Peer to give up his title and stand as a candidate for the House of Commons.

The Peerage Renunciation Bill had recently gone through Parliament and, due to an amendment which was passed in the Lords against the then Conservative government's wishes and advice, Peers could renounce their titles within six months of the Bill receiving Royal Assent.

The Bill originally said that it should come into force at the Dissolution of Parliament – in two years' time. Someone put down an amendment saying that it should come into force at Royal Assent – in other words, in July. The arguments went flying back and forth. What if somebody dies between now and the Dissolution of Parliament? What happens if a person renounces his title or then gets ill and cannot stand? He is excluded from both Houses. What happens if somebody gets run over – or his son dies? What happens if …? What happens when …? The arguments went on and on. 'Let us be clear, and do it straight away' seemed to be the most persuasive argument and it won the day.

We were at a fringe meeting in Brighton on some relatively boring subject, which was addressed by Lord Hailsham. At the end of his speech and after he had been thanked, he stood up again and said that he thought that we should know that he was 'putting his hat in the ring'. Well, the place went wild. They clapped and cheered and stood. Hailsham was a very exciting, entrancing, vibrant character. People loved him. We were actually there. I shall never forget it.

The news of Hailsham being a contender against Rab went round Brighton with the speed of a bush fire. At all the meetings people came dressed with favours on their jackets – up with Hailsham. Up with Rab. In some ways it was quite embarrassing because this was the crown which

Rab had always been expecting to receive, and there was now a vigorous attempt to snatch it away from him.

Iain McLeod was the Chairman of the Conservative Party. With fever pitch at full throttle, he told a packed Conference not to worry. We will take very careful soundings and opinions within the party – which was the way in which Leaders of the Party were chosen in those days – to determine who would be the most appropriate and the most wanted leader, and 'then we will all rally round behind him.' Stout stuff.

A few weeks later, Alec Douglas-Home was chosen and Iain McLeod said that he would not be part of his government. That was an appalling volte-face, and it was a very unkind thing for a highly influential member of the Conservative Party to do to an unexpected newcomer to the Leader's chair. I never really respected Iain McLeod after that.

Alec Home never wanted to become Prime Minister. He was persuaded to so because the party was split down the middle between the unexciting, pedantic but experienced Rab Butler on the one hand and the charismatic, brain-storming, exciting but unpredictable Lord Hailsham on the other. It was all because of the astonishing fact of the date on which the Peerage Renunciation Bill had come into force. Had the government's original intentions remained, neither Hailsham nor Home could have resigned their titles when they did, nor offered themselves as potential Prime Ministers. Presumably Rab would have become Prime Minister. History would have been different. Meanwhile the other astonishing fact is that Alec Home is the only person to have been Prime Minister when he was in the House of Lords, when he was in the House of Commons and when he was in neither the House of Commons nor the House of Lords. Quite a remarkable feat. Who says that the House of Lords does not have any effect?

In 1964, when the election was eventually called, Alec asked all his Ministers into No. 10 to have a farewell drink. Everyone knew that he and the Conservatives would be trounced at the polls. He thanked everyone for what they had done and said, 'And, if we get returned, my word, we won't half have a party.' So typically light, welcoming and encouraging to everyone. He very nearly did get back. Everyone expected a landslide victory for Labour. Alec missed being returned back by only four seats.

During the time when Alec Douglas-Home was Prime Minister, the front bench in the House of Lords decided to ask him to dinner in the Cholmondeley Room. Being about the most junior member of the government, I found myself with the privilege of sitting next to him. The most senior member, Lord Carrington, sat on his other side. I shall never forget two things. One was his opening remarks in his after-dinner speech which were, 'I cannot tell you what pleasure it gives me to come back to this oasis of civilisation.' It said mountains.

The other was his description to me at dinner of his first speech as Prime Minister from the Despatch Box in the House of Commons. Here was this man who had been plucked out from the House of Lords, who had to find a Parliamentary seat, who had caused a by-election and who then was, as it were, dropped by parachute into the House of Commons. The House of Commons is a pretty aggressive place at the best of times. It was then. I remember Lord James of Rusholme, who was High Master of Manchester Grammar School and who had been Second Master at Winchester when I was a boy there, referring once in a House of Lords debate to 'the gentle rustle of sharpening steel' in the Commons.

There was the House of Commons, full of pride, aggression, determination, personal ambition, all masquerading as 'the public interest' having to accept someone from outside as their Leader, their Prime Minister, who was a Peer. What was the matter with all these benches of testosterone-filled young Turks – and the older men too? Why could they not supply a leader and a Prime Minister? There were stacks of people there who would have fallen over themselves to have been given the chance. But no. They had to put up with an outsider. An Earl, too.

Alec told me that, when he rose to make his speech in the House of Commons as Prime Minister, the caterwauling and shouting that went on was unbelievable. It came, not just from the Opposition, but from all parts of the House where the frustrated politicians could give vent to their feelings with the happy knowledge that, so great was the whole cacophony, their own contribution was relatively incognito.

Alec said that the whole noise was awful. Terrifying. He stood at the Despatch Box. His knees trembled, and he felt that they were going to give way. The only thing to do was to stand up, not to give in and get

through the speech somehow. Anyhow. It did not matter what he said or
how he said it. Just read it and get to the end. That was a terrible indoc-
trination for one who did not want the job, who did it for his country's
and his party's sake, and which, after all, was the highest office in the land.

Alec had, of course, been in the House of Commons before when he
was Lord Dunglass, before he inherited his peerage, but that was different.

After the dinner in the Cholmondeley Room, and after Alec Douglas-
Home had left, Bertie Denham, who was then a Whip, suggested that
we all (eight of us or thereabouts) went off somewhere. What about the
Playboy Club, which had just opened up in Park Lane and of which
Bertie had been given free membership for a year.

I had been offered free membership for a year, too. I think that the
owners of the club hoped that, by this method, they might get some kind
of respectability to the club. I received my offer for membership in an
envelope within which was included a brochure indicating the advantages of membership – i.e. a number of photographs of extremely pretty
girls with unbelievable figures wearing the hugely sexy bunny clothes.

The trouble was that I left the membership form and the photographs on
my desk when I went out to see the farm. Annabel, meanwhile, came into
my study, saw what was there and went into a frenzy as she thought that
I had applied for membership. It took quite a while to persuade her that I
may be responsible for what I send to others in the post, but I cannot be
responsible for what others send to me. I had not applied for membership,
but had merely been offered it. The waters gradually became calm again.

So it was suggested that we all go to the Playboy Club. Peter Carrington, who was the Leader of the Lords, said OK. Michael St Aldwyn,
who was the Chief Whip, thought that it was important that he should
accompany the Leader on this dangerous foray in to the seedier side of
London night-life in order to make sure no harm came to him. Lord
Goschen, who was the Deputy Chief Whip, thought that he should
accompany the Chief Whip, in order to make sure that he was alright,
too, and that no harm should come to him, either. I wanted to join
in – just for the fun and for the curiosity of it all. So, off we all went.

We arrived in the foyer of the Club and there, on the wall in large
lettering, was a list of 'Members present here tonight'. Lord Denham's

name stood out in sharp relief and was there for all to see. I cringed with embarassment, and I thanked merciful Heaven that it was his name, and not mine, which was on display.

We went up stairs for a drink and sat at a round table. A bunny girl came up to ask us what we wanted. It is all very fine. You can argue the rights and wrongs, the moral side and every other consideration of the principle of bunny girls, but they *are* enormously attractive. Fishnet stockings which disappeared up the legs and out of sight, four-inch stiletto heels, a corset-type basque, which gave a great cleavage and an astonishingly nipped-in waist, together with white cuffs, a bow tie and rabbit ears and, to finish it off, a white powder puff, depicting a rabbit's tail, on the bottom. It was just an amazing – and, I must say, a wonderful – sight. As the bunny girl was walking away from our table with the order, Peter Carrington turned round and watched this astonishing apparition disappear. He exclaimed with total amazement, 'This is not true. It is *just not possible!*'

I remembered that evening with more pleasure and accuracy than I remembered the many Bills which I helped to place on the Statute Book over the ensuing years. It was all good clean fun. But you could not do that now – oh no. The newspapers, the paparazzi, all the nasties would concoct horrible and defamatory stories all about an innocent night out. Things were different then.

***

As a Whip in opposition, one's duties in those days (1964–71) were quite light. Nothing in the mornings, so I used to bring all my farm books and papers up in a huge great suitcase together with what was then a very modern Olivetti calculating machine. It was huge and heavy and had a large handle which you drew down to make the equivalent of an entry. I think that it cost £30. In comparison with today's small, light, simple electronic calculators, this seems like something out of the Ark – and just as heavy. But it was efficient and, in those days, modern.

I went to Nigeria on a Commonwealth Parliamentary Association visit in the autumn of 1964. There were about eight of us drawn from all three parties. We met the Prime Minister of Nigeria, Sir Abu Baka Tefawa Beluwa. He was a good and intelligent man, and he had known my Uncle Eric Hussey when Eric, Dukie's father, was involved in education in Nigeria, and he was thrilled that I was his nephew. He told me that there was a Hussey College named after him. Uncle Eric was the husband of Mummy's sister, Christine Hussey, father of Dukie and Helen, and he had been in the civil service and had been responsible for education in Nigeria. He was highly regarded there.

When we went to Nigeria, Ian Smith had just issued the Unilateral Declaration of Independence in Southern Rhodesia. Everyone in Nigeria was furious and rebuked the British government for doing nothing. Jeremy Thorpe, the Leader of the Liberal Party, had unhelpfully and impractically said that we should bomb Southern Rhodesia, and thereafter he became known as 'Bomber Thorpe'. In Nigeria they were in a state of apoplexy about the UDI and saw it as the White Man refusing to give the Black Man any say in his country.

So incensed was everyone in Nigeria that, if you got on to the subject at the soup course, you continued through the fish, the meat, the pudding, the lot. When Sir Abu Baka was asked by us, at a private meeting of our delegation, what his views were on the British reaction to the Unilateral Declaration of Independence, he looked very solemnly and quietly at the floor. 'Blood is thicker than water. You cannot fight them.'

I always thought, rightly or wrongly, that he looked so solemn then because he knew that Nigeria, which was the showplace of the Commonwealth for Independence – it was an example of just how Independence should come about – was bubbling with unrest. About six weeks later, after we had left, the whole place devolved into a bloody massacre. Sir Abu Baka was killed. The Sardonna of Sokuto, the Premier of the Northern Region, was killed, as was every other leader. It was terrible.

Now, some fifty years later, the place has still not got back to where it was. Before Independence, Nigeria was totally reliable. It just goes to show again that, under the much reviled colonialism, the infrastructure of the country actually worked, whether it was trains, roads, justice or education. Those who, for understandable reasons, wanted change for political purposes, unsettled and, to a great part, destroyed the fabric of their country, which would take years, and even decades, to recover – if ever.

The modern equivalent of Nigeria is Zimbabwe, a once glorious country with a thriving and prosperous agriculture. It has been brought to its knees by Robert Mugabe with inflation rising to the incomprehensible figure of 5,000 per cent and abover. People have been killed, insurrection encouraged and the indigenous population, or those parts of it which are close to the rulers in the party, have been encouraged to occupy – by force, if they wished – the farms which were owned by white Rhodesians. The country has become ruined, derelict and bankrupt. It is now a travesty of its former proud self.

When in Nigeria, I went to church in Ibadan. The church was full – full of Nigerians. It was quite something to hear a full church sing 'Onward Christian Soldiers' in Yoruba. They sang at the tops of their voices.

We went into Zaria, a town in the northern region of Nigeria, to see a Durbar. The organisers had filled our programme far too full with the result that we were late for everything everywhere. We arrived in Zaria to be greeted by hugely impressive Nigerians on horseback with turban-like headdresses and vast long pipes, like Swiss alpine horns, booming out long low notes. The other two occupants of my car were Sir John Fletcher-Cooke and John Litchfield, both Conservative MPs. John Litchfield had been in the Navy. Discipline still oozed from him. As we drove up to see the Emir, John Fletcher-Cooke said, 'How much behind time are we?' John Litchfield replied, 'About ten minutes and a thousand years.' What a wonderful reply!

We always had fun in the Whip's Office. That was important. They were long hours – from 2.30 in the afternoon until 10.30 plus at night. Mild, schoolboy humour was, fortunately, usually just around the corner.

We had a room with four of us in it: Bertie Denham, Charles Mowbray, Grey Gowrie (and later Janet Young) and me. There was a secretary in the adjoining room. Bertie's desk was opposite mine. Two things were imprinted in Bertie's diary at the beginning of each year – one was Cheltenham where he liked to go racing, and the other was Scotland where he liked to go fishing for two weeks. It did not matter what the business in the House was, whether the government was going to be defeated, even when he was government Chief Whip, these dates were sacrosanct. I never knew how he managed it.

One Thursday before Bertie was due back from Scotland from his fishing trip, I bought a herring and put it in the front drawer of his desk with a note saying, 'This is the one which got away.' When Bertie fluffed that something was wrong on the following Tuesday, the said herring had had a little maturity added to it which was accompanied by an exceedingly strong smell. Bertie was horrified, screamed, removed the herring from his drawer and, rather childishly I thought, put it into my drawer.

I, in turn, screamed, pulled the herring out of my drawer and threw it at Bertie. He screamed, the secretary screamed, everyone screamed. The secretary disappeared into her room and slammed the door. After a bit of, as you might say, 'tennis' with the fish, I eventually put it into Bertie's open brief case amongst his papers. That was just too much. It triggered an almighty bellow, such as a lion might emit and the game came to an end.

It was all good clean – if childish – stuff. I liked to think that that kind of thing stopped us from getting too pompous.

I remember telling one young Minister who was objecting to being kept up there late into the night saying, 'I want to get out of this bloody place and go home.' 'Never say that,' I said. 'This is the most wonderful place and is the most lovely building. Some people would give their right arm to come here just to see it, whereas it is your place of work. Don't complain.' That shut him up.

**

In about 1975 I became involved with the Norwich Union Insurance Company.

Desmond Long was President of the Norwich Union Insurance Group. In this case, the President was the equivalent of the Chairman. In America, President was an honorific title for an older person who had been put out to grass, rather like 'Emeritus'. That was definitely not so with the Norwich Union. The title was changed later because people in other countries did not realise that the President of the Norwich Union was, as it were, boss-guy – very much in charge.

Desmond was quite keen that I should join the Board of Norwich Union but he thought that I was not sufficiently widely known, so he asked me to propose the adoption of the year's accounts at the next Annual General Meeting. He had asked me once, if not twice, before and I had been unable to come. This was a pity, not only because it looked rude but also because I might be prematurely extinguishing any flames of opportunity which might have been there. But, on this occasion I could come. So I accepted. The AGM was a very civilised affair with it all running on very well-oiled wheels.

I was sent the accounts of both the Life Society and the Fire Society. I did not understand a word, and so I had a telephone call with Basil Robarts, the very efficient, slightly dry, but charming Chief General Manager. I reported the conversation in my speech to the AGM, which went something like this:

'Chief General Manager. I have looked through all the figures in the two books but I cannot see anywhere where they refer to the Life Insurance Society or the Fire Insurance Society.'

'Oh', said the Chief General Manager. 'The figures under the heading of Long Term Assets refer to the Life Society. Those under Short Term Assets refer to the Fire Society.'

I thought 'Well, why couldn't they say so?'

I went on: 'In all the figures, I cannot see where the profit appears.'

'Ah, well, we don't make profits.'

'You don't make a profit? An insurance company does not make a profit?'

'No, well you see it is called 'an increase in assets' – and you will find that at the bottom of page 19.'

And so it went on.

It was all deeply confusing to the amateur, but I repeated my memory of the conversation in my speech to the Annual General Meeting. Fortunately, the audience loved it. They roared with laughter. So, mercifully, did the Chief General Manager and the Board. They all laughed and, although I say it with some modesty, people remember it to this day.

As luck would have it, I became a member of the Board a few months later. It was a very happy organisation of which to be a member. When Desmond Long asked me to come on the Board, he said, 'I don't want you to go in and out at each change of government, and I would like you to give me an undertaking that you will not do so.' I said that I thought that that was very unlikely as my political days were virtually over.

'But I cannot give a promise. Suppose some bomb was dropped on Westminster and killed all the members of the government and that somebody said to me, "You must come and be Prime Minister." I could not very well say, "I cannot. I said that I would not leave the Norwich Union." Unlikely, I know, but I could not give a guarantee. Desmond understood that. What happened, though? I went in and out, just like the weatherman on a Swiss clock. Unintentionally, but that is the way that the cookie crumbled.

About that time I became more involved with the Trustee Savings Bank. Originally it was the East Anglian Trustee Savings Bank. Then we joined up with some others and it became known as the Trustee Savings Bank of Eastern England.

In those days, it was the poor man's bank. It had backing from the Treasury and the deposits were 'copper-bottomed'. Therefore, the bank could do practically nothing – certainly not without the approval of the Treasury. There was the Ordinary Account into which people put their money. The interest was peanuts, but if you had more than a certain amount, £2,000 I think, you could put some money into the Special Investment Department, where you received a higher return – 2 ½ per cent. Think of that – 2 ½ per cent! The TSB did not have cheque books. That was much too like a High Street Bank. Instead, the TSB had Passbooks. You went to the local branch and drew out some money and the transaction was noted in a pass book. It was a government backed bank which could not go bust and, therefore, it protected the interests of the working man.

The trustees were all unpaid local worthies, the good and the respectable. We met periodically for non-arduous meetings which were preceded by a good lunch. Our manager was a delightful and very efficient man, John Evans. He was tall, imposing and courteous.

The TSBs, and their boards, tended to be very insular. They looked after their own affairs and did not bother too much about what the other

Trustee Savings Banks did. I was lucky enough to become chairman of the TSB of Eastern England. Gradually, the banks did more. They were allowed to issue cheque books – a huge milestone. In the fashion of the day some Trustee Savings Banks amalgamated with each other – from fifty-two to sixteen – to make fewer and larger banks. This was always a bumpy transition. There was too much 'parish pump' consideration.

The Central Board of the TSB was formed. It consisted of a Chairman and the Chairmen of the sixteen Savings Banks and other representatives. I was on the Central Board, and I enjoyed it, even if it was ponderous.

A new part of the bank was set up called Trustcard, which dealt with card transactions in a similar way to Barclaycard. I was lucky enough to be on the Board of this brand new company from the day when it first started. It was fascinating to be part of an organisation which was set up from scratch to deal with credit cards. We chose Visa. Subsequently we had Mastercard as well.

The Central Board was not all that happy a place. Andrew Rintoul was the Chairman – a nice enough man but perhaps deficient in dynamism. Tommy Bryans was the General Manager, Irish, full of fun and jokes and laughter. Competent too. But the Board members were all pretty insular, not wanting to join up, to co-operate or to move into the new exciting era of the mid and late 1900s. 'I'm alright, Jack,' was the general, although unmentioned, attitude. That did not do too much good – either for them or for their bank. Tommy Bryans said of one of the chairmen, in a withering character synopsis, 'He has never been out of the village.'

It seemed to me obvious that there ought to be fewer banks. Sixteen was still far too many, but most people thought that they must retain their territorial links. To bring them down to one bank would be making yet another colossus and it would ruin the whole raison d'etre of the bank. The point of Trustee Savings Banks was to look after the local man or woman who did not understand, and who did not want to under-stand, the reasoning, the philosophies and the operations of the great big national banks.

We were having one of those acrimonious discussions at a Board meet-ing, where all the parish pumps were being pumped with vigour when one member referred to me as 'One Bank Ferrers'. This was supposed to be a huge insult. I found it rather funny and I recall the piece in the Bible where it said, 'They were first called Christians in Antioch'.

What happened in the end after I had left to return to government? All the Trustee Savings Banks were merged into one. The curious part was that no one knew to whom all the capital belonged. The Trustee Savings Bank had no shares. They only had the money which had been accumulated from depositors over the years, but many of the 'shareholders' were dead. Like all these things, a way was found round this problem, and the new bank was called, not the Trustee Savings Bank, but TSB. Eventually, it was merged with Lloyds and it became Lloyds TSB.

In the late 1970s things began speeding up in the TSB world. Rintoul was going to retire. I knew that some (but I have not the slightest idea how many) considered that I might have been a candidate for his replacement. The nearest I got to knowing anything was when, during a coffee break at a meeting, Rintoul took me over to the window and asked me what my 'ambitions' were. It was a curious question and it was not an easy one to answer.

One of my great drawbacks is that I have never really had ambitions, other than the general one that I wanted to do something useful in my life and, in a somewhat altruistic way, leave my patch a bit better off as a result of my having been there. Wrongly, I think, I have never said, 'That is the job I want, and I will go like hell to achieve it.' I have always waited – and hoped – that someone would say, 'Would you come and do this?' Like that, one would receive, in retrospect, achievement without the objectionable side of self-assertion or self-aggrandisement. Modesty with me could have done with a sharper cutting-edge.

Ambition is a good, if not necessarily a nice, driving force, a motivator. It makes people move and get places. Ambitious people, though, are not always very pleasant people. The achievement of their ambitions frequently – but not always – comes about by them treading all over people and pushing them to one side, on the way up.

At that time – 1979 or so – I knew that there were, as it were, three horses charging towards me. One was the possibility of being Chairman of the Central Board of the TSB which, by then, was a paid position. Another was the possibility – albeit a very remote one – of being Chairman of the Norwich Union Insurance Company. I had been sounded out in a very general way, but the front runner was one who knew far more about the Norwich Union than I would ever have known and who eventually took over as Chairman, Michael Falcon, and who did it extremely well. The third was the possibility of being a member of the Conservative government if it won the election, with the smallest, but nevertheless factual possibility, of being Leader of the House of Lords and therefore a member of the Cabinet.

Faced with these horses, all uncertainties, as it were charging towards one out of the mist, it was difficult to know how to answer the question, 'What are your ambitions?'

In a funny kind of way, I had felt that, if I was asked to help the government and refused, I might always regret it. There was the Labour Party saying, 'What shall we nationalise next – the banks, the insurance companies, the chemical industry?' And there was Margaret Thatcher, the last hope for the country of stopping the 'irreversible ratchet of social-ism'. If she were to say, 'Will you come and help row in this boat?', and if I were to reply, 'Thank you very much but I would rather earn a bit of money,' I might always regret it. It would seem selfish and materialistic.

Knowing of this dilemma, I asked John Hill, a great friend of mine who had been our Member of Parliament in South Norfolk for years and of whose Conservative Association I had been both Chairman and President for many years, what he thought. He said, 'If you were to be asked and you were to refuse, I think that you will always regret it.'

My mind was almost made up. I thought that I would ask another person for whom I had a huge respect – and of whom I always felt in great awe – Sir Edmund Bacon. He was Lord Lieutenant of Norfolk, Chairman of the British Sugar Corporation and of many other things. He said, 'No doubt about it. Don't mess about with being a Minister. Anyone can do that. If you are given the opportunity, do something in business.' I was bowled over. Here was this hugely impressive man for whom one could only have enormous respect, telling me to do the reverse of what all the others had advised me to do, and to do the reverse of what I was considering that I should do.

In the end, rightly or wrongly, I rejected Mindy Bacon's advice and, when asked, I went into government, eschewing the other possibilities. I have often wondered whether it was the right decision. I think that it probably was. To have done something in the business world would have almost certainly provided more money – and that, to me, was always an important factor – but politics is the widest life of all. I may not have been in the highest echelons of decision taking – indeed, I cannot think of hardly any decision which I took off my own bat – but I suppose that one adds something to the smell of government incense, and politics does bring you into contact with all 'sorts and conditions of men'. It is wider, more exciting, more unpredictable and, in the end, more important. People in business whom I have met have always said that business is quite a narrow road down which to travel, but that politics is more interesting and more essential.

The other really funny thing about politics is that it is so like being at school. There are the seniors – the prefects. Then there are the clever guys. There are the silly clots, too. Like football, you do the best that you can when the ball comes to you in order not to let the side down. At Question Time, if you can score a point or make them all laugh, it is very satisfying. The schoolboy ethos is never very far away – and that is good. It keeps it simple. It keeps it flippant and it stops everything from being too pompous.

When one Minister was replying to a question at the Despatch Box, I found a drawing pin, and placed it on the red leather bench next to me, where the Minister was going to sit in order to resume his seat. John Belstead, who was Leader and saw what was about to happen practically had an apoplexy. He screamed sotto voce, if one can do such a thing, 'No. No. No.' I removed it just in time.

I was made Parliamentary Secretary to the Ministry of Agriculture in 1974. Jo Godber was the Minister, a nice affable man with clear-rimmed spectacles. He would never set the place on fire, but he was good to work under. Peggy Fenner, later to be Dame Peggy Fenner, was also a Parliamentary Secretary.

Much to my horror, Jo Godber sent me off to Brussels for an Agriculture meeting of the EEC. The general election was approaching. He had to stay at home to go electioneering. So I had to go on my own – with, of course, officials from the Ministry of Agriculture. I had never been to an EEC meeting before. It was terrifying. It was becoming clear that there was going to be a row the next day because the United Kingdom had failed to give advance warning to Brussels that we were going to raise the price of milk paid to farmers by a shilling a gallon. Of course, by the time that I went to Brussels, we had done it and I was going to be at the fire side of the toasting fork. I rang Jo from Brussels and told him that he must come. There was going to be a fearful row and he must be here. 'I cannot. You will have to do it on your own.' I did. There was a row, but somehow we got through it.

It left, though, a marked impression on me. I had never been an enthusiast for the EEC on the good old British principle that Britain was a fine country and we can perfectly well manage on our own. Yet, now, here we were all arguing around a huge table – the UK, France, Germany, Italy and all the others. Only a few years ago they had been bombing each other, knocking hell out of each other, and fighting and killing each other ferociously and unnecessarily – as they had done for 500 years. Yet here they were all arguing frantically about the price of a pat of butter. It seemed so bizarre. It changed my view totally. Of course, we ought to be part of this great organisation whose prime purpose was to stop this terrible history of fighting and hatred from continuing and from happening again.

When Margaret Thatcher became Prime Minister in 1979, she asked me to go back to the Ministry of Agriculture as Minister of State. Peter Walker – who was about fifty – was to be the Minister. We subsequently became great friends and he was kind enough, some years later, to ask me to be godfather to his now lovely daughter, Marianna.

At that time, Alan Webster, Dean of Norwich, later to become Dean of St Paul's, asked me to be High Steward of Norwich Cathedral. I was deeply flattered. They usually had some eminent, titled, Norfolk land-owner to take on this responsibility. I was not Norfolk born and bred. I was a transplant. I came from Leicestershire, although I now lived in Norfolk. I was, therefore, deeply flattered to be asked to be High Steward of the Cathedral and I have loved the position and the Cathedral ever since. I did it for twenty-eight years.

It carried a salary with it, the same as it had been since the mid six-teenth century or thereabouts – now £6-13s-6d. At one of our morning meetings at the Ministry of Agriculture I told Peter, 'By the way, I have taken up paid employment.' 'What on earth do you mean?' I said that I had been asked to be High Steward of Norwich Cathedral and that it carried a salary of £6-13s-6d per annum. 'Well we had better clear it with No. 10.' I said, 'Don't be so silly,' in terms which were probably more deferential at the time. 'Well, you never know, there may be a conflict of interest.' No. 10, of course, said that it was alright for me to take this on.

How right Peter was. At the first meeting of the Friends of the Cathedral, which I attended in my capacity as High Steward, all hell was let loose because the government, in the guise of Geoffrey Howe, the Chancellor of the Exchequer, had altered the terms of tax relief, and this affected the covenants which had been given to the cathedral. The result was that Norwich Cathedral was now going to be several thousand pounds a year worse off. And it was all the government's fault. And here was I, the High Steward, and also a member of the government which had dealt this savage blow. Immediately a conflict of interests. People, though, were very understanding.

In the same year, 1979, I was asked to be President of the East of England Agricultural Society's Show at Peterborough. It was a fine show, and a huge one, as a result of the combination of some seven local shows. It was run by a charming, very efficient and exceedingly nice secretary, Roy Bird. There were endless stands, the biggest tractors you had ever seen, the best and the most enormous equipment and everything geared towards the large arable farmers of the Eastern Counties. The Grand Ring was full of the most exciting tableaux – soldiers on motorcycles, a military band, beautiful horses and the Grand Parade of Cattle. I was showing a beautiful Chartley Bull, large, perfectly marked and hand-some, but where was he to go in the parade? There were no classes for Chartleys. One person said, 'There is only one place for the President's bull to go, and that is to lead the parade.' And he did.

The commentator gave such a full and lengthy description of the bull and the breed that, when he had finished, everyone, all the way around the ring, clapped. I felt very proud. It was a very smart show. All the ladies turned up in their best summer dresses, and all the stewards wore grey bowler hats. Twenty-five years later, the stewards still wear grey bowler hats, but the show has, sadly, gone badly downhill. It is now called 'a country show'. Very few animals. No parade of cattle. No stands with unusual, big machinery. Mostly raincoats, umbrellas, boots, furniture and a rather miserable flower tent. But they still seem to attract a lot of visitors – I cannot think why. The East of England Show used to be quite superb, and they are kind enough to ask us both back each year. Meanwhile, the Norfolk Show was puny in comparison. The Norfolk Show now knocks the spots off the East of England Show. It is miles better.

***

Peter Walker, the new Minister of Agriculture, was then a young, determined, highly competent and totally articulate politician who had made his name firstly by starting up a very successful company in the City, Slater Walker, then by being a very young Secretary of State for the Environment, and a very young Cabinet Minister. He made planning history when a request came before him to knock down and rebuild Wellington Barracks in the heart of London. It was out of date and needed replacing. It also happened to be a fine old building, part of the landscape of that area of London, and the centrepiece of the Brigade of Guards. Peter said that they could do what they like with the interior, but the exterior, the façade, must be kept.

I think that was the first time that that kind of stipulation had been put on a planning document. It was a huge success. Honour was satisfied all round. Later, a similar request, and a similar result, came when there was a request to redevelop Coutts Bank in the Strand – a building of great character and significance. Again, do what you like on the inside, but leave the façade alone.

I always thought that those were quite important decisions as they were a substantial brake on the 'knock down the old and rebuild it with new' philosophy which was then rampant.

In contrast to the Department of the Environment, Peter Walker found the Ministry of Agriculture a doddle. 'You could do it all from home, really' was his philosophy. As one who found wading through the tide of bureaucracy and paperwork like swimming through treacle, pretty daunting, I admired his sensible view, although I found it difficult to share. His officials were always on tenterhooks about what he was going to say. He never followed a prepared speech, but always spoke off-the-cuff. His officials, therefore, never knew what he was going to come out with next, which totally alarmed them.

The other Ministers were Alick Buchanan-Smith, a nice young, very competent and articulate Scot. He was also a Minister of State, in charge of fishing, and was really Peter's No. 2. Peggy Fenner was then rather a dry person, who always, remarkably because of the distance, used to go back to her home in Kent each night. But she was charming and we still speak of the 'old days' with affection. Jerry Wiggin was Parliamentary Secretary. He did not fall into the same league of competence as Peter or Alick. He had a very pretty wife and, when his marriage came to an end a few years later, I shall never forget him saying to me, pathetically, 'I have lost my wife, my house and my yacht all in a week.' Tragedy is never very far around the corner for anyone.

As a Minister of State I was technically senior to Jerry Wiggin, who was a Parliamentary Secretary, but we never thought of these things in a hierarchical fashion. We were colleagues together. I was, though, always conscious of the fact that I was a Lords Minister and not a Commons Minister. I had not been elected. The others had been. It was in the Commons where all the power lay. We, in the Lords, merely had to process what the Commons did. Of course, there was a little more to it than that but I always felt that, if there were a dispute, my Commons colleagues should get their way.

I was sent off to Brussels to negotiate the price of agricultural commodities. Me? Negotiate? I had never negotiated anything in my life more vital than a packet of sweets. Anyhow, I was taking a very competent negotiator from the Ministry of Agriculture, Freddie Kearns. He knew it all backwards.

They were all sitting round the table with the great big, charming, beer-swilling Bavarian, Herr Ertl, in the chair. I had my folder out. We took ages discussing wheat and barley. Then, Herr Ertl said, 'There is nothing much in the rest. I think we can go through that quite quickly.' Then we came to clementines. My brief said, 'Resist'. I turned to Freddie Kearns and said, 'I can't resist this. There are only 80,000 tons (or whatever the figure was) involved anyhow.' 'Minister, you must resist.'

I put my hand up rather gingerly and said, 'I object.' 'The United Kingdom objects?' 'Yes.' Jacques Chirac, who was later to become President of France, but was then the French Minister of Agriculture, breathed fire across the table and said, 'Does the United Kingdom not realise that there are only 80,000 tons involved?' I slid further into my seat. They meant a lot to France, as they produced most of them.

It was the only time that I met Chirac. He was tall, impressive, distinguished, had a great personality and he spoke good English. I liked him. After it was all over, he got up and came around the table. Help, he is coming for me. Not a bit of it. He knew how these negotiations work. He disregarded me as if I was a bit of fluff on the wall and he went straight to Freddie Kearns. They talked for about ten minutes.

On the way back to the British Embassy in a very smart large limousine, I said to Freddie, 'There you are. I told you that we should not object over the clementines. You made me look a complete idiot.'

'Oh no, Minister. Clementines in themselves are not that important. But I wanted to negotiate with France over sugar and some other commodity. Chirac was quite happy with my suggestion over sugar and this has saved the United Kingdom £x million. So it was all worth it. The clementines stay as they are. France is happy and the United Kingdom is happy.' But I still felt an idiot – and certainly a fall guy. Freddie loved negotiating. It was in his blood.

That is how these funny decisions are arrived at. And sometimes Ministers are used as mincemeat.

***

Two of Mrs Thatcher's burning enthusiasms in the election were to save public money and to cut down on Quangos – Quasi Autonomous Non Governmental Organisations. They had sprouted like cress and were, in effect, an extension of government and certainly of government expenditure. The Prime Minister had asked all her Ministers to a drink in No. 10 shortly after the election. I took the precaution of finding out how many quangos there were for which the Ministry of Agriculture was responsible.

It was a lovely summer's evening and one felt the huge privilege of having a drink in the garden of No. 10. The Prime Minister came round to our group, which consisted of mostly young nervous Lords Ministers. We were chatting about some inane subject. She turned to me and said, 'How many quangos are there in the Ministry of Agriculture?' 'Thirteen, Prime Minister' I replied. She said 'get rid of them,' and walked on. The irony was that, at the end of her period as Prime Minister, there were more quangos than when she started. Which only goes to emphasise what I have inadequately called Ferrers' Law, which is that 'Everything has the Reverse Effect of that intended'.

When I was at school, I learnt all about Ohm's Law, Boyle's Law and Faraday's Law. I subsequently constructed my own law, which modesty compelled me to call Ferrers' Law. I give three examples of this. When in the earlier days of the marketing of eggs, the British Egg Marketing Board decided that all eggs should be subjected to rigorous testing before being offered for consumption; they had to be washed, counted and inspected to make sure that there were no blood spots or meat spots or cracks or any other kind of miserable irregularity in them. Having passed all these tests, the egg was stamped with the mark of approval of the British Egg Marketing Board, a Lion. But, by the time that the egg came on to the shop shelf, it was old. What was the result? Nobody liked them. The Lion was not an accolade of perfection, but an indication of age. Everyone said, 'Give us an egg with a good bit of old muck on it, then we will know that it is fresh.'

The second is that when the United Kingdom was going through one of its periodical financial crises, Jim Callagan, who at that time as Chancellor of the Exchequer, said, 'In order to protect the pound, nobody must take more than £50 abroad.' What was the result? More people went abroad than ever before. All the Travel Agencies said, 'Hooray for the Chancellor of the Exchequer. Now everyone can see how cheap it is to go abroad.'

The third example is that, when the government bought the Goya painting of the Duke of Wellington, they hung it in the National Gallery, so that a grateful nation could see a wonderful painting. It might be hard to believe, but somebody stole it. There was the most appalling row in the newspapers. The result was that more people went to see the place where the painting used to hang than ever went to see the painting when it hung there.

So that is the stuff of Ferrers' Law – everything has the reverse effect of that intended. It is surprising how often that proves true.

***

We had to order new headed writing paper in the Ministry of Agriculture. The proposal came to me which was, in effect, to renew the contract with Her Majesty's Stationery Office who had always supplied the stationery. I agreed and signed the submission.

It must be remembered that this was an era when everything was being questioned. There were too many ruts into which government and bureaucracy had fallen. They must be got out of this. I was, though, surprised when Peter Walker called a meeting to discuss the purchase of stationery. I went along too. Peter was in a relaxed mood in his armchair. The official was there, too. Peter's questioning of him was devastating. 'Why do you want Her Majesty's Stationery Office to provide the stationery?'

'They always have.'

'Just because they have supplied stationery in the past, why should they continue to do it in the future?'

'They know what we want and how to do it.'

'Have you asked any other companies for a quotation?'

'No.'

'Why not?'

Then came the terrible answer, 'I haven't had the time.'

Desperate, pregnant pause.

'You haven't had the time?' Peter asked in scathing horror, 'Give me samples of what we require and I will get some alternative quotations.' The official was in despair. The atmosphere was electric. I sank into my chair and hoped that it would disappear through the floor. There was nothing nasty or improper or antagonistic in the questions. They were just devastating.

***

A submission came up to me to increase the funding for research from £42m to £48m – I may have the figures wrong, but not the principle. As the diktat from on high had been to cut government expenditure I put a note on the submission that I thought that the expenditure ought to remain at £42m if not be decreased. I wanted to speak to officials.

So a meeting was called. To my surprise, extra chairs were brought in. Then, all the officials came in one after the other, about eight of them, ending up with the Permanent Secretary, Sir Brian Hayes. He was a very nice, hugely competent person who used a special font on his typewriter – they were typewriters in those days – so you could see the Permanent Secretary's opinion easily. They were always read – by me anyhow – and they were always good.

I laughed and asked why it was necessary to have so many people to the meeting. 'You want to cut the research budget, Minister?', said the Permanent Secretary.

'Yes, but the government wants to cut costs.'

'Do you really want to see all the research departments closed, research work ceased in its tracks, research workers made redundant?'

I whimpered that I did not. 'But you are asking for a huge increase.'

'Minister, by the time that we have argued with the Treasury, who will demand cuts, and by the time that we take account of inflation, we will be back at the figure which we want, which is the current figure plus an allowance for inflation. Research will go on uninterrupted.'

I laughed. I said, 'This is just like *Yes Minister*.' So it was. No one else laughed. But they got their way. Quite right, too.

***

My office in the Ministry of Agriculture was looking very shabby. The walls needed painting. The windows needed cleaning. So did the anti-bomb-blast net curtains. We couldn't have the windows cleaned because that would mean a huge great paraphernalia being erected on the roof with pulleys and platforms. Too expensive. Then, alright, the curtains must be done. Nothing happened. It was the responsibility of another Department. I said that the curtains were filthy and, if the Ministry of Agriculture would not get them cleaned, I would take them down myself and put them in the washing machine. 'Is that a threat?', asked my Private Secretary, alarmed. 'No. Just a fact.' The Department cleaned them.

Then my Private Secretary came to say that the room could not be painted – government cuts. I said that it must be painted as it was a disgrace for any visitors, especially from overseas, to see Ministers living in such squalor. No, it could not be painted. There was no money because the government was imposing strict restraints. Eventually a compromise was reached. In the summer recess, the walls would be washed. Hooray. But, all that the washing did was to highlight the really unspoilt places like where the clock and the previous pictures had been, and all the rest was markedly dirtier. So that was not a huge success. But one had to be thankful for small mercies.

Later I was given the great privilege of being made a Privy Counsellor, one of the most senior and cherished positions in public life. It is not an honour, but an appointment, therefore it is technically wrong to put PC after one's name. The fact that you are a Privy Counsellor is recognised by the prefix The Rt Honourable before one's name. It is an organisation whose duty is to ensure that nothing untoward comes against the Monarch, and any information can be passed from one to another under 'Privy Council terms'. One member of Parliament commented to me, in the light of my appointment to the Privy Council, that it was the most respected position that anyone in political life could receive.

I had to go to see the Clerk to the Privy Council to be instructed as to what to do when I went to the Palace to be enrolled as a Privy Counsellor. At the end, the Clerk asked if I would like to see the Lord President's Office on the floor above. I agreed with alacrity. It was a beautiful room with high walls and a magnificent ceiling and majestic plaster work. *But* – the walls were bright puce pink. I could not believe my eyes. I thought it was dreadful and an offence to beautiful architecture.

The Lord President of the Council was Norman St John-Stevas, who later became Lord St John of Fawsley. He was noted for having less than orthodox views on some subjects of which interior decoration was obviously one. I asked the Clerk, 'How on earth was it allowed for this room to be painted in such a fashion?' He replied that Privy Counsellors have the right to have their rooms painted and that the choice of colour was entirely theirs. My ears pricked up. 'Privy Counsellors can have their rooms painted?' I went back to the Ministry of Agriculture and said, 'Privy Counsellors can have their rooms painted. Can I have mine painted please?' It was. But not pink.

***

I was sent out to Bangladesh for a conference of Ministers of Agriculture. Bangladesh was teaming with people, almost all on rickshaws, pedalled by very skinny people. It was arduous work. The average life expectancy for rickshaw drivers was forty-five. They just wore themselves out.

We were taken down the Ganges on a very rusty old steamer. People had their houses and brick kilns scattered all over the place between all the little rivers. I shall never forget being told that, when there was a storm, the flooding could be so bad that the position of the river can move *eight* miles. I found that hard to believe. I still find it hard to believe. But I was told categorically that it was true.

Whilst there, I met Dennis Norman, the Minister of Agriculture in Southern Rhodesia, and his wife, June. They were charming people. The next time I met them was in the Prince's Chamber in the House of Lords in London when they were guests of Henry Plumb in 2007. They immediately recognised me and remembered my name – but that was twenty-five years later. Not bad going.

On the flight back from Dakar to Singapore, we went first class by Thai Airways. It was superbly comfortable. I shall never forget sitting next to, and having a conversation for the duration of the flight with, one of our Foreign Office officials who had been on an overseas posting in Bangladesh. We were kept perpetually, and liberally, topped up with champagne by an extraordinarily attractive and gracious air hostess with a staggering figure – but then, they are all like that – who always called one 'Excellency'. It was pretty heady wine!

I remember the conversation so well because the official said how, earlier in his career, he had been a District Officer in an outer region of Nigeria. His daughter had been going through a rather bolshy phase, saying how awful it was that the British should go and run other people's countries, and virtually take them over. The official (such a nice person whose name unfortunately I have forgotten) explained to his daughter that they were running the country as best they could and for the benefit of the country.

These were the District Officers, often living in remote parts of the country, taking decisions which would affect the local population. They had no guns. They had no soldiers to back them up. They had no one who could force their views on to an unwilling population. The local people could come up and kill them if they wanted to. But they did not, because they realised that it was all being done for their benefit.

The official explained how sad it was that these expatriate people, who had been working for the benefit of other countries by giving them growth and stability, should be nowadays portrayed as wicked, oppressive colonialists, sitting on top of a bewildered and oppressed people and working against the interests of the people for whom they were responsible. It was just nothing of the sort. These were good people doing their best for the countries to which they were sent.

Why is it that the do-gooders nowadays manage to get everything upside down and impugn the motives, actions and successes of previous generations? Despite all its controversy, the old colonial style had much of which to be proud, of which one at least was stability. Of course, there has to be change. That is life. But has it really proved to be for the better?

The President of Bangladesh was a great admirer of Mrs Thatcher and, at a reception in Bangladesh, he pulled me to one side and sat me down on a sofa to speak to me. He asked all about Mrs Thatcher, how she was and what she was doing. I felt very privileged.

The next time I saw the President was at No. 10. Annabel and I had been asked to a lunch which was being given for him by the Prime Minister. I had been down to Hampshire that morning to see some strawberry growers who were moaning about the Common Market and the influx of cheap strawberries from Spain and Italy. 'The EEC don't care about us at all. All they want to do is to sell all their produce to us and undermine our market.' It was an uncomfortable time. There were about twelve of them encircling me like vultures. I suddenly thought of a question. 'What car do you run?' There was silence – and a lot of embarrassed faces. They squiggled and squirmed. They drove Renaults or Citroëns or Volkswagens – all European cars. 'You are quite happy to buy their cars. Why should not we be able to buy their fruit?' End of conversation.

We shot back to London. I got changed. Annabel was collected and we went off to No. 10. I had not had time to look at what we were doing in the House of Lords that afternoon. During the pre-lunch drinks, the Prime Minister signalled for Annabel and me to go over to her. She turned to the President of Bangladesh and said, 'Mr President, this is Lord Ferrers. Lord Ferrers is Deputy Leader of the House of Lords. Lord Ferrers, what is it that the House of Lords is discussing this afternoon?' Horror of all horrors. I had not the slightest idea. I tried to turn the answer round to what we had discussed yesterday. I was mortified. So was Annabel. I wanted the floor to collapse underneath me. So did Annabel. It was awful. The whole of the lunch was completely ruined for me. I felt that I was carrying a placard around my neck saying 'I have bogged it.'

The Prime Minister was a very frightening person. I have always admired her hugely, but she – quite rightly – expects everyone to be on top of their job. Still in a state of nervous agitation, I went to the House of Lords for Question Time and sat next to Christopher Soames, the Leader of the House of Lords, on the front bench. I said, 'I am in a terrible state.'

'Why?' he asked.

'I have bogged it with the Prime Minister.'

'Why? What has happened?'

'She asked me what the House of Lords was doing this afternoon and I did not know.'

Christopher roared with laughter.

'What is funny about that?' I asked.

'She knew perfectly well. I told her myself this morning.'

***

I went for a two-day visit to the north of England to see, amongst other things, land rehabilitated after opencast coal had been removed, and a place where lettuces were being grown in warm water from the cooling towers of a power station. It was during lunch that my Private Secretary had a call from the Ministry of Agriculture saying that Peter Walker wanted me to go back to London to do a press conference. Why could not Jerry Wiggin do it as he was in London? But Peter wanted me to do it. So, off we went back to London. We did the press conference, turned round and came back to the north of England again. On a train. The wonders of modern travel. You really can get about when you need to. We had a very good dinner on the train after an arduous day.

***

I had a letter from a Labour Member of Parliament containing a letter from a constituent who was out of her mind because of some pesticide store belonging to the Ministry of Agriculture which was ten yards from her kitchen window. It was plastered with yellow and black stripes and notices such as 'Keep out', 'Highly dangerous', 'Inflammable', 'Toxic', 'Don't enter'. The poor constituent was terrified of being in her house, and so were her grandchildren who did not want to come and see her any more.

   I received a very indifferent draft reply to send. 'Don't worry. It is all perfectly alright' was, in effect, what it said – but it all smelt fishy to me. So my Private Secretary, Gareth Steele, and I flew up to Darlington, or wherever it was, one Friday. There was the house, and there was this inflammable store about ten yards away from her kitchen. I quite under-stood why the lady was so worried. I would have been, too. I said that they must find another place to put all this inflammable stuff. The lady was hugely relieved, and I received a very grateful letter from the lady's Member of Parliament, a Labour member. It was these sorts of occasions where you felt that you can really do a bit of good, even if it only brings a bit of humanity to a bureaucratic way of life.

***

In the August of 1979, when I had just joined the Ministry of Agriculture, I was sent out to Nairobi to attend the Kenya Agricultural Show. Annabel joined me a few days later.

It so happened that Alan Lennox-Boyd, who used to be the Colonial Secretary and who was now Lord Boyd of Merton, was there staying in the same house. He was a huge, tall, impressive person and a very nice one too. Many years earlier, when we were farming the whole time at Hill House, I was milking the cows for the third time at 8 p.m. (we did that crazy kind of thing in order to get more milk out of the cows – but I do not think it was very sensible and it was certainly very laborious). Annabel came rushing out to the cowshed and said, 'Quick. Come quickly. It is the Colonial Secretary on the telephone.'

I could not think what this could all be about. What did the Colonial Secretary want with me? I rushed to the house and grabbed the telephone. What was it? He wanted to know what was the inscription over the west door of the chapel at Staunton – about doing the best things in the worst times and hoping them in the most calamitous. I told him. I wondered what on earth he wanted to know that for.

Many years later, in August 1979, we were having dinner in the same house together in Nairobi. Alan told me that, when he telephoned me, some twenty years earlier, he had to open a new Town Hall in Nairobi, and yet there was the most appalling civil war going on with the Kikuyus. He thought, 'What kind of a country is this when, whilst you are having the most dreadful civil war, killing people all over the place, you go and build a new town hall?'

Alan had to open it, and he thought that the quotation at Staunton Harold was the most positive contribution he could make. 'To do the best things in the worst times and to hope them in the most calamitous.' The next day he took me down to the town hall and showed me where he had made the speech and, later, he sent me photographs of the occasion. He was a very kind – and a very impressive – man.

Some years after that, when Alan was Prime Warden of the Goldsmiths' Livery Company in London, he asked me to lunch. I felt very flattered.

He said that they had just had a Court Meeting, and that I must meet the members of the Court which I did, going down the line. 'This is Mr X. This is Mr Y. This is Mr Tarratt.'

'How do you do.' I moved on to the next person and then turned round and said,

'Did he say Mr Tarratt?' I asked of the gentleman.

'Yes,' he said.

'Mr Tarratt of Leicester?'

'Yes,' he said.

'You made my wife's wedding ring.'

'Yes I know.'

That was twenty-five years earlier. What an amazing coincidence. The ring, if my memory holds me correct, cost £3. I remember at the time thinking that it was not very expensive. 'Oh yes,' said Mr Tarratt. 'It is engagement rings which are expensive. Wedding rings are quite cheap.'

When out in Kenya, I thought that we must do what people do in Kenya, which is to go deep sea fishing.

I was told that there was a man who was an expert on this and his name was Martin Thompson. Little did I realise that he was the person who had married Matilda Matheson, whose parents, Fergus and Jean Matheson lived just opposite us in the Old Rectory at Hedenham in Norfolk, and who would later return to England and set up the Ultimate Travel Company.

When Annabel arrived in Nairobi, I told her with pride that I had fixed for us to go deep sea fishing. 'That will be very exciting,' I said. 'That is the great thing to do if you are in Kenya.' Annabel was a bit quiet and not all that enthusiastic. 'I am not sure about that.' 'Oh yes, it will be lovely. Everyone who comes here does it,' I said. She looked increasingly less enthusiastic. Eventually she came out with the punchline, 'I don't want to be drafted for deep sea fishing.'

Matilda showed us the very simple and comfortable sandals which people wore in Nigeria. She took me down to a shop in Mombasa where I asked if they could make me a pair of sandals. 'Let me see your feet.' I put them up. They all roared with laughter. They had never seen anything quite so big. They made me a pair, for the next day, for £2.

We had spent a lot of our time seeing different aspects of agriculture in Kenya, including staying a night on safari where you could see animals coming in to drink. The outside was floodlit and, if the animals came to the watering hole in the night, a bell would ring in your room and you could get up and watch them from the veranda. Some people went mad about it, but I did not find it all that exciting.

At the end of our visit, my back was very painful having been bumped up and down in a Land Rover travelling down all the unmetalled roads. I said to the High Commissioner, with whom we were staying, that I would much like to see an osteopath. He smiled. 'You won't get an osteopath here. There aren't any.' I felt distraught. But he told me that there was a faith healer just down the end of the road on which the High Commission was. Faith healer? I was a bit apprehensive about this. What are faith healers, and what do they do? I was told that she was a very respectable lady, called Michaela Dennis. She used to do wildlife programmes on television with her husband Armand. Armand had died and she kept his ashes in an urn on the mantelpiece in the living room. The High Commissioner arranged for me to see her after dinner and said that I would be taken down in his car. 'I can easily walk,' I said. 'You will do no such thing. It is not safe. If you don't come back in an hour, I will come and look for you, otherwise you may land up in an urn on the mantelpiece too!'

Michaela Dennis was very nice and very helpful. She explained that there is no faith involved in all this, but she just has healing qualities which sometimes helped people. It was remarkable. I removed my jacket. She told me not to talk. She put one hand on my forehead and one on my back. I could feel the heat come from her hand and through my shirt. It was most surprising. I suppose that it took, in all, half an hour. When I returned to the High Commission they were all in a fairly jovial mood enjoying their post-prandial brandies and coffees. They asked me how I got on. 'Look,' I said, and bent down and touched my toes. No pain. It was amazing. Unfortunately, it did not last for all that long, but it was a remarkable alleviation of pain for the time being. Michaela had said, 'If the pain comes back, think of me. That sometimes helps.' It did. I did. But it didn't.

Above left, Admiral Washington
5th Earl Ferrers (1722–1778). He
redesigned Staunton Harold to its
present shape. Above right, Anne,
wife of 5th Earl Ferrers.

Left, 10th Earl
Ferrers at school
in Cheam.

Below, 10th Earl Ferrers
– 'Two Back'.

Above left and right, Nenella and
Bill Carr, Annabel's parents.

Right, Mummy with Betty, Neppy and
me (aged three). Below, Neppy, Betty
and me, aged eleven, by the lake at
Staunton Harold.

The Queen inspecting the Queen's Body Guard, talking to Bill Carr.

Below, Staunton Harold in the snow.

Left, with Dukie on his retirement from the BBC. Below, Andrew and Tammy's wedding at Staunton Harold.

Left, Annabel at Staunton, 1950. Right, Annabel in the red evening dress at the Meynell Hunt Ball where we danced for the first time, 1948.

Left, Annabel arriving at our wedding at St Edmund's, Bungay, 21 July 1951. Below, the wedding reception, Ditchingham Hall.

Above, Andrew, Louise (on Tara) and Annabel, Hedenham Hall, 1979. Right, Robert and Andrew at Farleigh House Prep School, 1977.

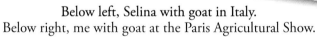

Below left, Selina with goat in Italy.
Below right, me with goat at the Paris Agricultural Show.

Right, Selina's wedding,
1988. Below, Selina with
Hermione Shirley, Georgina
Ellis, William Shirley and
Felix Descamps, 1988.

Below, before our
Ruby wedding dance,
Ditchingham Hall,
July 1991.
Below left, Sallyanne.

Above, with Harold Macmillan (Prime Minister) and the Earl of Home (Foreign Secretary) greeting the President of the Cameroons, Victoria Station, 1963.

Left, on a parliamentary visit to Indonesia.

Right, with Lee Kuan Yew in Singapore.

The opening of Parliament, 1989. Carrying the Cap of Maintenance.

Addressing the House of
Lords from the dispatch box.

Grand Prior of the
Order of St Lazarus
of Jerusalem.
Venice, 2005.

***

On one occasion, when I was going to Saudi Arabia, the Foreign Office asked if I could very kindly go to the North Yemen on the way. It was funny to be asked with such courtesy. I thought that one was normally just detailed to go. All Ministers apparently flew over North Yemen to go to South Yemen because there was more happening there, and North Yemen felt left out. So I said that I would.

It was a funny place. All the men looked like brigands. They shot anyone when they felt like it and they were transfixed by chewing khat, which is a curious green plant which contains, equally, some curious drug. One side of their cheeks sticks out as if they have a golf ball inside it, and it shows that they are chewing the wretched stuff. It eventually makes them dozy – not very nice when you are being driven in a car.

I saw one farm which had been set up by an Englishman. He was responsible for getting the cows, the milking parlour, the dairy, the vehicles, the lot – what they call a 'turnkey' job. He sets it all up, the owners move in and he then gets paid.

Everything, but just about everything, had gone wrong with the project, and here was a British Agriculture Minister coming to the North Yemen, so we will rub his nose in it. And they did. Look at the dairy – collapsed. Look at the lorries – rusted and in a heap. Look at the cows – there weren't any. Look at the dairy – a shambles. 'And it is all his fault. He has taken his money, and refused to come back and put in right. We will never do business with the United Kingdom again.'

I must say that it all looked dreadful, and I felt much sympathy for the Yemenis. I gathered subsequently that the other side of the coin – and there always is another side to any coin – was that there was a muddle up over the land tenure and that the land upon which this 'farm' was a part did not properly belong to the person who thought that he owned it and who had engaged the English company.

When I got back to the UK, I asked this entrepreneur to come and see me in the Ministry of Agriculture. He lived in Diss, only fifteen miles from my home. He was a farmer who, in addition, had become an exporter. I said to him, 'This scheme was appalling. It had never been finished. There had never been any after sales service and, if this is the way that we treat our overseas customers, we will never get another order. You must show good faith. Go back to the Yemen. Face the music, and put it right.'

The poor fellow explained his side of the story and said, 'I cannot go back.'

'What do you mean, you cannot go back. You have given the United Kingdom the most appalling reputation. You must go back.'

'I cannot.'

'Why not?'

'My wife won't let me.'

'What do you mean, your wife won't let you?'

'They say that, if I go back, they will kill me.'

Silence. Help. 'Oh I see. Then, you cannot go back can you?' And they *would* have killed him. Pompous Minister deflated immediately like the rapid expression of air from a big balloon.

We had a funny time leaving the Yemen. We were all collected from the hotel in a great convoy of cars with an outrider in the front. We soon got to the airport where we were very graciously met by the Minister who had come to say goodbye.

He and I sat down and chatted aimlessly about this and that, and suddenly my Private Secretary, who was not much good at the job and did not really like it anyway, came up and said, 'Minister. Have you got your briefcase?' I said, 'No. You have. It was with the bags in the hotel.' 'No I haven't.' The only thing to do was to take a car and whip back quickly to the hotel and get it. But it was not as simple as that. When we came to the airport, we had a police escort, and it was easy, like a knife cutting through butter. On the way back it was very different. It was rush hour and there was no police escort. It took ages.

The airport official came up to us and said that the aeroplane was now ready for us to board. No Private Secretary. No briefcase. The Minister, who was quite charming, said, 'Don't worry. We will continue to sit here for a while. There is plenty of time.'

The official came up to the Minister again and said, 'I am sorry, but I am afraid that they must all board because, if the aeroplane doesn't leave now, it will lose its slot for Jerusalem (or wherever it was going).' Still no Private Secretary. Still no briefcase.

So, we started to walk to the aircraft. The Minister was superb. 'Let us walk slowly, and be involved in deep conversation.' Which we did. We got to the steps of the aircraft. Still no Private Secretary. Still no briefcase. The Minister and I took a long time shaking hands and going slowly up the stairs and into the aeroplane. Inside the aeroplane there was complete silence. A deathly hush. All those poor blighters in the aeroplane had been sitting there in the heat with no air conditioning, waiting for us. I sensed an atmosphere of complete loathing towards me. Then, all of a sudden, there was a rush of tyres and a displacing of gravel and there was the car – plus Private Secretary and briefcase. I was pretty fed up with him by now. It is the Private Secretary's elementary job to look after the Minister's bags, and there was my briefcase standing in the foyer of the hotel. We set off, all feeling a bit jittery. The Private Secretary apologised to me, which of course I accepted.

I thought that I should send the pilot a note apologising for being late and thanking him for holding up his aeroplane. I called the air hostess and asked her to give the note to the pilot. When she had disappeared into the cockpit, the dour Minister of Agriculture official Brian Camp said, 'He will probably think that that is a skyjack note.' It had never occurred to me!

***

I was asked to be President of the Smithfield Show in 1979. This was a great honour. It was a unique Agricultural Show, held annually in December at Earl's Court in London and consisted entirely of machinery – the best in the land – and fat livestock – the best in the land. As with much which was so good, it now no longer exists. The prize fat bullock would go for thousands of guineas and the meat would be sold as coming from the prize winner of the Smithfield Show. It always seemed to me odd that people would take trouble for two years to fatten up an animal to perfection, to be the best in the country, and then promptly shoot it. You would have thought that they would want to preserve it as a prime beast or to use it for breeding. But that is not the way with that particular world.

The Queen Mother came to the show, as she always did, and it was my duty to take her round and then give her lunch. She was wonderful. She took such an interest in everything. We went upstairs in to the dining room and the Queen Mother had her normal glass of gin and Dubonnet and then a second.

We then sat down, some twenty of us, to lunch. When we came to the end of lunch, the port went round. I sent the decanter round a second time and offered the Queen Mother another glass. 'No thank you,' she replied. 'You are all very busy people and you have all got lots of things to do.' 'Oh no, we are not. We have nothing to do except enjoy ourselves,' I said. 'Oh, if that is the case, then I will have a second glass of port.' She did. We all did. It was fun. The Queen Mother knew how to combine duty with fun and to make everyone there do the same and enjoy it. It did not seem to do her much harm. She lived until 101.

When I took the Queen Mother back through the exhibition to the entrance of Earl's Court to her Rolls-Royce, all gleaming black and splendorous, I shall never forget the sight of all the people surrounding the car. Each one was smiling. I said to the Queen Mother 'Now you can see the pleasure which you give to so many people.'

***

I was lucky enough to go to several countries overseas when I was in the Ministry of Agriculture. The Prime Minister adopted a very thoughtful practice which was that Ministers on government business abroad could be accompanied by their wives at public expense on one occasion a year. It was a very 'sympathetic' rule. It made the visit much easier. It softened it. Because the Minister's wife was coming, other wives were asked to dinners, and the conversation was not stuck on boring old business the whole time. And it didn't cost the government that much. Usually, we were staying in Embassies or High Commissions. If we were in a hotel, usually it cost no more to have a double room occupied by two people than occupied by one. So, apart from the incidentals like food, the only real cost was the air fares. The difference it made to the whole visit by having one's wife there was enormous.

I went, amongst other places, to Burma, Sri Lanka, Thailand, Indonesia, North Yemen, Australia and New Zealand. I came to love the Far East. Apart from the climate, the food, history, culture and courtesies are all so interesting, and the people charming. The younger Far Eastern ladies have eye-shattering figures and are very beautiful. That also helps. The older Far Eastern ladies dress beautifully with the most exotic clothes and look very elegant. Behind it all is this great courtesy and respect for the other person. I find it quite fascinating and the Far East is, to me, infinitely more interesting than Africa.

I was to go to Burma, Sri Lanka and Thailand. I wanted Annabel to come too. The government on this occasion would not pay for her, so I said that I would pay for Annabel to come myself. I would be going first class and, rather unchivalrously, I said that I would not pay for Annabel to go first class, but I would pay for her to go economy. She was quite happy. She did not need the leg room which I need on a long journey – and, anyhow, Annabel was always superbly generous.

It was at the time when Mrs Thatcher had told everyone, including government departments, to 'shop around' and not just to deal with firms with which they had always dealt and accept their prices. Annabel had a hairdresser whose husband ran a travel agency. I asked him to quote. He did. He then said that if he could get the tickets for the whole of my party – five, I think – Annabel could go free, first class. This was electric. I told the officials. They were deeply suspicious. The price which the government agency would charge would be much higher. If Annabel can go free, there must be something fishy going on with discounts. If there were a discount available, it should go to the government. We could not have Ministers travelling around the world on cut-price tickets.

I thought the whole thing was quite absurd. I was doing what the Prime Minister had told us to do – shop around – and here were the officials bridling like a horse at it. Typical officials. They always do. Find a way of making things simpler – oh no. I must have endured thirty telephone calls. Little did I know that the hairdresser's husband had had the books of his firm, unbeknown to him too, gone through with a toothcomb to make sure that he was not selling tickets illegally. He was not... just.

So we could get the tickets through him – but Annabel could not go free. She could go on the same plane and with the same connections as mine, but economy. Done. Alright. Then, one day, the travel agent rang. 'I have managed to get your wife upgraded to first class at no extra charge.' So Annabel accompanied me all the way around the Far East first class for £500. It was a happy end to a bumpy saga.

Burma was a country to which not many Ministers had gone. I asked what its politics were. Is it pro UK and the West or not? 'It is totally independent,' I was told, 'It does not want to be aligned to anyone – to such a degree that it had resigned from the Organisation of Non Aligned Countries', because they thought that they were becoming too aligned.

The Burmese were charming people. They hate killing anything. One of the members of my party was John Mitchell, a charming, forceful man from ICI. He wanted to sell pesticides to the Burmese. The need for this became more apparent than expected when, at a formal dinner, after which I was giving my speech, a rat ran from one end of the wall behind me to another. I did not see it because the rat was behind me – but everyone else did, and nearly doubled up.

It was difficult to sell pesticides because, in the eyes of the Burmese, it was unfair to the pests to kill them with pesticides. I noticed at night time a number of what looked like bonfires on the corners and on the edges of the fields. I asked what they were for. To kill the insects. How do they do that? The insects are attracted by the lights and they fly into the flames. I said, 'I thought that you did not like killing animals.' 'Ah, that is different. With pesticides, you deliberately kill the insects. With fires, the insects are not forced to fly into them. They choose to do so of their own accord.' Lovely, logical thought!

We went to a school for a presentation. All the children, aged about seven to fifteen, sat outside very quietly under some trees. At the end of the presentation, I thought that I had better go and talk to the children.

'You have a lovely school.' No response.

'Do you like it?' No response.

'Do you like your teachers?' No response.

'Do you play lots of games?' No response.

Dead silence. I could get not a glimmer of movement from any of them – just a totally glum look from every child, but I suppose that a 6ft 6in foreigner must have looked to these tiny Burmese children like an ogre or something from a rather bad fairy tale. So I gave up and turned round. When I had walked for about twenty yards, they all suddenly burst into roars of laughter. I wonder what they were thinking. It was very sweet. So were they.

In our hotel they were very polite to us. Annabel had been out on an expedition with some of the wives from Burma, and I had returned earlier and had gone to the pool. When Annabel returned she was told 'The Lord is back'. She thought that that was very uplifting and supremely flattering.

***

There was quite a controversial Bill, introduced by the Conservative government, called The Wildlife and Countryside Bill. It was very much the responsibility of the Department of the Environment and, as I was in the Ministry of Agriculture, I did not have a lot to do with it, but the problem of bats did come within my purview.

The great thing, according to the Bill, was to protect bats. I thought that the government had gone mad. You were not going to be allowed to remove bats from your house or your church without the permission of the Local Authority. 'The bat has as much right to be in your house as you have,' some opposition Peers said. I replied, 'You tell that to someone who has just paid £50,000 to buy a house.' I had strayed from my brief somewhat for I do not like bats myself and my family simply cannot stand them. Have a bat in the house and everyone screams until it has been got rid of.

Lord Melchett was a bumptious young Labour Peer, about twenty-four. He had been an Agriculture Minister in the Labour government and he was then speaking from the opposition front bench. For some reason, he became exasperated with me. On one occasion from the Despatch Box he called me the Arthur Scargill of the Ministry of Agriculture. I never knew why or exactly what Peter Melchett meant, or with what he was trying to say about me, other than the fact that it was pretty uncomplimentary stuff but, on this occasion on bats, he found it all too much.

I had been making some non-sympathetic remarks about bats, and he said, 'I am quite sure that what the noble Lord is saying is not the advice of his officials or of the government scientists.' I said, 'No. The Noble Lord is quite right. It is from my own experience. If there is one thing which my family cannot stand, it is bats. The girls dive for cover. They shut themselves in rooms. They are terrified of the bats getting into their hair. The place is mayhem until the bats are removed. And, when it is suggested that the bats have the same right to your house as you have, I just don't agree.' It was not the government line. It was mine, and I felt that I was right – but I lost!

One of the tit-bits which I was told by Lord Melchett, not I think in the Chamber, was that the one thing which bats cannot stand are owls. The owls need not even be alive. Bats are terrified of them. A dead, stuffed owl in a church will see the bats off. I was talking to Lord Rippon one day in the Bishops' Bar. As Geoffrey Rippon, he was previously a member of the House of Commons, and had been responsible for the negotiations for Great Britain joining the EEC. He was complaining that he had had bats in his house and that he could not get rid of them. I passed him on the tip. 'A dead stuffed owl will get rid of them.' Some twelve months later I found him in the Bishop's Bar again. I asked him how his bats were. He told me how he had bought a Victorian stuffed owl from an antique shop in Brighton. He had paid £100 for it. He had put it in his house, but it had made no difference. The bats were still there!

***

On a visit to Indonesia, I went to Jakarta, and I was taken to see the Botanical Gardens at Jogjakarta, a few miles away from the Capital. We arrived in a long and impressive cavalcade of cars with me, as the Minister, in the front car with a United Kingdom flag on the bonnet. The driver was dressed in a beautiful white suit. I noticed that there were some trees ahead with what looked like large dead leaves or black hand-kerchiefs hanging from the branches. Much to my surprise, the dignity of the whole procession was eroded when the driver sat on the horn and continued to blow it intermittently for a long time. I thought 'What a funny thing to do on a pompous occasion like this.'

All of a sudden, all the black handkerchiefs fell off the branches and flew all over the place – huge, great big black 'birds'. These, I was told by my ministerial hosts, were Flying Foxes. Huge great big bats with a wingspan of 6ft. 'They are dreadful. They are the scourge of the place. They eat everything. We want to get rid of them.' They could not believe their ears when I told them that we, in the UK, were preserving them. They thought we were mad. So did I!

Every day, when we returned in our motorcade to the hotel, I used to get out of the car and went to the front to thank the Police outriders. I stood to attention, thanked them and bowed. They liked that. They had an extraordinary way of driving their motorcycles. They would blow their whistles and indicate that people should get out of the way by taking one of their hands off the handle bars and waving their hand as if they were swatting a fly. On some occasions, they would take both their hands off the handle bars and make these glorious gesticulations with both hands, the motorbike continuing at 40 m.p.h. It was the kind of thing that, as a boy of fourteen, one would do on a push bike. But not on a motorbike. It was very impressive, but I think that Health and Safety would have had a fit.

U-Than, the Burmese Minister of Agriculture, was a very nice man, and I got on well with him. When he came to London, I gave a dinner party for him at Lancaster House. They were mostly friends of mine from different walks of life, who I thought would provide interest and variety – instead of boring old politics and business. The one thing which he wanted to do was to visit Sandhurst again, where he was during the war and where he asked for *four* blankets! The poor chap was so cold after Burma.

***

I passed Bryan Hayes in the Ministry one afternoon. He was the Permanent Secretary in the Ministry of Agriculture. He was a very charming person and very efficient. 'Where are you going?' I asked. 'I am going to No. 10 to brief the Prime Minister on Muldoon's visit.' Muldoon was the Prime Minister of New Zealand, and was at that time supremely fussed about the UK joining the EEC, with the consequent loss of Commonwealth preference on agricultural imports to the UK, and the effect that would have on New Zealand lamb and butter.

I saw Bryan Hayes later that day. 'How did you get on?' I asked. 'I am exhausted. I have never had such a time. I was grilled solid for two hours and, at the end of it, the Prime Minister asked if I would like a cup of tea. I didn't want a cup of tea at all. All I wanted was a large whisky and soda.'

***

I had to take the Bees Bill through the House of Lords. It dealt amongst other things with a nasty disease affecting bees called Varroa. During the Committee Stage an amendment was put down by, of all people, the Conservative Peer Lord Hives, making a suggestion which was unacceptable to the government. He divided the House. The government lost. The next day Peter Walker said to me, 'Robin. The *only* Bill which the Ministry of Agriculture has this year is the Bees Bill. The *only* time that the government has lost a division in this parliament was yesterday. It was in the House of Lords. *You* were in charge of it, and the government were defeated by an amendment to the *Bees* Bill – put down by Lord *Hives*. Really.' He laughed.

Lord Hives was a charming, but stodgy-looking, middle-aged gentleman whom I thought had probably not done anything very remarkable in the whole of his life, but his forebear was Rolls of Rolls-Royce. I think that probably the entrepreneurial genes of Rolls had slipped through the net on the way down to Lord Hives.

Chapter 14

Out of Government

I LEFT THE government in 1983 as we were going to take on the task of moving to Ditchingham. I thought that would be the end of my time in government. Michael Falcon was kind enough to ask me back on to the Board of the Norwich Union, a wonderful and happy company.

I was asked to be Chairman of the British Agricultural Export Council (BAEC). I always thought that British agriculture ought to look outside its own territory instead of being inward-looking – and I was glad to do it, but it turned out to be a hornet's nest.

I had to sack the Chief Executive, John Thorneloe, and he did not like that. I did not like it either. I am useless at that kind of thing. BAEC had been Thorneloe's baby. It did not employ many people – about ten – but it had many companies subscribing to it, and hence providing its revenue. John Thorneloe knew everyone. Some people did not like the fact that, as Chairman, I was being paid £7,000 per annum – a novel idea. The Chairman used to be paid nothing. When the Members heard about this and that we were going to reorganise it all, they set up a splinter group called 'The BAEC Concerned Members Group'. I did not like that a bit. Eventually, John Thorneloe left, and Peter Sillars took over. He was a stalwart, and a charming person, previously the President of the National Institute of Agricultural Engineers. I had met him in Ministry of Agriculture days. I liked him. He was sound, good and had a charming and understanding character. He was always laughing and made any problem seem manageable. We became great friends.

We were always struggling to find enough money to keep BAEC going, especially as agriculture was beginning to feel the cold draught of recession, and companies hunted around to find costs which they could cut. Sometimes companies amalgamated, so two subscriptions became only one subscription. That might have helped them, but it did not help us. It was a difficult and, frankly, not very enjoyable time. Two real stalwarts were Francis Pemberton of Bidwells in Cambridge, and John Mitchell of ICI. They made life possible and worthwhile. They were total supporters, and they realised that change was needed. They were full of encouragement and could see beyond the end of their noses, which is more than most of the members could do. They were real buttresses for which I was very grateful.

In 1986, as Chairman, I went to China with the British Agricultural Export Council to AgChina 86, an agricultural exhibition. When the aeroplane on which we were flying – it was China Airways or some such – had landed in Beijing and was taxiing to the terminal, many of the passengers began to get up off their seats, as they do. The tough butch-looking airhostess, dressed in a baggy trouser suit, walked down the aisle hitting everyone with a roll of paper who was standing up and saying 'Sit down. Sit down.' I cannot imagine a British air hostess doing that and certainly not a Singaporean one.

Michael Jopling was Minister of Agriculture and he came with his stunningly pretty wife Gail. We had great fun going from Beijing to Shanghai and to other places on the way to Hong Kong. We laughed a lot. Oh! It is so important to laugh. In Beijing everyone wore that hideous green uniform and bicycled all over the place. They all looked dull and bored and boring. I somewhat irreverently wondered, how, or why, sexual intercourse ever took place – but evidently it did.

The hotels were very incompetently run. The further south that we went, though, and the nearer to Hong Kong that we got, the more things brightened up. The hotels became more efficient, and the girls wore pretty, bright clothes.

I also went to an agricultural exhibition in Moscow. One of the people whom we took was Jim Crossley who lives in Norfolk and is a friend of Angela's. He was trying to export Pea Viners, of all things. These are colossal great machines, the size of huge combine harvesters, and he wanted to take one over to Beijing, which he did.

I got two tickets for the Bolshoi Opera and I asked John to come with me. It was Verdi's *Masked Ball*. When we got there, the programmes were all in Russian and everyone talked in Russian, and so we did not know where we were. I said to John 'This is supposed to be about a wedding, yet it is just rather boring old singing. What do you think it is that we are watching? You can't tell from the programme.' John said, 'I don't know. What shall we do? My wife will kill me if I tell her that I have been to the Bolshoi but that I did not know what I saw.' I kept deadpan and said, 'Ask the chap next to you.' Much to my surprise he did, and much to both our surprises, he was an elderly American. 'I don't know, either. I haven't the slightest idea.'

In the interval all we could have was fruit juice, which was pretty dull and not the guarantor of a successful and enjoyable evening. We had seats at the side and almost over the orchestra pit. I shall never forget the sight of one colossal double bass drum, looking like the kind of drum that the drummer in a military band plays when they are marching – but about eight times bigger. I watched the musician. I think that he gave five whacks on it the whole evening. It was clearly an important part of the score.

Although we could speak no Russian, I was impressed by two things on the way back. Everyone was so helpful trying to tell us when to get off the tube and where to go. The other was how smart and well turned out the Muscovites were. They all had smart coats and these impressive fur hats. It may have been a communist country, but the tube was as safe as houses. No fear of crime there. A great change from Britain. Now, though, that the Russians have shunned communism, I gather that the tubes are less safe places.

That night I was writing in my bedroom in the hotel and the telephone rang. It was about 11.30. I wondered who on earth it could be. 'Oh darling, I love you. I must see you.' I was bowled over, and I realised that it was probably one of the local hotel 'girls' about whom we had heard so much. I gave what must have been the most English of all responses and said, 'I think that you must have the wrong number.'

***

The Ministry of Agriculture was a happy place in the 'olden days'. In 1979 agriculture mattered. Food mattered. The countryside mattered. Now, in 2010, agriculture doesn't matter. The farmers are accused of being scroungers, living off subsidies. Get food from abroad, it is cheaper. Farms, the countryside – they don't matter. It is just 'the environment' that matters – the bugs, the butterflies, the beetles and all that jazz.

But the bugs and butterflies and beetles all managed to live during the war and afterwards when agriculture mattered, when farmers, who knew about the land and cared for it, farmed the land. Now they are not called farmers. They are Land Managers, bossed around by an army of civil servants from the Department of Environment, Food & Rural Affairs – DEFRA – who know little about the land, but who are concerned with ticking boxes and filling in forms. Farmers no longer farm the land, the government does. The farmers are now contractors working for, and badly paid by, the government for doing what the government wants.

A huge new form of subsidy was introduced, called the Single Farm Payments Scheme where everyone's land has to be mapped out to perfection. One person, who lives near me, had two officials for four days on his farm measuring up the hedges and ditches to see if they agreed with what had been put on the form. If they did not, he could have been fined. And it is all watched over and logged by satellite. It is Big Brother, and George Orwell's *1984*, come to reality. What does it matter if the measurements are not strictly accurate – compared with the cost of checking it?

To do all this, the government installed a vast new computer costing £120 million or so, and it did not work. Farmers in England were not paid. Yet the farmers in Scotland, Wales and Northern Ireland were paid. Why? Because in Scotland, Wales and Northern Ireland they had different computers and different systems. Why did England have a system which was different to the others? Because the Secretary of State for the Department of the Environment, Food and Rural Affairs, decreed that this should be so. Who was the Secretary of State for the Department of the Environment, Food and Rural Affairs? Mrs Margaret Beckett.

It was a disaster. Farmers were not paid. Huge sums of money in interest and on default were demanded by the European Union from the government. Huge fines were paid to the European Union – £400m in one year, I think. Nobody resigned. Nobody does nowadays. Some senior officials were sacked. What happened to Mrs Beckett? She was promoted to Foreign Secretary.

Lord Carrington asked a lovely supplementary at Question Time to Lord Rooker who was answering questions on agricultural payments. Lord Carrington said 'Would the Minister care to speculate what the government would do to me if I owed the government what the government owes me?' Rooker understandably evaded the question. It was over £100,000. If anyone owed the government £100,000 they would be chased through the courts for it. But, when it is the other way round, and the government owes an individual £100,000, nothing happens. No politician gets the sack. Nobody resigns. They all continue as if it was 'just one of those things'. Farmers know the land best and they know how to run it. Civil servants don't. Their job is just to ensure that the systems, which the civil servants introduce in accordance with the wording of the Act or the European Regulations, are carried out to the letter.

***

In 1976 I was responsible for leading the Opposition against the Aircraft and Shipbuilding Bill, both of which industries the Labour government of the day wanted to nationalise. As a result, I was invited to the Farnborough Air Show. I was very excited. It was like any schoolboy's dream to go to the Farnborough Air Show and to see these magnificent aeroplanes showing off their capabilities – and at low heights and high speeds.

I shall never forget sitting at lunch next to the Chairman of De Havilland's (Canada). Canada had just *de*-nationalised its Aircraft Industry when we were about to nationalise ours. I complained that our government wanted to nationalise our aircraft industry and how awful that would be. The Chairman of De Havilland (Canada) said, 'Whatever governments may say, whatever assurances Ministers may give from the Despatch Box that they will not interfere with the industry, that when it is nationalised it will be like before and that the firms will run themselves just as they used to, it does not mean a thing. Ministers can say what they like, and they may mean what they say, but it will be the civil servants who will *badger the thing to death.*'

I have never forgotten him saying that. How right he was. The Act says this. The civil servants have to interpret what the Act says, and not what any Ministers might have said what is important. How many men have you got? How many did you have? How much money has been invested? Borrowed? Made? Lost? The questions and the ferreting will go on and on – not because the civil servants are being hostile or aggressive, but simply because they are doing, as they see it, their job – trying to ensure that the wording of the Act is carried out.

So it is with agriculture. It is the civil servants who have badgered the thing to death.

***

In 1984 Annabel and I were confronted with the appalling problem of Ditchingham. We were going to have to leave and sell our house at Hedenham, Hedenham Hall, and we were going to take on this large, impressive and beautiful house Ditchingham Hall. But Ditchingham needed much doing to it – a large part of the back needed knocking down, the whole house had to be re-roofed – in lead. It needed new electricity, water and heating supplies. It was, in all ways, a magnum opus. I could not just leave it all for Annabel to do. Apart from anything else, that was not her forte. To be interested, to help, to be involved, yes. But not to be responsible for the whole panjandrum. Nor did I feel that I could do that and do a government job, too.

So I decided that I would have to drop out of government, and give some time to my family and my family responsibilities.

I had seen Staunton Harold go and I had minded it – and I still mind it – quite enormously. This was an opportunity to pull us all together again – a lovely big house in a beautiful setting. Only one large house and not *two*, which had made all the effort on the estate appear to go into a two-forked tree. In a funny way – and it was a way which was not of our making but it just happened – it bought the Landless Title and the Titleless Land together. The happy confluence happened to be Annabel and me. Now everyone would be able to dance around one single maypole. But it required effort and thought and, I suppose, leadership. I still, of course, remained in the House of Lords, but on the backbenches.

I left the government in 1984 and went back in 1989. Bertie Denham, who was then the Chief Whip, had asked me if I wanted to come back into government. I was then sixty and I thought that my life was closing in and that I would never have anything proper to do – other than to chase cows which had got out or wringing oneself to pieces over trying to make a farm pay when the tide was flowing in the opposite direction. So I said yes.

About a week later, Bertie telephoned me at home and said that Willie Whitelaw was ill and had had a stroke and would I come back to the government in a position of importance. I said 'What is that?' 'I can't tell you,' he replied.

We had just had a shooting weekend and had said farewell to our guests, one of whom was Quintin Hailsham. Annabel and I were packing up to go and stay at Shrubland Hall for ten days, a health farm near Ipswich, to try and unwind and lose some weight. John Belstead had taken over as Leader of the House of Lords from Willie Whitelaw, and he rang me and said, 'You must come. You never know what may happen. Look at me. I am now Leader of the House of Lords. I never expected that to happen.'

There were we about to go to the health farm and yet having the prospect of our lives being turned upside down by joining the government again. My first instinct was to ask Quintin his views. He, of course, was out of contact because he was on his way down to London. Drat! That was wildly frustrating. Angela and Robert were quite excited by this turn of events. 'No secrets, Daddy. Keep us in the picture,' they said.

I eventually got hold of Quintin when he had returned to London. I told him that I had been asked back into government. What should I do? Am I too old? Will it be too much of a family upheaval? Is it a good idea to go back when you have left? Quintin was crystal clear – as he always was. 'Provided that you can make arrangements for Ditchingham to be looked after, it is your duty to go back.' Duty? Help! I had not quite thought of it like that, but Quintin was of that age and social structure where duty mattered.

I rang Bertie and said that I would come back. 'Don't tell anyone,' he said. It was as if one were involved in some clandestine terrorist operation. But I had to speak. To tell one's children, for example. What about Michael Falcon, who was Chairman of the Norwich Union and who had come to dinner with Quintin the night before? I could never look him in the eye again if I had just walked out of the Norwich Union without letting him know what was happening. When I told him, he said that of course I must go. What about the British Agricultural Export Council of which I was Chairman, which was going through one of its traumatic periods? I could not say nothing and let them read it all in the papers the next day that I had buzzed off. So I had to tell those people, and all was alright.

So Annabel and I cancelled our visit to Shrubland and headed to London.

Chapter 15

Government Again

I WENT BACK into government in 1988 as Minister of State at the Home Office and Deputy Leader of the House of Lords. I was given a great welcome back in the House. When I went into the Home Office, one of the first people to come and see me was the Permanent Secretary, Sir Brian Cubbon. He said that the trouble with the Home Office was that it dealt with everything which impacted closely on people: the police, the fire service, law and order, prisons, television and the BBC. Everyone in the street was a potential Home Secretary and ready to criticise and give voice to their opinions. I had never thought of the Home Office like that before.

I went to see the Home Secretary, Douglas Hurd, who was sitting in a comfortable chair in his office. He gave me a lovely welcome and told me that I was to look after the police, the fire service, charities and the Channel Islands. Apart from Douglas Hurd there were three other Home Office Ministers in the Commons, Douglas Hogg, Tim Renton, and John Patten. One looked after immigration, another one prisons and crime, another one the BBC and Sunday trading. In the House of Lords I had to answer, not just for my responsibilities, but for the responsibilities of all the other four Ministers too.

A few days after I had started, Douglas Hurd took me over to a police dinner at the Savoy. In his speech, he introduced me as the new Police Minister and I shall never forget his memorable words: 'I have told Lord Ferrers that, as long as he has responsibility for the police force, he will die neither of hunger nor of thirst.' How right he was.

The police were 'good doers'. As was the fire service. I enjoyed being associated with both. They were disciplined forces – not militaristic but disciplined – and they had the ethos which went with smartness, receiving orders and carrying out difficult, and sometimes unpleasant, tasks. Compared with the Brigade of Guards, their marching was a shambles – but at least they tried.

The police at that time were going through some fairly major changes, one of which was to make the police more 'user friendly'. There were those who wanted to stop calling it the police force, but to call it the police service instead. But I liked smartness.

I remember visiting the Sussex Constabulary. The Chief Constable was Roger Birch, an ex-RAF officer and a charming person who oozed authority from every pore. As we drove away, there was the Chief Constable on the steps of his office, standing upright and giving a very smart salute.

That was in marked contrast to a visit which I paid to the Thames Valley Police, whose Chief Constable was Charles Pollard. He was one of the younger Chief Constables. He was considered very bright, up-and-coming, and avant-garde, and he did not like military-style policing. When I left, he bent down to the car window and waved a cheery goodbye. I thought 'There goes your hail-fellow-well-met policeman.' I did not like it or respect it. You can have military smartness without militaristic attitudes.

There is an annual tug of war match between the Lords and Commons on the green opposite the House of Lords in order to raise funds for Macmillan Nurses. It is always a social and fun occasion with Members of Parliament, Peers, secretaries and everyone else turning up and cheering for whichever side they fancied.

I was asked to be a cheerleader for the House of Lords. I was not quite sure what a cheerleader was or what he was supposed to do. I was told to appear in some outrageous get-up and prance up and down on the edge of the arena invoking everyone to cheer for the House of Lords. There was somebody else doing it for the Commons. It was on a Tuesday.

The Thursday before, I was at a dinner of The Association of Chief Police Officers (ACPO) with all senior police officers present. I said over a drink after dinner, 'I want to find someone with a bit of initiative around here.' 'Why, what do you want?' asked Roger Birch, the Chief Constable of Sussex. 'I have got to be a cheerleader for the Tug of War on Tuesday, and I have to dress in something outrageous. I want some Morris Dancers' Bells.' I thought that I had asked for the Moon. 'Leave it with me,' he said. 'They will be on your desk on Monday morning.' They were. Roger Birch was supremely efficient even over the things which did not matter. The fact that they did not matter, in a funny way, made them matter.

I had to have a hip replacement operation in 1991. I went to the wonderful King Edward VII hospital. I had been there so frequently that I now even got a kiss from the Matron. I really felt that I had arrived! Caroline Cassels, the Matron, is very good, kind, competent, understanding, professional, efficient, cheerful – and pretty. In my book, that is all just wonderful. It is such an efficient hospital, calm, welcoming, personal and unfrightening. I do not think that there is any particular magic in it. I just wonder, if that is so, why NHS hospitals could not take a leaf out of King Edward VII's book and try to do the same. And it is not the most expensive.

During my convalescence, I was obliged to attend and address a police meeting. It was at that time that there was considerable controversy about the introduction of the side-handled baton for the police. The normal truncheon was smallish. It was held in the hand and used to thwack the baddie. The side-handled baton was considerably bigger. As its name implies, it had its handle on the side with part of the length of the truncheon continuing upwards on the arm, rather like a crutch. This gives much more leverage and much more power. Some said that it was too offensive and brutal for the police to use. As I stood on the podium with my crutches fitted around my arm, I raised one of them and swung it about and said 'Now I understand why you police officers want the side-handled baton.' It went down well.

I always felt sorry for the police, although they would not wish to be on the receiving end of such sentiments. They were there, doing their best to keep the Queen's Peace and to keep order in society and, if anything is done wrongly or a policeman acts incorrectly, the Tower of

Babel falls on him. Some of the police work on the fringes of crime. They have to. Incognito. It is not surprising that the odd one slips. In fact, it is surprising that more do not. And if they do, the public outcry of 'bent copper' is deafening, with the inference that all the police are like that which, of course, they are not.

I once went down to the cells in a police station. I never really liked doing that as it was a little like looking at lions in a cage. People who were, at least, suspected of doing wrong invoked one's wrath. Yet here they were, so to speak, entrapped in a cage and that evoked one's sympathy. I always found that one's feelings and emotions got disoriented on occasions like that. I saw one poor man in a cell, dressed in scruffy T-shirt and jeans. I asked him why he was in there. 'I am a police officer,' he said. I reeled. He had been an undercover officer, catching shoplifters in a supermarket. Whatever next?

On one visit to a police station, I asked a police officer what he was writing at his desk and what he was doing. 'Is there anything you can do about this?' he asked. 'I don't know. Tell me what you are doing,' I said. 'Well, I am having to fill this form out thirteen times about a person who is not even going to be charged.' It is a shocking waste of time and effort. Everyone thinks so. Yet, bureaucracy – and we see it everywhere – is like a cancer. Once you get it, it spreads.

You can say that bureaucracy is unfair, unnecessary, a waste of time, a waste of money and ought to be stopped. Yet it seems virtually unstoppable. It will take a superhuman Prime Minister to reverse the engines. Poor John Major tried to do so with the Deregulation and Contracting Out Bill, which was supposed to remove all of the out-of-date statutes from the Statute Book. Yet the Bill itself was two inches thick. It produced a whole host of *new* regulations which had to be introduced in order to get rid of the *old* regulations. You don't ever seem to be able to win.

The great thing about the police was that, almost to a man, they loved being in the police force. There was great loyalty and *esprit de corps*. They felt proud of what they were trying to do. And I felt proud of that.

I used to tell them not to worry too much if the newspapers and others periodically had a go at them, 'Remember,' I said, 'you are in public life, and everyone in public life has periodically to accept ridicule, offensiveness and outright dislike. It is just the same in the House of Lords. But, at least no one is suggesting trying to abolish the police force, which is what they want to do to us in the House of Lords.' I think that that gave them a modicum of comfort.

It was fun visiting police forces. It was always a little unnerving because one appeared like the GREAT I AM and one was always met with due deference, but I was always terrified about the questions which one may be asked and how one would answer them and what the answer ought to be.

Part of that concern was personal pride but part was that one did not want to let the questioner, his superiors or the Home Office down. I did not want to leave the impression that 'the silly old Minister did not know what he was talking about' or that one was arrogant and non-listening. Heavy criticism is always just around the corner. It was important for the whole edifice that the Minister should conduct himself properly and that the police (or the fire services because the two were not dissimilar) should feel confident in, and have respect for, the office of the Minister, whoever might happen to be holding that office at the time, as well as for the intellectual integrity and the stature of the Minister himself.

On two occasions I went to the Northumbria Police. The first was when they had had terrible riots with houses and vehicles being set on fire. Some of the residents were understandably terrified. They were grateful for the help of the police, although there was inevitably some criticism. I went to see one couple in their house. They had made some lovely, huge sandwiches and a cup of tea for me. They had had bricks thrown through their window and pieces of burning wood chucked in, too. One just wonders how they survived – mentally apart from anything else. John Stevens was the Chief Constable, a 6ft 5in broad-shouldered man with stacks of personality and a great sense of fun. He subsequently became the Commissioner of the Metropolitan Police and very good he was at it. He also became a great personal friend of mine.

I went up to Northumbria six months later to see how they had got on. The change was astonishing – in atmosphere and attitude as well as in the physical environment. The people were so pleased with, and were so grateful to, the police. Small units of police had been seconded out to various parts of the once troubled area. The policemen got to know the people, and the people got to know the policemen. There was trust all round and contentment. That was what true policing should be.

That evening the Chief Constable had set up a small dinner for me with a few of his senior officers. After dinner one of the officers gave me a present by which I would be able to remember the Northumbria Police. What was it? A walking stick, of all things. A beautiful one, yes. With a carved head. Yes. But a walking stick! Why on earth does he think that I want a walking stick? What do they want to give me a thing like that for? I am not that doddery. Now, twenty years later, I love it. It is beautiful. I admire it, and it is admired constantly by others. I use it the whole time at home and in London too. One of the police officers, Sgt Wilf Laidlaw, had taken up stick-dressing, and the head was carved out of a Dorset Horn's horn. He then carved it in the shape of a trout with the fins and tail and body being exquisitely moulded and carved. The eyes were small, round bits of ebony surrounded with a little copper to make them shine.

I was so touched by that present. Members of the police force seem to abound in hidden skills of all sorts.

I once visited the police in Dorset. We were due to leave the train at Weymouth. As the train drew in, there was the Chief Constable and the other senior officers, all togged up and on the platform waiting to meet us. Very smart they were, too. But the door of the carriage would not open. My Private Secretary, Barbara Nicholson, and I tried to push and shove at the door, but it was totally obstinate and, much to our horror the train started to draw out of the station. There were we still in it, and there was the reception party, still on the platform. We would just have to wait till the next station and get out there. As we drew in to the next station, who should be on the platform? – but the Chief Constable, the senior police officers and the reception party, all standing ready to greet us as before! They had raced from Weymouth to the next station and were there to meet us. Very efficient, very amusing and great fun.

I was lucky enough to go to Singapore on a number of occasions. Douglas Hurd was nervous of me doing that, wondering what kind of signals that would give out – people disappearing off the street and not being seen again? Would people think that that was going to happen in England? In fact, the Singapore police are very impressive and very efficient.

Martin Narey, my Private Secretary, said, 'I will get the tickets then – British Airways?' I said, 'No. Singapore Airlines, then Thai Airways, then Malaysian Airways, then Cathy Pacific and then British Airways. In that order of preference.' 'Oh, don't you like British Airways?' 'Not particularly, but Singapore Airlines are superb as are most of those Far Eastern airlines.' So Singapore Airlines it was.

We set off on 31 December and when we arrived in the aeroplane, it had some holly decorating it and they were playing Christmas Carols – all very romantic. We were going first class. Unbelievably luxurious. An exceedingly attractive air hostess came up and offered us champagne. We accepted willingly. As we settled into the comfort of our seats, Martin turned to me and said, 'Lord Ferrers, I don't want you to get me wrong. I am very happily married but, my word, these girls are attractive.' 'Of course they are,' I said. 'Why do you think that I told you that I wanted to go by Singapore Airlines?'

We had a meeting with Lee Kuan Yew, the charismatic Prime Minister (or First Minister and then Senior Minister of Singapore). I had met him on a number of occasions, and I found these meetings sensational. The conversation is pretty one-sided – but that does not matter. That is what it is for.

We got on to Gorbachev. 'Gorbachev is a fool,' said Lee Kuan Yew. I practically fell off my chair. 'How can he be a fool?' I said. 'He has brought Communism to an end.'

'To get to the top of the hierarchy in Russia, you have to be a very clever person. And to plan to dismember the state of Communism but having nothing to replace it with is madness. You will have states fighting between each other and within each other.'

I was amazed to hear this diagnosis of Gorbachev when I thought – and still do – that he had done so much.

On another occasion I asked him how he achieved splitting Singapore away from Malaysia. They were always inextricably tied up together. And yet, here we were with a small island which, nevertheless, has to have its own forces, its own Foreign Service with Embassies and Ambassadors and yet the whole place still has to make ends meet. 'How do you do it?' He replied, 'You can either sit at the bottom of a tree and wait for the coconuts to fall off, or you can climb up the tree and get the coconuts yourself.'

On a second visit, I reminded Lee Kuan Yew of what he had said and he smiled, 'Oh yes. But there is another method. Get somebody else to climb up the tree and get the coconuts for you.'

***

The Police and Magistrates Courts Bill was one of those Bills going through Parliament which are bound to cause great controversy. One of the parts of it was to allow the Home Secretary to approve the Chairman of the Police Authority. This caused an almighty uproar. 'This will enable the Home Secretary to control the police' was the great – and forceful – argument. The police have always been locally run in order to stop us from having a national police force, which can so easily turn into a government police force. The idea of having the Home Secretary approve the Chairman of the Police Authority insinuated that only people sympathetic to the Home Secretary's views would be approved. In short, the police force would be run only in the way in which the Home Secretary approved. In other words, almost government-run.

Everyone was speaking against this in the House of Lords and getting very worked up – Jim Callaghan did. So did John Boyd-Carpenter. So did Willie Whitelaw, the highly respected Conservative ex-Home Secretary. I was in charge of this wretched Bill and I was up against the ropes. I said that, in view of the very considerable level of feeling in the House and without giving any commitment as to the result, I will take the first two clauses back and give them further consideration. Relief all the way round. It was like popping a balloon. Everyone said how wise and sensible and correct I was.

Callaghan said that he was grateful that I had respected the view of the House and had quite properly taken the clauses back. He said, 'It would be churlish of me to do anything but congratulate the noble Earl. Some doubts were expressed as to whether he had the capacity to influence the Home Secretary.' He added, much to my horror, 'We now know that it is he, and not the Home Secretary, who is in charge of the Bill. He has had his way over this matter. He undertook very clearly to represent all that we had to say. Undoubtedly, he represented it to the government and he has won. I salute him and congratulate him on his great victory on behalf of us all.'

I was getting deeper and deeper into the red leather of the benches. What will Michael Howard say? Roy Jenkins had also made a fiery intervention, to which I replied:

> The noble Lord, Lord Jenkins, then said that he did not want to fire any shots into the back of a routed army – not very nice – that the procedure we had proposed was pointless and farcical and that it was humiliation by instalments. I found these pretty tough words to accept. However, the noble Lord is a tough operator and I suppose that he is entitled to put forward those views. But we were trying to get over a problem that we had all encountered. This is not a question of humiliation; it is a matter of Parliament saying what it thinks about the Bill and the government saying that they will try to take note of it. I have to say that it is remarks like those of the noble Lord that make Ministers a little more obdurate than they may naturally want to be, for fear that, if they try to give a bit to meet the point, they will be castigated by someone with the power of the noble Lord, Lord Jenkins of Hillhead. I hope he will feel that, on reflection, that was not perhaps one of the most helpful of the many observations that he has made since he has been in your Lordships' House.

Then Lord Harris from the Liberal Democrat benches got up and said what a good thing it was that I was taking the clauses back but did I realise that if I was taking back the first two clauses, I would have to take back the first eight as they were all dependent one on the other. Of course, I had not realised this, but I agreed to take them all back and just hoped that Michael Howard would not blow his top. He did not, and he was very understanding.

After due consideration had been given, Michael said that the clauses must stay as they are – and we had to prepare for the whole fandango again.

When the Bill returned almost as it was before, everyone was very upset. Callaghan, who had earlier praised me for taking it back said,

> I thank the noble Earl, Lord Ferrers, for the way in which he has steered the matter through this Chamber. I would only add that, if such an elaborate farce has been staged, the noble Earl is entirely acquitted of any responsibility for it. He told me last time that I was quite out of order to suggest that he had any responsibility for the Bill. I fully appreciate that. Indeed, I believe that the noble Earl is very wise to say so. As regards the noble Earl's rebuke to me when I suggested that he might have had something to do with the Bill, the plain truth is that when history comes to be written the further he can distance himself from the provisions of the clause the better it will be for his reputation, which stands so high.

They were tough operators on this Bill – Lord Callaghan, Lord Jenkins of Hillhead, Lord Whitelaw, Lord Renton, Lord Peyton. They were experienced war horses and it was quite nerve-racking to have to take them on – and always to be courteous. But it was quite fun and the Bill got through in the end.

***

The Simon Wiesenthal organisation produced a report saying that there were a number of German war criminals who had escaped from Germany and from prosecution and who had come to reside in England and elsewhere and were now living perfectly normal lives but under a different name – incognito.

There was a political row over this with plenty of people saying that this was intolerable. Douglas Hurd, who was the Home Secretary, decided to introduce the War Crimes Bill. This was to allow the police to chase up, find if possible, and bring to justice those people in the United Kingdom who had in the past engaged in criminal activities in Germany and elsewhere. They could have been prosecuted for these were they in their old country, but they could not be prosecuted in Great Britain for crimes which they had, or might have, committed in another country.

This was controversial stuff. Many Jewish people were greatly in favour of it. Margaret Thatcher, the Prime Minister, supported the principle partly, I suspect, because there was a large Jewish community in her North London constituency of Finchley. What was done, not only illegally but in a heinous way some years ago, went the argument, should not be allowed to go unpunished simply because of the passage of time.

The other side of the argument questioned whether it was right to spend vast sums of money following up these possibilities, and chasing people who were now elderly, money which would have been better spent on catching the present-day criminals? How can a man of eighty swear in Court 'Yes it was 3 January when that happened – and not 4 January?' A lot of water had flowed under the bridge since those terrible days and, as Alec Home, by then Lord Home of the Hirsel, put it so succinctly, 'Old men forget.'

I found one of the most impressive arguments was made by a Bishop in Second Reading who said 'One never knows. Some of these people might be full of remorse for what they did and may have been trying to make amends by trying to live new and fresh lives in a decent way and forgetting about the past. Is it wrong to allow people to repent?'

I had to take this Bill through the House of Lords. I did not like the Bill – brought about, as it was, by political pressure. Why cannot we leave people alone? What is the virtue in stirring up trouble for people who have been trying to live better lives for the last fifty years and who are now in the twilight of their lives and in putting the fear of God up many more? In most cases these people, anyhow, at the time of the crimes would have been only in their twenties, and were probably acting on the orders given to them from above.

After all the rigmarole and investigations, apprehension, prosecution and possibly the obtaining of a conviction, what do you do with the poor eighty-year-old? Send him to prison for the rest of his life – five years? Who has gained what? How many people are likely to be prosecuted and, of these, how many are likely to be convicted? It all seemed to me to be an absurd waste of time and money and a good way of generating hatred.

However, I had to take the Bill through. My officials had kindly drawn up an excellent speech and, as we were going through the draft, it said at the end words to the effect of 'I know that this Bill is controversial but, in the cause of justice, I believe that it is important. And, my Lords, you know that I would not say that if I did not believe it.'

I said to the official, 'I am not going to say that.' He said, 'It is government policy and you are a member of the government.' I said, 'I dare say, but I am not going to perjure myself like that. I don't mind saying that the *government* thinks it is right, but I am not going to say that I think that it is right. I don't.' So, we had a few jolly minutes altering the speech to show that this was the government's view, but not mine – in the nicest possible and least obvious way!

The War Crimes Bill had an unusual passage. It was passed in the House of Commons by a large majority in June 1990, but it was thrown out at Second Reading in the Lords – an unusual practice.

David Waddington became Home Secretary and reintroduced it into the House of Commons when, again, it was passed by an enormous majority. Unusually, the Second and Third Readings were held in the House of Commons on the same day, 18 March 1991.

By the time that the War Crimes Bill had come to the House of Lords for discussion, David Waddington had given up being Home Secretary and had been sent to the House of Lords as Leader of the House and as Lord Waddington. So, as he had reintroduced the Bill in the House of Commons and had taken it through, he had to deal with it in the House of Lords (and not me – thank Heavens).

The House of Lords rejected the Bill and it was passed through *under the Parliament Act* and was given Royal Assent on 9 May 1991.

It was odd that, of the two Houses, the House of Lords contained the older people, some of whom had been locked up in Colditz and other concentration camps, and who had been involved in all the beastliness of war, and who you might think would be in favour of hunting the criminals down. But no. On the whole, the House of Lords was against it. Yet the House of Commons, which was full of many young men who had never been near the war and who, you might feel, would say, 'Forget it. This is a thing of the past. Let's move on', did not take that view. They were the ones who said, 'Hunt them down. Bring them to justice.'

As David Waddington was speaking from the Despatch Box, I was sitting next to him, and I could not fail to notice that one of the pages of his speech was one whole paragraph. I could not manage like that. One unbroken mass of words. To me it would be like looking through wire netting. I would get hopelessly lost and could not bring the necessary emphasis anywhere where it was required. It is odd. Everyone has their own attitudes and techniques.

***

Annabel and I had a spectacular visit down the Thames on one of the fireboats. Gerry Clarkson, who was the Chief Fire Officer for London asked me and my family down. We took William and Hermione (Robert's children), aged about ten, and Charlie and Georgina (Angela's children).

Before we went down the Thames, I was asked to inspect part of the London Fire Brigade. I took Annabel and some of the grandchildren as well as Michelle, the very pretty and kind secretary who was in my Private Office. We met at the fire station and I was asked whether I would like to go up in one of those things which look like extending ladders with a box to stand in, from which the firemen can direct their hoses on to the tops of houses. They go up a tremendous height – and at a tremendous speed.

'It is perfectly safe,' the Chief Fire Officer said. Oh yes. Apart from having no head for heights, I knew what they would do. Having got the stupid Minister in the cage, they would propel it up at great speed to an enormous height and then would show the versatility of the machine by shaking it to the left and to the right and generally destabilising the poor Minister and making him feel sick. I was not born yesterday, and so I declined the invitation after many attempts at persuasion. Michelle, meanwhile, said that she would love to go up. So she went up with two of the grandchildren. They had soon had enough, and were allowed down, but Michelle went up much higher. When she came down she was grey and felt sick!

We then went down the Thames on one of those great fire tenders. And then the hoses were activated – enormous spouts of water going high up into the air and quite a long way across the river. It was great fun. The grandchildren loved it, and they were allowed to hold and aim the hoses, but Hermione was a bit frightened and held for comfort the hand of the formidable Chief Fire Officer who, in his long double-breasted thick overcoat, looked like a Prussian General. When she wrote her thank you letter to him, she said, 'Thank you for letting me hold your hand.' He loved it. There is something endearing and captivating about the innocence and dependence of children. Why cannot we enjoy it and wallow in it instead of dismissing it on the altar of unnecessary protection?

***

Shortly after I returned home after the hip replacement operation, the burglar alarm went off one evening. It frequently – and maddeningly – did that. I went hobbling off to switch the alarm off and Annabel said, 'Do be careful. There may be someone in the house this time.'

As I was switching the machine off, I heard something go thump, thump, thump down the landing, and there was I face to face with an intruder. Now what do you do? If I had done nothing, he would have whizzed down the back stairs. Yet there was I in a bright red dressing gown, my grey hair standing straight up on end, and on a crutch looking, I suspect, a fairly formidable sight. What does one do? Hit him, I thought. So I did. On the shoulders. That put him on the floor, and I gave him another two whacks for good measure. I asked him what on earth he thought he was doing. He said that he was looking for his father. I said that it would surprise me if his father was here.

I told him that he had better come and sit down. That was all very fine. This young man could have scarpered any time. I could not have stopped him with my replaced hip and crutch. I thought, 'What do pilots do with a skyjacker? Keep talking.'

So I led him to a big chair at the top of the stairs where we sat down. After quite a lot of meaningless chat, he said, 'Tell me, are you a Magistrate's Justice?' I said, 'No.' 'Oh, thank goodness for that,' he replied. 'I thought that you were somebody important.' I did not like to tell him that I was a Minister in charge of the police. I thought that that would be pulling rank. 'I will go now,' he said. 'Sit down,' I shouted. It was basically a case of personality. I could not have stopped him going off. Where were the police? One always wants them immediately, but the poor fellows had to speed for about twenty miles to get here.

The trouble was that the young man's father had given him some Magic Mushrooms, which are an hallucinatory drug like LSD, and so he had not the slightest idea of what he was doing. His father seemed a pretty unorthodox person at the best of times. I found out later that, for some reason, he had filled a scaffold pole full of sugar and weed killer. This is a very explosive concoction and it blew the scaffold pole up and took off one of his arms. Anyhow, the young lad was taken into police custody and that was that.

I think that the incident had happened in November, and I was telephoned in May by *The Times* correspondent, Sheila Gunn, whom I happened to know. She had been having a drink in the House of Lords with a Peer and she said how nice it was to see me back after my hip operation. 'Yes it is,' replied the Peer. 'You know what he has been doing whilst he was away? He hit a burglar.' 'He what?...'

Sheila Gunn rang me up and said that she was going to write an article about it. 'For goodness sake, don't', I said. 'After all, *The Times* prides itself on writing news. This is old hat – six months old.' 'That does not matter and, anyhow, if I don't write about it, some other newspaper will.' Persuasion was no good. 'I tell you what,' she said. 'I will write the article and show you the draft and you can alter it as you wish.' That was very generous of her.

She did write the article. I did alter it, and it was published. It was very fair. But then, all hell was let loose. The press rang up constantly and asked me questions. One photographer appeared at the front door and said that he wanted to take a photograph of me outside my house jumping up and down waving a stick. I politely indicated that that really was the bottom. He said that he went to the same church as Annabel and that he had to come as his boss told him to. 'I have done what I was asked to do,' he said smiling. 'So I will go away.' That was kind.

The press, unfortunately, missed the best quote of all. When they asked if I had hit the burglar, I said 'Anyone who comes into my house gets what is on the menu.' I thought that it was a gem – but, it was never used.

The police, meanwhile, loved all this. To think that a Minister actually did what they all long to do but are not allowed to – hit a miscreant. They revelled in it. Whenever I went into a room, they all smiled. The more senior the police officer, the greater the smile. When I met Her Majesty's Chief Inspector of Constabulary, he just smiled from ear to ear.

***

Quintin Hailsham is one of the people whom I have enjoyed and whom I have admired most in politics. He was the most brilliant and clever person. He was very articulate, crystal clear, exceedingly funny and there seemed to be no subject in the world about which he did not know. On two occasions I was asked to carry the Cap of Maintenance at the State Opening of Parliament. I thought that I had better find out exactly what it was. I looked up all the appropriate reference books, but they said very little. Ask Quintin, and out it all came. It was like a history lesson – and in detail. I shall not rehearse what he said here because I shall get it all wrong. I did disappear and write it all down on a piece of paper – but I then lost the piece of paper.

Quintin became a great friend of ours in about 1977. He and his wife, Mary, went to Australia on an official engagement when he was in opposition, having been Lord Chancellor, which position he was to hold again. His hosts asked him if he would like to go riding. He said, 'Yes, and can Mary come too?'

They were mounted on carefully trained police horses early in the morning and, with their hosts, they set off. Mary's horse for some reason panicked and bolted off at high speed down the tarmac road. They all set off in pursuit, but Mary fell off on to the tarmac and broke her skull. When the others, including Quintin arrived, Mary was dead.

The sight, the shock, the immediate removal of one's loved one, the hideous realisation that for one all was over, was too much for Quintin.

He was an emotional and emotive person at the best of times but this, understandably, devastated him and pulled him inside out.

When he had returned to this country, I thought that I ought to say something but I did not know quite how to. After all, here was this very erudite and important ex-Lord Chancellor and I was only a junior, even if we were part of the same team on the Opposition Front Bench. If I said anything, would it make it better or worse? But I could not just say nothing. Then the opportunity came. I was walking down the passage in the House of Lords one day just outside the Whip's Office, and Quintin was coming along on his own towards me. We stopped, and I said how sorry I was to hear of what had happened to Mary. Here was this great man, a warrior in all circumstances, and he just burst into tears, and said, 'I never knew that God could be so cruel.'

When I went home, I told Annabel all about this, and I said that we must do something for Quintin. The poor man was devastated and lonely. He had no wife and he was in pieces. Let's ask him down for a shooting weekend.

'What?' said Annabel. 'Have the Lord Chancellor to stay? I would be terrified. I shan't know what to do, and I will be all nervous.'

'No, you won't. He is a lovely person, and he is at the moment very, very sad and very, very lonely. He needs some help and friendship.'

Quintin came. He was wonderful. He enjoyed the whole weekend and it cheered him up hugely, as it did us. Thereafter, every year for about fifteen years he came to shoot.

We always used to go to Norwich Cathedral for the service on Sunday, and Quintin used to say the Lord's Prayer in Latin. One Sunday, the preacher was Canon Beswick, one of the Canons of the Cathedral and, in his sermon, he referred to Lord Hailsham's new book – Lord Hailsham said this. Lord Hailsham said that. Lord Hailsham said the other. I began to slide further and further down my misericord with embarrassment wondering what was going to come out next. He obviously did not realise that Lord Hailsham was in the congregation. When Quintin went up to receive communion, I think that the poor priest nearly dropped the Ciborium.

***

There was one day when we Ministers were all sitting in Douglas Hurd's room in the Home Office discussing some matters at the time when Aids was at its scariest. Douglas Hogg was in charge of prisons and said, 'Aids is terrible and can quickly spread in prisons as there is no outlet for the sexual urges of prisoners other than other prisoners. We must protect against this and we should issue condoms to prisoners free.' I said, 'You cannot do this. There really are limits. Just think what the press and the voters will say – the government is giving out condoms free to prisoners so that they can bugger each other.' Douglas Hogg replied, 'Oh I know, and they will have to be heavy duty ones too.' I said, 'Look. This is intolerable. You simply cannot do that kind of thing whatever the risks.' As far as I know, it was never done, but I dare say that it was more than my contribution which quashed the idea.

After I had been in the Home Office for about three months because of my responsibilities for the fire service I went to the passing out dinner at the Fire Service College. Those were people who had been on a course of three months and were passing out.

It was a smart occasion. Dinner Jackets, Mess Kit – the lot. In my speech I said how impressive it was that, after three months, they had all passed out knowing exactly what to do. 'It is funny,' I said. 'You came here at the same time that I went to the Home Office. Yet, after three months, you have all passed out with Flying Colours knowing every-thing. And yet I am still trying to find out what on earth is going on in the Home Office.' They liked that.

When I was being briefed in the morning by Peter Bolton, the Home Office official who was responsible for my speech, with my Private Sec-retary, Barbara Nicholson, I said that I was reminded of an occasion in Malaya when our whole company had to spend a night on a tea estate. The officers and the company headquarters had taken over a wooden hut. In the night it all caught fire and we had to evacuate it quietly. Ralph Anstruther, who was our Company Commander, got out of his portable bed in his pyjamas (he always wore pyjamas even on opera-tions), scratched his head at all the flames billowing up around us and came out with the most appalling expletive which was, in effect 'Christ All F...ing Mighty. This is no joke.' An exaggeration and understatement all in one.

'Oh you cannot possibly use that Minister,' said Peter Bolton. When the time came, I thought that I would tease him. I gave my speech and, at the appropriate moment, I inserted my story. Peter Bolton was nervous. As the story progressed his neck got redder and redder with impending embarrassment. The poor man was almost doubled up with confusion when I said, spinning it all out slowly, 'I shall never forget the memorable and distinctive words of Ralph Anstruther, my Company Commander, when he saw us all caught up in the inferno. Those words have remained embedded in me all my life.'

Peter Bolton's neck was now bright puce. 'Goodness gracious me. This is no joke.' They all roared with laughter. They all knew what his words were likely to have been and they knew that they were not those. Mr Bolton and Barbara were mightily relieved and the colour of Mr Bolton's neck returned to normality.

The West Midlands Fire Service band was playing for the dinner dance. They were very good. They played 'Hootin Annie', a really infectious tune. I said, 'I am going to conduct the band.' And I did. Brian Fuller, who had been Chief Officer of the West Midlands Fire Service and was now Commandant of the Fire Service College and who was our host, was talking to Annabel, and suddenly looked up and said to the photographer, 'Look, what is going on? Go and take a photograph of Lord Ferrers conducting the band.' He did. It was a lovely photograph. I was sent a copy of it. I cherish it. The only sad part was that every musician was looking at his score. No one was looking at the conductor!

They used to have functions periodically in the Fire Service College at Moreton-in-Marsh in Gloucestershire, and I used to be asked quite often to go down there and I was frequently accompanied by Annabel.

My Private Secretary before Martin Narey was a girl. One day she said that she had been asked if she would like to bring a partner for the forthcoming dance and was it alright if she brought her current boyfriend? I said, 'Yes. Of course.'

She accompanied Annabel and me to the hotel and, when she checked

in, she said, 'Two Double rooms. One for Ferrers, and one for 'Smith'
(not her proper name).

I could not believe my ears. Nor could Annabel believe hers – a double
room for her and her boyfriend – all paid for by the Fire Service College.
She was going to have a night out all hunky-dory with her boyfriend
ending up no doubt with a bit of rumpy-pumpy, when she was supposed
to be attending to me on official government business.

This upset Annabel no end. Me too. When we attended our next
Ministers' morning meeting on Monday, I spoke to Tim Renton, who
was then a Minister of State in the Home Office with me. He was very
sound and always had a twinkle in his eye, 'What am I to do? We went
down to the Fire Service College and my Private Secretary shacked up
with her boyfriend whilst supposedly looking after me.' Tim smiled in
a gorgeously relaxed and knowing way and said, 'Well, I think that it is
always best on these occasions to have it out with the person concerned
so that everyone knows where they are.'

I said, 'That's all very fine for you to say that, but I don't find it a very
easy thing at all to do.' Tim said, 'Well, that is what I would do.'

So, I went back to my office all of a judder. The Private Secretary came
in to see me and fortunately closed the door behind her. 'That was a
jolly good party on Friday, wasn't it?' she said. I sensed my opportunity.
'Yes,' I said, 'but I was a bit surprised that you took a double bedroom
and shacked up with your boyfriend when you were supposed to be on
official duty looking after me. Apart from anything else, it embarrassed
my wife hugely.'

She was deeply and genuinely apologetic. She even had the good grace
to ring up Annabel and to apologise to her for causing embarrassment.
I gave her full marks for that. I gave myself pretty good marks, too, for
having been brave enough to raise the matter!

On one of my visits to the Fire Service College, when Annabel was not
with me, I was dressed in my dinner jacket. Brian Fuller, the Commandant of the ire Service College, had a message during my after-dinner
speech. When I sat down he told me, 'There is a fire in [wherever it was].
It is a twelve-pump fire, (which in fire service speak, means one which
is being attended to by twelve fire appliances). I have got to go. Would

you like to come along too?' I agreed – and that means that my Private Secretary, Barbara Nicholson (who was in a smart long evening dress) would have to come too. Sir Reginald Doyle, Her Majesty's Inspector of Fire Services, a tall, tough, fine, good-looking man, thought quite rightly that he should come too.

Brian Fuller went to his car and changed into his smart protective gear, whilst we stayed on in our evening dress. When we went to the scene it was pretty good chaos. Everything was pitch black. One sometimes forgets that all the electricity is off on these occasions, except for the fire service's very bright portable lights.

'Follow me,' said Fuller. We did. Up into the roof, over the charred beams. 'Mind that water down there. Be careful of that charred beam over there.' We went all over the place, bumping one's head, and not being able to see anything. I did not know where we were. And there was the faithful Barbara Nicholson in her evening dress and high-heeled shoes, trying to pick her footsteps carefully in the mess, but faithfully following her boss. We eventually returned to the Command and Control Centre.

After about ten minutes, Her Majesty's Chief Inspector of Fire Services turned up. I said jokingly, 'Chief Inspector. Where on earth have you been?' 'Trying to catch up with you, Minister!' They were fun times and fun people.

Whenever I visited a Fire Service, the Home Office was very keen that I should ask the question, 'How are you getting on with recruiting women?' This was a policy with which I was not enamoured, but it was government policy, so there we were. It was also a policy with which not all Chief Fire Officers were greatly enamoured either, so they needed a bit of prodding.

One Chief Fire Officer told me that they were getting on well and the women were very good.

'Where do they sleep? In rooms at the end of the dormitory?'

'Oh no. In the same room as the men.'

'In the what...? Don't you get a fearful amount of misbehaving going on?'

'Not nearly as much as you would get if the women slept in rooms on their own!'

He had a point. But we do seem to make things so difficult for our-selves on the altar of Equality, Fairness and Progress.

The General Secretary – or leader – of the Fire Brigades Union was Ken Cameron, a communist. No one in the Home Office could stand him. I thought that I would try and soften things up. He was a character, a rogue, but he had charm too. He was always blabbing off to the press at the most inconvenient time – but trades union leaders do that – which irritated everyone.

We had a big meeting of some thirty-five people and, that morning, there appeared in the press an article all about the forthcoming meet-ing, full of information. It was pretty clear that this had come from someone, and most people had a good idea from whom it had come. Before we started the meeting, I referred to this article and said, 'It looks as if someone has been chatting to the press. Does anyone know where the information has come from?' Silence. 'Have you any ideas, Mr Cam-eron?' 'Oh no!'

I did refer to the fact that, when we have a meeting like that, Mr Cameron often goes and has a chat with the press first. 'He is rather like my wife's Jack Russell. It goes out and has a jolly good bark and then feels quite content and comes back to bed.' He took it all very well.

On one occasion he brought a delegation from the Fire Brigades Union to see me because they wanted to have the arrangements about pensions changed. If a firefighter was killed on duty, his pension went to his widow. Cameron said that, on some occasions, the marriage had broken up and the firefighters may have been living with another woman for years, who was sharing all his responsibilities and life with him as a wife, and it was pretty galling, not to say unfair, that, when the firefighter died, all the pension went to the person from whom he had split up years ago and who no longer had the responsibilities of a wife.

That was an understandable argument, but I did not like the idea of it. I said to Cameron, 'You mean to say that, when a woman has been married to a firefighter, has had children with him and has given all her effort to the marital home for many years and, if he then goes off with a young girl like Fifi, you think that Fifi should get all the pension and not the one who has borne all the burden and heat of the day?'

I knew that I was on weak ground, but we continued to discuss the problem. 'All the other departments have made this change. Do you mean that the Home Office is the only one who won't? Would you put this in writing?'

About six weeks later I went to a party given by the Association of District Councils, or some such, and there was Cameron with a lady. He came up to me all smiling and said, 'Good Evening, Lord Ferrers. May I introduce you to Fifi.' We had a good laugh.

***

One of my responsibilities in the Home Office was the Channel Islands and the Isle of Man. So, of course, they had to have a ministerial visit.

We went to the Channel Islands one August. That was fun. We went to Jersey, Guernsey, Sark and Alderney. Annabel came too. We stayed with the Governor of Guernsey, Lt General Sir Alexander Boswell, colloquially known as Sandy Boswell. Before I left London I was given a briefing by an exceedingly nice intellectual civil servant who, it turned out, had been to Winchester, called John Stephens. He had done his own homework before briefing me, and found out that one of my ancestors had been Governor in 1300 or thereabouts. Needless to say, I knew nothing about this and was amazed.

When I came to give my speech after a dinner, which was attended by all the movers and shakers in Guernsey, I started off by saying, 'It is so nice to come to Guernsey and, as it were, to come home again,' and I explained that my forebear had been Governor in 1300 and something. Everyone was amazed, including the Governor. On the way home he said, 'Do you really mean that your ancestor was Governor in 1300?' I replied that I understood that to be the case. 'Well, we will soon find out, because I have a list of the Governors on the wall in my study.' I felt – help, supposing that this is all wrong. He will think that I am a most terrible imposter.

When we arrived at his Residence, we went into the study – and there was the list of Governors on the wall and there was my forebear amongst them, near the top. I felt relieved, and a little proud.

We went to the Guernsey Agricultural Show on a perfect day – lots of Guernsey cows and calves and goats. Annabel was in her element. We bought some bric-a-brac including a lovely round black velvet draught excluder to put by a door. It had the face of a cat, and so Annabel and I called it 'Pussy'.

When we went to the airport, the Governor was accompanying us over the tarmac to the aeroplane, and Annabel and I were rather bowed down with our hand luggage and purchases and Pussy.

The Governor very generously offered to help to carry something. He looked down and said, 'But I am not carrying Pussy!' He was such a charming man.

I was warned that we would not like Alderney. There were too many dreadful war stories about it and the place had a most unpleasant atmosphere. So we were prepared, but we did not find it that way at all.

We went to have a formal lunch in the hotel, some forty people. We went upstairs. For some reason, during lunch, the subject came up of how one can climb through quite small openings.

I said that it was possible for a person to go through a coat hanger. Absurd. Impossible. 'Well, let us put it to the test,' and I asked one of the waitresses if she could kindly get hold of a wire coat hanger. By this time the whole lunch party was enthralled, and the conversation at the far end of the table had stopped. The waitress came back with the coat hanger. Now, who was going to be the sacrificial Ox? I suggested the Governor's ADC, Captain David Hodgetts. He was a young man of 35 or so and was very efficient *and* slim – and, anyhow, that is what ADCs are for.

He took off his jacket and waistcoat – this was in the middle of lunch – then put his head through the coat hanger and it slipped down to his waist. Fine. But would it get over the hips? It nearly got stuck there – they always do – but he managed to get through it all. Cheers went up all the way around the room and the lunch party was made. Thereafter, instead of being stuffy, it was a huge success. I had not planned it. It was just one of those things which happens.

Sark was a lovely island. No cars. It was a good place to go on holiday. You can take a horse, a trap or a bicycle. It was run in quite a feudal way by the Seigneur of Sark. During the War, his mother, the Dame of

Sark, ran it. When the Germans occupied the Island, they came to her house to find the Boss of the Island. The senior German officer found the Dame sitting at a table at the far end of the room. She made the officer walk all the length of the room before she spoke to him. When the officer reached her she told him that she expected her people to be looked after by the Germans with courtesy and respect. That was a brave act of dignity and defiance to an invading power. She was a powerful, formidable lady.

***

The problem of homosexuality used to appear, in various guises, about once every three days in the Home Office. Everyone tried to be prim and proper and not in any way outraged by the problems, whatever they happened to feel. The most extraordinary vocabulary was used, which one was more used to hearing in the Sergeant's Mess, but in the Home Office those words were used as if they were common parlance. They were always discussed in a genteel manner like having tea with granny with a couple of cakes and sandwiches.

One day, I had a submission all about homosexuality. Needless to say, I cannot now remember what the submission was about, but I took pretty good care to consider my thoughts and to put them down for the Home Secretary – and others – to see.

Martin Narey, my wonderful Private Secretary, said to me, 'Lord Ferrers. Please don't send that.' I said, 'Why not? These are my views and it is important that people should know the views of Ministers.'

'Yes,' he said. 'But please don't send it. It won't do you any good.' I did not send it. He was right. I was wrong. And I have always been very grateful to him for warning me off.

The important point to me has everlastingly been that it showed the right relationship between Minister and Private Secretary. The one can guide the other away from falling into an elephant trap of gargantuan proportions.

***

I once succeeded in changing the Law of the Country single-handed. And by mistake. That is not a bad achievement, especially as it was not intended – and, even more so, because nobody could put it back.

Douglas Hurd was the Home Secretary and he introduced the Licensing Bill which was to allow pubs to be open at all times, but that this relaxation in the licensing hours was not to apply to Sundays. It was just too controversial and, if we were to start trying to have a free-for-all on Sundays, we would get no Bill at all.

The Bill was to start in the House of Lords and, as it was a Home Office Bill, I was in charge of it.

I made it perfectly clear that the Bill deliberately did not refer to Sundays. All went well until somebody put down an amendment saying that pubs should be allowed to be open all day Sunday. I did my stuff and said, 'No. No. We cannot accept this amendment because we have always said that the Bill is not to refer to Sunday.' A lot of Peers stood up and supported the amendment. None supported the government view.

So, the amendment was put to the vote. The Lord Chairman of Committees said, 'Those that are in favour say Content.' There was a great roar of Content. 'To the contrary Not Content.' The Whip and I were the only two to say Not Content. I sat back and waited for the Division, knowing that everyone would come in, and the Conservative backbenchers would back the government in the division lobby.

Because there were so many people saying Content and only two saying Not Content, the Lord Chairman decided to put the question again. 'I think that the Contents have it.' No objection. 'The Contents have it.' I had switched off and had been waiting for the Division. I should have said Not Content again, but I did not. I suddenly sat up and realised what had happened. The Holy of Holies had been violated and the amendment had been accepted. Pubs were now going to be able to open on Sundays.

I attended Douglas Hurd's morning meeting the next day in the guise of a worm. I profusely apologised for this terrible disaster. He roared with laughter and took it all quite happily.

They then had to decide what to do when the Bill went to the House of Commons. The government could put an amendment down reversing the Lord's decision. The trouble with that was that it was such a popular amendment that the government did not believe that the members of the House of Commons would want to reverse it. And that would look worse – the government putting an amendment down and then being defeated by its own side. So they decided to let it go and to let the Lords' amendment remain in the Bill. It was then that Douglas Hogg said in the House of Commons, somewhat indelicately, of the Lords' Amendment, 'There was either a conspiracy or a cock-up. We are content to believe that it was a cock-up.'

The fact was, though, that I had changed the law of the land single-handed and by mistake. And no one could put it back.

***

Mrs Thatcher's government decided to change the law on Sunday trading. It was in a complete mess. Nobody took any notice of what the law was, even if they knew what it was. The Local Authorities could not take much action because, if they took anyone to court for allegedly breaking the law, the Local Authority always lost because the courts found that the law was so uncertain that they could not convict the defendant. The Local Authorities always lost and had to pay all the costs, and so they lost all heart in trying to protect the unprotectable.

There were absurd anomalies, like the fact that you could buy clotted cream on a Sunday, but you could not buy tinned clotted cream, but you could buy tinned unclotted cream. A church was not allowed to sell a Bible on a Sunday, but it could sell a pornographic magazine.

On and on the absurdities went, so the government decided to do something. Nothing had been done for forty years, principally because there was no agreement in the Commons on what should be done. There was a strong Church lobby which said that Sunday was a special day and that any change in the law would only mean more trading on a Sunday – and that, in their eyes, was a bad thing.

There had been a Shops Bill introduced into Parliament in 1981. It was a Private Member's Bill and Baroness Trumpington was in charge of it. It was dropped after the Third Reading.

So, the government tried to introduce its own Bill. A Home Office

Bill. And, I had to be in charge of it in the Lords. The Bill managed to get through the House of Commons – just – and then it came to us. It was exceedingly difficult to get the MPs to agree to anything. They were like a sackful of ferrets, but eventually some kind of reason prevailed. It was very interesting because there were just so many views. Garden centres was a typical example. Families want to go out together on a Sunday to a garden centre to buy plants. That is understandable, but some of these garden centres sell tables, chairs, loungers and things for the house as well as for the garden. It would be unfair to allow those garden centres to open to sell these things, but not to allow other shops, like furniture stores, to open which sell the same thing.

It is all very well for people to say that families want to go to shop together at a garden centre on Sunday, but what about the families of those who are working in the garden centre on a Sunday? They cannot spend Sunday together. Then will those who do not want to work on a Sunday be penalised, and eventually find themselves out of a job during the week for not agreeing to work on Sunday?

So the arguments went on and on. We were just getting towards the end of the Bill when up jumped the Conservative Peer Lord Onslow. He is a funny fellow. He has a fairly high opinion of himself which is not necessarily shared by others. He said, 'I have just thought of this and I think that this may be the solution to the problem.'

I felt irritated. I remember saying something like, 'My Noble Friend is like a schoolboy sitting at the back of the room and putting his hand up and saying, 'Please Sir. I have got a better idea.' I am bound to tell my Noble Friend that it does not matter how good his suggestion is it will not have a snowflake's chance in hell of getting through the Commons.' That shut him up!

***

I was always nervous at government reshuffles; most Ministers are, other than the supremely confident and ambitious ones – and there are not too many of these who do not receive unexpected jolts. One moment you are one of Her Majesty's Ministers, with an office, private secretaries and car – a pillar, one hopes, of society with the appropriate respect attaching thereto. The next minute one is out. Scrapped. Finito. Terminado. Nothing. A Has-Been and, like newspapers, there is nothing more dull than yesterday's newspaper. It really is a lottery. One minute you are in. The next minute, you are out. Having been in the Home Office for six years, I had got used to having survived reshuffles, but I suppose that the more of them you survive, the less likely you are to survive the next one.

The inevitable day came and I was asked to go to No. 10 to see the Prime Minister. People had been going in and out all day. I had thought that I had escaped trouble. But no. Horror of all horrors, I had been sent for. I was terrified that I was going to be given the heave-ho. But, fortunately, I was asked if I would go to the Department of Trade and Industry.

I was very disappointed to leave the Home Office. It was a lovely Department and a very efficient one, despite its size. I fear that in those days the Home Office was much nicer and better and more efficient than it is now. It seems to have been hit by every conceivable problem, including now the continuous loss of computer files of people's personal affairs. Its standing in the country has dropped. Even one Home Secretary, Dr John Reid, now Lord Reid, said that the Home Office was not 'fit for purpose' – a terrible and wounding description, which has now become part of the English vocabulary if you want to slag somebody nastily.

When Her Majesty's Inspector of Constabulary came to say goodbye to me, he said, 'Why on earth are you leaving? Did you not enjoy it here?' I said, 'Of course, I did, but the Prime Minister said that he wanted me to go to the Department of Trade and Industry. So off I have to go.'

In the six years during which I was in the Home Office, I served under five Home Secretaries: Douglas Hurd from 1986–1987, David Waddington 1989–1990, Kenneth Baker 1990–1992, Kenneth Clarke 1992–1993, Michael Howard 1993–1994; and I served with three Permanent Secretaries: Sir Brian Cubbon, Sir Clive Whitmore and Sir Richard Wilson, now Lord Wilson of Dinton, who went on to become the Secretary to the Cabinet, Master of Emmanuel College, Cambridge and Chairman of Hoare's Bank.

They had been happy days. Of all my time in government, I think that I look back on the days in the Home Office as the most fun, as well as being the most prestigious and the most respected and the most hard work. There were usually four Commons Ministers in the Home Office, but only one Lord's Minister. In the Lords one was responsible for all Home Office matters: police, fire service, the Channel Islands, charities, prisons, courts, crime, sentencing, levels of sentencing, immigration and broadcasting, the lot. It was not surprising that I used to say, 'I don't know half of what is going on in the Home Office, and I have forgotten the other half.'

Many years later, in 2008, when Gordon Brown formed his first government, somewhat flippantly called GOATS (the Government of All the Talents, because he had brought in outsiders to help), Lord West of Spithead, previously Admiral Sir Alan West, told me that Gordon Brown asked him if he could come and help in the Home Office as he knew so much about security. 'Well,' Alan said to me, 'I do know quite a bit about security as that has been my job, but Gordon Brown never said anything about me being the only Home Office Minister in the Lords and that I would have to answer all those questions about prisons and murders and every other matter which was a Home Office responsibility and which cropped up in the Lords and about which I knew nothing.'

When I was in the Home Office, I was asked if I would go, with Annabel, to Venice, to sign some International Document. Annabel, being half Italian, needless to say adores Venice. We agreed and we were put up very comfortably. They asked us if we would like to go to Murano, and we were taken there by a most luxurious launch to see the glass which they make. Quite fabulous.

We had been there before when Angela was seventeen – about seventeen years earlier. On our first visit, we had seen some lovely champagne glasses in red and emblazoned with gold. 'How much are they?' 'A million lire' – or whatever the price then was. Anyhow, they were wildly expensive and we did not buy them. We constantly regretted not having bought them. On our second visit seventeen years later, we went to the same place. Had they still got those glasses? Do they still do them? We went through one room. No. Then another room. No. And then – 'Yes, there they are.' What was the price? Now two million lire or whatever it was.

What was the point of six glasses? Smash one and the set is useless. So we bought twelve. They were very expensive – hideously expensive. The point is that I cannot remember what we paid for them. All I know is that they have given us huge pleasure ever since.

There is a moral there somewhere.

Chapter 16

Department of Trade and Industry

IF I HAD to change job, the Department of Trade and Industry was the favourite. I also thought that it would be a Department in which one might bump into people in the business world who, apart from anything else, might offer me a job when ministerial life came to an end. That particular prospect was advancing rapidly and it was only prudent and inevitable to think of what might or might not happen after that.

Michael Heseltine was the President of the Board of Trade, a lovely title which they had rescued from the dustbins of government in place of Secretary of State. Michael was a remarkable communicator. It was said that he did not read briefs very much, but he always knew what they said and what was happening. He was a fascinating person to listen to – tall, extremely good looking and with a thick mane of fair hair, a voice of substance and clarity, and a personality to match. He always made things seem obvious and that what he said must be right, even if in one's heart of hearts one might not think that it was. I always felt in awe of him.

I was given Small Businesses to look after. I did not find that much fun. I enjoyed going out and seeing people who were struggling away, managing their own small businesses very often in a remarkable way. But, as the name implies, there was little common thread to draw the businesses together which would enable the businesses to speak with a unified voice or with a unified approach – unless, of course, it was to vilify the government.

When I went to the Department of Trade and Industry, the main 'project' which it had on was the privatisation of the Post Office. I thought that that was quite mad. People liked the Post Office, and the delivery of letters, and the postmen, and its ubiquitousness in the villages and towns. To disrupt all that, and to invite furious hostility both within the Post Office and in the country itself, seemed to me like walking voluntarily into a tub of boiling oil. But Michael explained it to me quite gently and carefully, and I understood and, in the end, not only did I understand it, but I agreed with the idea.

The short answer was that the Post Office is hamstrung by being owned by the government. It had to go to the government for everything. If it made a profit, most of it had to be handed back to the government. On top of that, the Post Office was going to be open not just to national competition but to international competition. In order to be competitive they had to modernise and not to be tied up with government restrictions and qualifications. If they did not modernise, other companies across the water in Holland and elsewhere would come in and cream off the most lucrative part of the business for themselves leaving the dull and unprofitable pieces with the Post Office. The Post Office would get poorer and the service across the country, which it could offer, would get worse and worse. And one must not forget the original agreement with the Post Office, which is still in place, that it will guarantee to deliver letters anywhere in the country for one standard price.

It was not just a government looking round and saying, 'What can we denationalise next?' but it was a fairly forward looking government trying its best to enable the country's postal system not to fall in to the elephant traps which lay in front of it.

But was that controversial? I will say it was. The House of Commons was up in arms. The countryside was up in arms. The country was up in arms. Everyone loved the little post offices in the countryside. They liked to get their pensions there. They liked the cosy people who ran it. They liked everything about them. So did we all. But would they work in the future or was this Bill running the Post Office into disaster? The rural people bashed their Members of Parliament, and the Members of Parliament bashed the government. Talk about stirring up hornets' nests. Economics, facts and emotion found no meeting place. But still the government plodded on with determination, until all of a sudden – they dropped it. It was just too controversial by half and the poor Conservative Party which, by then, was full of internal bickerings, was split all ways.

I was told some years later by Martin Narey that he had been told by one senior official in the Home Office that the reason why I was moved to the Department of Trade and Industry was that I was the only person who was thought to be able to get the Bill to privatise the Post Office through the House of Lords. That was, of course, enormously flattering and my ego went flying up the Richter scale for a brief moment when he told me that. But I do not know whether there was any truth in it and, even if there were, I doubt if I would have made much of a fist of it. I was never very good at giving answers to fiendishly difficult questions – unless someone had told me the answers beforehand.

I had a delightful Private Secretary in the Department of Trade and Industry, Ian Gibbons. He was a craggy faced man, full of fun and happiness. Very competent, very thorough and very efficient. He was always in the right place and he was impeccable at looking after one's interests. I had only been at the Department of Trade and Industry for a year when there was a reshuffle. Help. I think that I am OK. I haven't been sent for. And then Ian came into see me. 'The Prime Minister wants to see you in No.10 at 4.30.' I was terrified. I thought that I was going to get the sack. At the last minute, Ian said 'Minister, would you like me to come with you?' It was a wonderful offer. I wanted someone to lean on. The answer was a big 'yes'!

When we got to No. 10 we had to sit and wait in the hall and then I was told to go in and see the Prime Minister. Much to my surprise and relief he did not sack me but he asked me to go to the Department of the Environment. I wondered if I had been about for too long and if the Prime Minister would really like a vacancy, and anyhow I had been moved about a bit in the last two years. I asked him straight, 'Prime Minister, would you prefer it if I were to leave the government altogether?' John Major is an exceedingly gracious man and a kind man and he said the nicest thing to me that any Prime Minister could ever say. He said, 'Certainly not. The House of Lords without you would be like having Trafalgar Square without Nelson's Column.' What a lovely thing to say! I still ruminate on those wonderful words if I am having a down.

Despite that, I did not really want to go to the Department of the Environment. I had heard about Ministers arguing their case to go to a certain Department. So I thought, 'Why not me?' I had forgotten that they were senior and pretty arrogant people who did that and that I did not really slot into either category.

I was happy at the Department of Trade and Industry and I had not been there that long. The Department of the Environment seemed to me a Department reflecting the long-hair and sandals brigade and trying to keep and protect all the bugs and beetles and insects which I tended to find a menace. They were always putting, or so it seemed to me, a whole host of curious things on the endangered species list which I did not think should be on the endangered species list at all. Instead of being thankful that I had not been sacked and after such a supremely gracious remark, I rather cheekily questioned the offer, in the hope that an alternative may come up. John Major said understandingly and charmingly, 'Go away and think about it and let Tom Strathclyde know.'

When I got back to the House of Lords I went to see Tom Strathclyde who was the Chief Whip. 'Well, are you going to the Department of the Environment?' 'I don't know. I don't want to. Can't I go somewhere else?' 'There isn't anywhere else.' 'Well, I shall have to go and think about it.' The first thing I wanted to do was to ask Annabel. She was out. Typical.

After a quarter of an hour, Tom came back. 'Have you made up your mind yet?' 'No. I can't find Annabel and I want to ask her first.' 'Oh, for God's sake man,' Tom said. 'Make up your own mind for once instead of asking Annabel. No. 10 is pressing me for an answer.'

I continued to stew about it and I wondered whether I should say no and leave the government. But that seemed a bit of a churlish thing to do, and it was, after all, all quite fun and, by any standards, a great privilege.

Another quarter of an hour later, Tom came back and said 'Have you made up your mind yet?'

'No,' I said. 'I simply don't know what to do. What do you think?'

'I cannot make up your mind for you, you idiot,' he said, 'and you must make up your mind quickly because No. 10 are ringing me every five minutes for an answer.'

'Well, give me more time to think about it.'

Tom said, 'Alright, I will go for a walk around the House for ten minutes so that, if No. 10 rings up, I am not at my desk.'

That was a wonderful thing to do – the act of a real friend. He is such a charming and lovely person. When he came back, I said yes.

I then went back to the Department of Trade and Industry, with Ian Gibbons, to collect my things – totally shattered. As we went into my room, Ian said, 'I think a whisky and soda would be a good thing, don't you Minister?' 'Yes,' I replied and he added, 'A large one?' 'Yes.' We sat down and enjoyed a very good drink and chat together. It was one of those special occasions, and I shall never forget it.

Ian knew how to deal with the tensions of office and he knew when the tensions were being exerted. I had felt stripped to pieces by all this, and it was a wonderful calming private secretary act, and I have never ceased to appreciate it and to be grateful for it.

***

I once went to Dubai for the Department of Trade and Industry. There was a great fair on and a number of British companies were exhibiting, and I went to give some encouragement and to be a 'presence'. It is an extraordinary country. A few years ago – say fifty – it was just sand. Now it is a thriving country, heaving with activity. Brand new roads, huge skyscrapers, modern airy buildings, even the golf course was new and perfectly watered.

Along the edge of the airport were two huge Russian jets. 'What are these?' I asked. 'They come in regularly from Russia with businessmen who buy loads and loads of television sets, radios and all kinds of goods because it is cheaper here and they take them back to Russia and sell them.'

There is no doubt about it but even then, 1994, there were plenty of very rich people in Russia. That seems odd because one always thought of Russia and the Russians as being very poor and down at heel, but it was when that great communist country decided to follow the UK and to *de*nationalise their big primary industries – steel, gas, coal, electricity and so forth – that some of the people, who were in the know and who knew their way about these things such as senior civil servants and engineers, made a killing and some became fabulously, even notoriously, wealthy.

I went to the Trade Fair with the Ambassador and we saw the various British stands – and there, pride of prides, were two gleaming, sparkling Rolls-Royces. I looked and inspected them and felt, rather absurdly, a surge of British pride. The Ambassador got talking with somebody and I, together with my entourage, went on looking at the other stands.

Some half an hour later, the Ambassador reappeared.

'Where have you been, Ambassador?' I said 'I thought that we had lost you.'

His eyes sparkled. 'I have just sold a Rolls-Royce.'

'You couldn't have,' I said. 'How hugely exciting.' And then after a slight pause, I added 'Ambassador, if you had been doing your job properly, you would have been looking after your Minister and we would both have been on the stand, and it would have been *I* who would have sold the Rolls-Royce, and not you. Just think what that would have done to my credibility back home!'

One afternoon I went with Ian Gibbons down to the gold market. He wanted to buy something nice to bring back home. I found a lovely pair of earrings for Annabel and I started the inevitable haggling with the salesman. Then I found something else to add to it. More haggling.

Meanwhile, Ian had got bored with listening to me haggling so went off and found something that he wanted. He haggled and he reached an agreement. He came over to me. 'How are you getting on?' I had been infinitely more successful in my haggling than Ian had in his. 'Well, good heavens,' he said. 'We had better send you off to argue the Department of Trade and Industry's case with the Treasury at the next annual government expenditure round.' I liked that!

Chapter 17

Department of the Environment

I WAS VERY apprehensive about going to the Department of the Environment. 'The environment' is the in-thing. If you are doing something for 'the environment', ipso facto that means that you are a good person and taking your responsibilities for the planet and the country and the bugs and the beetles seriously.

Of course, that is a load of old rubbish. People and government interfere far too much in everything nowadays. The world has been going for hundreds and thousands of years and one wonders why, just now in the year 2011 or thereabouts, everything is suddenly collapsing and there is impending disaster. Frankly, I don't believe it, but obviously we have to be prudent about what we do.

The reasons invented by government to interfere or boss you about are endless. Protect the beetles. Protect the butterflies. Don't burn old tree stumps or logs or wood because you will be destroying a habitat, never mind the fact that people have been burning dead bits of wood for centuries and, despite this, the bugs and beetles have managed to live. Don't eat butter because it contains fat. Don't eat margarine, either, because it contains chemicals. Don't spray your crops because spray contains chemicals – yet, when we are unwell, we rush down to the doctor who prescribes what? A pill. What is a pill? A chemical. So it goes on and on, and I feel, and I have felt for a long time, that as a country and as a society we are being grossly over-bossed.

Of course, there is the other side. There must be control. New drugs have to be certified as being acceptable to the public without undue risk.

Agricultural chemicals have to have a rigid testing regime for the same purpose. But you will never eliminate risk altogether. The main test is whether the benefits of the drugs and sprays are likely to be substantially greater than the risk of them. On the whole, the ones that we use are.

If one tries to limit all risk, you eliminate all progress. The fashion now is to say that cars are dangerous and therefore their speed must be limited – to 70 mph, 60, 50, 40, 30 or even 20 mph. Controls. Controls. Controls. And if you exceed them, you are punished, like a boy at school, with a fine or worse. The logical conclusion is that, if you want to avoid accidents from cars all together, do away with cars. But that would not work. You would be back to horses and carts. Who is going to remove the muck, and where are they going to put it? How are you going to feed the horses? No, that would be a denial of all progress. One has to accept cars – and their downsides, too. And cars are fun. It is such a pity that the Powers That Be will try to boss around and control everyone mercilessly – on the self-righteous basis that 'Nanny knows best'.

A typical example is when a government is introducing a 'nannying' Bill, when the Bill says, for example, that homosexuals should be treated the same as others. Fine. Most people would agree with that. The Bill is passed.

The civil servants then have to make the regulations in order to make the Act work. The kind of thing which then happens is that a couple may wish to let two of their rooms out on a board-and-lodging basis. They find that the regulations make them bound to accept two homosexual people, who wish to share a room together, who perhaps fornicate in their house, and walk around the house together in front of their family. The owners are left to clean the rooms, wash the sheets and generally tidy up.

If the owners understandably do not wish to see their home used in this way, and refuse to accept this couple, they may find that they have broken the law and can be subjected to court proceedings, a fine or even a prison sentence.

Whatever the arguments may be, in my book, that is just not right. But that is so often what happens when apparently reasonable Acts of

Parliament get turned into practical law. The civil servants will say that they are merely putting into practice what Parliament has agreed to put in the Statute Book.

That is why we should be careful about State Interference. Ferrers Law can be found to work all too frequently – 'that everything has the reverse effect of that intended'.

The great advantage of going to the Department of the Environment was that the Secretary of State was John Gummer. John and I have been friends for ages. He lives in Suffolk near us and was MP for Suffolk Coastal. He has a very lively mind, is very articulate and has a wild and impish sense of humour. His wife, Penny, is sweet and gentle. John is, of course, very green indeed and we had many fun jousting matches about 'the environment' in which I was always the loser. The first thing that he said to me when I arrived was, 'When I told Penny that you were coming to the Department of the Environment, she jumped with joy.' I felt so encouraged, and my ego momentarily went flying up the Richter scale – only to fizzle out again like an expended firework.

Everyone carries on about climate change. I find it very difficult to get worked up about it. Change happens the whole time. In a rather stubborn, block-headed way, I just feel that it is odd if the world has been going for 150 million years – or whatever it is – that it is all going to fold up in 2011.

I do not believe it, but there is no doubt that the weather has changed. In the 1940s, we used to skate on the lake at Staunton and take chairs to hang on to for those who were not reliable on their own. Maurice, later Neppy's husband, walked across the lake to see Neppy during the war – all very romantic. Winters were much colder.

Equally, we do not seem now to have the often very oppressive heatwaves in the summer that we used to have. During the 1940s I remember catching the train at St Pancras to go to Staunton. We took our jackets off, flapped our handkerchiefs around like windmills, stood by the window, and longed for the train to start so that we would get a breath of fresh air. Inevitably it ended in a monster thunderstorm. Of course, we have air conditioning now – but we do not have summers like we did in those days.

When I went to the Department of the Environment, CFC gases (chloro-fluorocarbons) were all the concern. When CFCs were first discovered a few years earlier, everyone was very excited because they replaced the chemical which made the aerosols of those days highly inflammable and dangerous. CFCs were thought to be the cat's whiskers. They were in refrigerators and deep-freezes and in all sorts of things. When refrigerators were dumped, all the gas – the CFCs – came out. They were also in containers and aerosols.

Later, it was discovered that CFCs, when released into the atmosphere, contributed to the hole in the ozone layer. The ozone layer is the layer of gases high up in the sky, which, amongst other things, prevents dangerous rays from the sun, like ultra violet rays, from getting through and causing skin cancer and generally upsetting the climate, including increasing global warming.

This was all an alarming problem and these wonderful CFCs were contributing to it and so they had to be discontinued. This was all new territory to me and, we were sitting around – John, the officials and some other Ministers and me – just after I had arrived. I said rather incredulously to John, 'Secretary of State, are you telling me that, when a girl goes into the hairdresser to have her hair done and when, at the end, the hairdresser sprays her hair with lacquer or whatever, the spray goes out of the window, goes up a couple of thousand feet, turns left, travels for 500 miles and then goes up and makes a hole in the ozone layer?' John replied, 'Yes. That is exactly what I am saying.' I said, 'Well, I just don't believe it.' John, in no way offended, just turned to his officials, smiled, and said, 'Oh dear, oh dear. We have got a lot of work to do here!'

One of the animals that it was proposed that we should protect was the dung beetle. I got quite worked up about this. Who on earth wants to protect a dung beetle, and why? Most people don't know what a dung beetle is, or what it looks like, anyhow. If you were to see a beetle walking across the kitchen floor, how would you know whether it was a dung beetle or another of God's many creatures – unless you have been reading a leaflet showing you what a dung beetle looks like? If you conclude that it is a dung beetle, then you must not kill it – or you will have

committed an offence. But who is going to know that you have killed the dung beetle and, even if they do know, are they going to shop you to the police? And is it seriously suggested that the government should carry out an intensive advertising campaign showing people about some dung beetle which, by its rarity, they are obviously unlikely to come across in order that, should they come across it, they should not kill it? I think that we have all gone bonkers.

In my view, the whole thing is totally absurd. I said so to Matt, the wonderful cartoonist in the *Daily Telegraph*, when we were having lunch together. When he sent me a thank-you letter for the lunch he enclosed a spectacular Matt cartoon, depicting a miserable-looking dung beetle with his eyes sticking out of his head like organ-stops and carrying a placard saying, 'Dung Beetles say "Save the Hereditary Peers"'. It was wonderful. Matt always hits the nail right on the head.

Matt and his wife, Pascale, came to a drinks party which we were having on the terrace of the House of Lords and to which we had asked a number of friends from all sorts of different strands of our life in order to celebrate our golden wedding anniversary. It was quite a big party and it was great fun. The terrace of the House of Lords is such a dignified and gracious place and it makes a superb setting for a reception. The fact that all the waiters and waitresses are from the House of Lords gives a lovely family feel to it. Annabel and I had previously driven down to Chalons-

A letter from Matt after our Golden Wedding party at the
House of Lords, July 2001

en-Champagne in our Audi to pick up the magnums of champagne.
Matt's letter of thanks was a superb cartoon.

I have a deep hatred – and it is getting deeper – of public interference
and of regulations. The Department of the Environment was always
looking for ways of 'protecting the environment' and showing how good
it was to be in the swim – and in the van – of public opinion. Over
animals, bugs and protected species in general, there was a fairly simple
process which was used. Some Body or authority would suggest that an
animal – bird, bug or anything else – ought to be protected. The Body
writes to the Secretary of State suggesting a list of species which ought to
be put on the 'protected' list.

The Secretary of State cannot, of course, take such a decision on his own. What does he know about said bird, bug or anything else? So he has to 'seek advice'. How does he do it? He writes to a whole list of organisations which may be interested, thirty or forty of them – Local Authorities, English Nature, Natural England, RSPB, the Ramblers, Friends of the Earth, the Water Authorities, and every other conceivable organisation which may in some way be thought to have an interest.

It is funny how pretty well all of those organisations are government-funded. If they are not government departments or their offshoots, many of them are quangos, many of them have government grants, or the chairmen of the board receive salaries or expenses which emanate from government. In other words, by one way or another, many of these bodies which are consulted by government are, in fact, funded by government. Many of the organisations will be written to with the basic question: 'Scientists think that the following birds, bugs or whatever, should be added to the Endangered Species List. Have you any views?'

The majority of organisations feel that, if scientists have proposed this, who are we to object? Then, after the statutory consultation period of three months or whatever it may be has taken place, the Secretary of State declares that he has been out to consultation with the thirty-nine (or whatever) bodies and none has objected to the proposal. So the Secretary of State makes an Order which he presents to Parliament. All these august bodies have agreed to this proposal and anyone who might have an objection thinks what chance has my little voice got against some proposal which by now is virtually set in concrete?

I once wrote to John Gummer and said, 'If you want some perfectly good common-sense advice, why don't you ask someone like me – instead of all these public bodies which feel that they must agree unless there is something really bad being proposed?'

As a result, we get on the Endangered List all sorts of curious species. And it doesn't end there. The Local Authorities then say that you must not burn wood between two dates in order to let some bug, which sits on the bark, breed. Bureaucracy and interference increases again, coupled of course with the threat of legal action and fines and, if necessary, a criminal record against you should you inadvertently not comply.

But the old bugs used to live alright despite the bonfires. What has happened? Knowledge, environmental concern, and the desire that the State should have complete authority, and that individuals must be subservient to the so-called 'will of the people'? It has got wildly out of control. It is a transformation for the worse.

Now farmers or landowners cannot burn logs, trim hedges or do that which they have always done in the way in which they have always known and at a time when they have always done it. Now, they are told that they cannot do it until a certain date – by which time they will be in the middle of harvest or some other occupation and will be unable to do it.

All this has, of course, nothing to do with the will of the people, which is the great maypole around which we dance. It is the diktat of the civil servants. It is they who have to operate the written letter of the Statute Book. Otherwise they, in theory, will get into trouble. It is an example – and there are hundreds of them – of the operation and the growth of the machine of Bureaucracy.

***

One of the little bits of fun which one used to have in the Department of the Environment was that one saw all sort of memos, submissions and suggestions which were proposed by civil servants, other Ministers and even people from outside – even if the subject matter did not relate to one's specific portfolio of interests within the Department. If one wished one could then write one's views, usually concisely, and send them to the Secretary of State. These prized snippets of departmental life had a fairly wide circulation amongst the senior civil servants in the Department, and sometimes lower.

When I was worked up about the dung beetle and the proposal to protect it, I wrote to the Secretary of State, John Gummer, as follows (the etiquette was that one's Private Secretary would write to the Secretary of State's Private Secretary conveying one's views):

From: Anne Hemming, Private Secretary to Earl Ferrers

26 January 1996

Mr Bendall

Biodiversity

Earl Ferrers was grateful for your paper of 23 January on the importance of biodiversity. The Minister found the paper very interesting and has commented as follows:

'I really think that we must lift our heads higher than the dung beetle, the moss and the lichens.

If we wish to conserve everything let's go back to the seventeenth century when there were lots of these little things and plenty of rats and disease as well and life expectancy was forty-five years.

The decline in the rabbit (which most people think was a good thing) was largely due to myxomatosis and it may have resulted in fewer ants and fewer woodpeckers. But the terrible destruction caused by the rabbit far outweighs the benefits provided by the ants and the woodpecker. Anyone who might suggest that there ought to be more rabbits in an area to ensure that there are more woodpeckers might be described as being off his proverbial trolley.

I am sure that the National Union of Farmers and the Country Land-owners' Association ensured that their members' interests were "taken into account". That does not mean that they were necessarily reflected in the conclusion.

I just think that all the time and effort which is being spent by intelligent people ferreting around in trying to find how important a bug or a lichen is to 'biodiversity' and to human life could be better spent on trying to find how we can feed another 3,000 million people in the world in the next twenty-five years and give them houses and jobs.

I regard most of this as an obtuse misdirection of effort fanned by public opinion, who feed on it as much as they are alleged to create it.

Do let us keep our feet, if not on the ground, at least somewhere near it.'

The Minister would like to discuss the paper and this office will be in touch in due course to set up a date.

Anne Hemming

***

On another occasion, I was worked up about the stag beetle.

Secretary of State

Wildlife and Countryside Act 1981: Third Quinquennial Review

I have now had the opportunity of discussing with officials the recommendations of the JNCC's Quinquennial Review.

I am concerned that it is proposed that a further 33 species should be added to the protected lists or be given further protection. Only 1 is being removed.

There seems to be a virtue, misplaced in my view, that the more 'things' which are protected – whether birds, plants or mosses – the better. There must be a limit. And presumably, having been protected and allowed to multiply, some are no longer rare and should be removed from the list.

I can see little attraction in protecting, for example, the Stag Beetle. They are horrible, nasty things which bite. I had the unforgettable privilege of sharing the inside of a mosquito net with one in Malaya. It was a disagreeable experience. Even the JNCC describe them as of 'fearsome appearance'. I cannot conceive of anyone in their right mind wanting to protect them. Maybe it is in order to stop traders from exporting them. My view is, if they do export them 'bully for them'. The fewer we have of them the better.

Then there are objects like the Southern Damselfly, the Allis Shad and the Royal Bolete. Most people do not know what these are nor whether they have one. Nor would they know if they are likely to remove one or destroy one, unless this is all to be accompanied by a comprehensive publicity campaign.

The cynic might question the value of an expensive publicity campaign which would be designed to inform people about a number of species which, because of their rarity, they are unlikely to meet.

These lists of protected species get progressively longer to the satisfaction, mainly, of the purist or the specialist. Once on the list, it seems impossible to get a species off. Cormorants can hoover up every fish in sight – to the despair of the angler. The population of sparrowhawks consume 35 million songbirds, 2 million pigeons and 1 million blackbirds each year – but no one can get them off the list.

The list of those who are to be consulted on these matters is a list of those who have a vested interest.

There seem to be few people to be consulted who might represent what might be called the 'common sense' point of view (which, by definition, means people who hold views similar to me!).

I do think that we should take a very firm line on not adding anything more to the lists than is absolutely necessary, and that we should remove from the protected lists those which no longer need to be on them.

Ferrers

***

On one occasion, I met the Prime Minister, John Major, at a function and he referred to a piece of jolly correspondence which we had had in the Department about bats. He asked to see this. I was alarmed. I felt that it was like the headmaster asking to see what it was that you had been writing underneath the desk.

I sent the memo to the Prime Minister together with another letter which my Private Secretary had sent to Mr Plowman. Mr Plowman was a charming, delightful, clever and witty civil servant. I had suggested that the House of Lords should become an SSSI – a Site of Special Scientific Interest – an accolade which is distributed around the countryside like confetti to any part of it which is considered to contain something of biodiversity interest (whatever that may be) and which should be preserved.

Mr Plowman's reply is a gem. It is a spoof. It is a glorious dig at the House of Lords, at biodiversity, at the Labour Party and at everything else in sight. It needs, though, a little interpretive glossary:

- Strappedocashus means Strapped for Cash.
- Walworthroadiensis refers to the Labour Party's Headquarters which were, at the time, in Walworth Road.
- There is a dig at Peers who go for a drink in the evening in the

Cholmondeley Room and who go to their country estates at the weekend and who go abroad to warmer climates in the summer. There is a charming dig about acronyms.

• Item 7 refers to three options for a name. The three refer to Faith, Hope and Charity.

• Item 8 refers to 1 Corinthians XIII: 'And the greatest of these is Charity.'

When I told the delightful Mr Plowman that, at the Prime Minister's request, I had sent him a copy of the note about bats and rabies, but that I had also sent him a copy of Mr Plowman's tongue-in-cheek and superb submission on moths and SSSIs, Mr Plowman smiled gently and said to me, 'Oh dear, oh dear. There ends a glittering career!'

Prime Minister

As you requested, I am sending a copy of the memo about bats.

I am also venturing to enclose a memo about making the House of Lords a Site of Special Scientific Interest. The reply is a gem.

I should point out that other memos also circulate within the Department, usually of the more sombre and traditional variety.

F.

***

Mr Plowman

Bats and Rabies

Earl Ferrers has been alarmed by the recent press coverage of a bat, which has bitten a pregnant woman, and has been found to have rabies. He has commented:

'The United Kingdom always carried out a rigorous protection policy against rabies – in order to protect the population from a most disagreeable and violent form of death. When foxes were considered to be infected with it they were shot.

Now that bats are found to have rabies the position appears to be that, if a person kills a bat, he is fined £5,000. If a bat kills a person then nothing happens.

How do officials recommend that we crawl out of this absurd hole?'

Anne Hemming

***

Mr Plowman

Biodiversity

Earl Ferrers was glad to see your minute of 2nd February to PS/Secretary of State about Biodiversity. He was, though, somewhat alarmed by both prospects in your minute. These were:

- that there were 100 million clothes moths in the United Kingdom,
- if they were not 'pseudo', the Minister's clothes cupboard might become an SSSI.

Both prospects worried the Minister, although, in view of recent announcements, he wondered whether it might not be more appropriate now to make the House of Lords an SSSI. It now contains, in hereditary peers, an endangered species. He considers that they ought to be protected.

As would be required of an SSSI, the premises are already open to the public, the work undertaken there is 'transparent', 'cost-effective', 'coordinated' and 'cohesive'. But this part of our heritage could be destroyed by deliberate vandalism.

The Minister wonders if, as English Nature has the responsibility for preserving the flora and fauna of our country, and as hereditary peers might be regarded – without accusation of immodesty – of being two rungs higher up the 'hierarchy' than the dung beetle, the Secretary of State might be advised to lean upon English Nature to take action.

Anne Hemming

***

From: J P Plowman
Wildlife & Countryside
N14/16, 2 Marsham Street
APS/ Earl Ferrers

Anthropomorphic Diversity

Your minute of 9th February raises a number of important questions to which reference to Bagehot and Erskine May would probably be more valuable than Darwin and Bob May. Nonetheless, never let it be said that this Directorate shirks from giving honest advice on matters of great public concern.

1. Taking this issue from first principles, we must establish whether members of the House of Lords would qualify as an endangered species. According to the most authoritative treatises on species of this kind (Burke and Debrett) there are thought to be some 2,000 Peers. These divide into several categories, the two most important of which are the pure bred hereditary species and the feral kind (Life Peers) whose life cycle, like that of the dragonfly, is colourful, energetic but short.

2. Word has it that pairs of Hereditary Peers breed at about the same rate as that of the population of humankind as a whole, with each pair having an average of 2.4 offspring, though for unusual genetic reasons species rarely survive down the female line. As there are no known predators, it seems probable that long-term survival is assured.

3. There are reports that a new virus (STRAPPEDOCASHUS WALWORTHROADIENSIS) that turns blue-blood red, is gaining hold but we have no evidence to substantiate this.

4. So, survival of the species itself is probably not in question and it cannot therefore be regarded as endangered.

5. The next question therefore is whether, even if the species is not endangered, its habitat is. Recent observations by Parliamentary ornithologists suggest that flocks of Peers cluster round such watering holes as the Cholmondeley Room at dusk. There seem to be food supplies in abundance. Regular weekly migration to well-established feeding grounds, often purpose built by conservationists such as Repton or Brown, are commonly observed. Migration further afield

to warmer climes in the summer months can also be observed though ornithologists are puzzled by the apparent need to migrate at the hottest time of the year.

6. A question remains about the future of the building which houses the Peers. As it does not house an endangered species and human beings are not covered by the Wildlife and Countryside Act nor by earlier wildlife legislation, there is something of a dilemma. Relief may be at hand, however, if the Minister of Agriculture is successful in his negotiation of animal welfare provisions at the Intergovernmental Conference to revise the Maastricht Treaty. Mr Hogg has defined animals in one context as 'sentient beings'. We have it on good authority that Peers qualify in this category and it therefore seems only appropriate to apply at least the spirit of the Wildlife and Countryside Act to their Lordships' House.

7. For the reasons given above, however, we cannot describe the House as a site of scientific interest. A 'site' is something that building contractors live on, not the Mother of Parliaments. The 'interest' can hardly be described as 'scientific', whatever else it may be. The matter has therefore been referred to the Government Acronyms Committee (GAS) whose chairman (Les Majesty) has proposed three possible names to cover the special designation of the House of Lords:

i) Formally Ancient Institution, That's History (FAITH)

ii) House of Peers (Extinct) (HOPE)

iii) Could Have had A Royal in There Yesterday (CHARITY)

8. I am advised by higher authority that the greatest of them is the third.

J P Plowman
16 February 1996

***

I regard this as the real classic of all my correspondence in any Department. It is *so* important not to get bogged down with the boring things in life. Ministers and civil servants ought to elevate themselves above that. John Plowman did.

We are so lucky that, despite endless criticisms of the Civil Service, it is comprised of people of outstanding ability and intelligence and who can see the funny side of things, too. When I showed this correspondence to a senior legal friend of mine he said, 'The Civil Service is unique. You would never get that type of correspondence in business.'

***

In 1996 BSE – Bovine Spongiform Encephalopathy – was in full swing. It was a disease of cattle, and the way in which the government tried to stop its spread was to slaughter all the animals within the area surrounding the outbreak.

This was a very risky and highly controversial policy because many perfectly healthy animals were being destroyed, and people's livelihood and lifetime's work was being exterminated.

Once it was certified that the animals on a farm should be destroyed, the system went into action. Animals were killed and high-lift tractors and bulldozers pushed the carcasses onto a pyre where they were burned. It was a grotesque site, with dead animals with their feet sticking up in the air in the undignified position of sudden, imposed death. The smell was terrible and the emotional devastation experienced by those who had known and loved their animals, was immense. Fearful stories appeared in the press about how some animals, usually small ones, understandably tried to run away from it all only to be chased by young men on motorbikes with rifles dangerously firing in all directions, trying to shoot them. It was bizarre, almost inhuman and, in all ways, disagreeable. It was all, though, in an effort to prevent the spread of an ugly, new and relatively unknown disease.

I wrote a note to John Gummer airing my concerns:

Secretary of State

I am disturbed at the course on which the Government appears to be embarking over BSE.

The idea of destroying 4 million cattle seems almost beyond comprehension. The United Kingdom has the best dairy and beef stock in the world, and we seem to have been whipped up into a manic hysteria of self destruction – all on the basis of 'restoring public confidence' in meat.

The fact that even when meat prices are halved, the shops are sold out shows that people's alarm is only skin-deep.

When cattle were destroyed in the Foot and Mouth scare of 1968, it had a traumatic effect on those who had looked after them. But those animals were diseased. These are not.

I have no doubt that, when the television shows pictures of cattle being incinerated, public opinion will turn like litmus-paper. But by then it will be too late. The machine of destruction will have been set on an unstoppable course.

And what of the undernourished in the Third World? They will be horrified to see us destroy what they would willingly eat.

This is not just the destruction of cattle. We will be embarking on a course of loss of exports, increased imports, unemployment and violent damage to the economy. This is far deeper than just an animal health problem. We are in jumping-down-the-well territory. I fear that the consequences of the kind of action which is being canvassed now will be far greater than has begun to be thought of.

I just hope that some way will be found of avoiding our embarking on this course.

I am copying this to Robert Cranborne.

F.

4 April 1996

***

Another of my pet hobby horses was – and still is – the length of government papers, submissions, reports and general government, and other, documents.

There is a theory that everything must be written down in glorious detail and then everyone knows where they are. But this is a fallacy. The point of writing something down is in order that people should read it. If it is long or boring – or *unattractive* – to read, the writer falls at the first fence. The reader does not want to read it, and the points which the writer is trying to make get vaporised.

Now, all businesses and commerce are falling into the same trap.

They are writing endless documents, Reports and Annual Reports, all produced on very expensive paper with coloured photographs. I suppose that they are all trying to make their document more attractive than the others so that, when the reader is inundated with all the others, he will read the one which at least appears to be attractive to read. That is fine. But there is too much of it.

Even after I have been out of government for thirteen years, so all the Reports, Annual Reports and the rest come flooding onto my desk. Despite the glory of the publication, I am afraid that the majority go straight into the waste-paper basket.

When I was in government I used to avow to the fact that, when I left government, I would set up a business to make documents, letters and papers easy to read. Needless to say, I did not do so – and, as a result, I then lost out on what might have been a lucrative retirement career.

The first overriding principle is that, if you write something down, you want it to be read. The following points seem to me to be desirable if you want this principle to work:

- The type must be sufficiently large for ease of reading. I was once sent a lobbying document the print of which was so small that one could hardly read it. They asked for comments on the paper. I told them that the print should be larger, as it was virtually unreadable. I never heard from them again.
- There must be plenty of paragraphs. No paragraph, unless for exceptional reasons, should be more than seven–nine lines in length. With too long paragraphs, it is like looking through wire-netting. You do not know where you are.
- Spaces between paragraphs should be larger than spaces between lines.
- Unfashionable I know now, but new paragraphs should be indented in order to break up the mass of verbiage.
- Documents should be short, sharp and to the point. Not a compendium of essays.
- Rubbish words so loved by civil servants, but which actually mean nothing, should be avoided like the plague, such as:

Joined-up Government
Seamless Government
Cohesive
Co-ordinated
Meaningful
Underpinning
Overarching

The list goes on.

I readily acknowledge that it is easy to write this, but that it is far more difficult to comply with it. You may wonder why this dictat has not been followed in this book. The answer is that printing books is a 'science' all of its own and does not always take kindly to good suggestions. Not everything, though, is books. There are letters, documents, memos, reports, and all sorts of instructions, each inviting the reader to read. The more inviting they are to read the more people will be likely to read them. Most could be improved by these suggestions. If people only, though, tried to keep along these simple lines, I think that the practice of reading and absorbing what the writer is trying to get across would be much easier and much more fun. I wrote my thoughts to John Gummer as follows, and the circulation list was fairly formidable.

Secretary of State
DEPARTMENTAL PUBLICATION

I get worried about the number of publications which the Department issues – and their length. I think that every effort should be made to cut down on both.

   Ministers are often asked to 'approve' documents for consultation or Guidance Notes which are hopelessly technical and accordingly – to the layman anyhow – often incomprehensible. I sometimes pity the poor fellows who have to read them.

   As the documents are often in the advanced stages of preparation and up against a deadline, by the time that they get to the Minister, it is difficult for him to determine what should be cut and where. The whole process would end up in turmoil.

A discussion document, for example on Landfill Monitoring, runs to 277 pages. One questions whether that sort of length is really necessary. Likewise, do we need to have such copious Annual Reports? And there are many other examples.

Thousands of hours of officials' time must be spent in drawing together all the material for the huge variety of different documents which the Department produces, and then writing them. They then get passed on to others who receive them with a heavy heart, realising that they are supposed to read them.

I am aware that this is a very difficult area, and I put forward these ideas with a sense of humility, being myself a bad succinct writer. But I think it important that there should be fewer documents, that they should be shorter, and that they should be more attractive to readers.

F.

I took up the cudgels about the nannying state and its interference when I saw that they were going to ban a spray, used by gardeners, called Roseclear (alleged to be unsafe). I wrote:

> The article claims that Roseclear is being banned because, when it was squirted into the eyes of rabbits, not surprisingly, it caused irritation. Not one case of human eye irritation has been caused in the 40 million times in which the spray has been used ... It is not surprising that it is found to be an irritant. So it would be to human beings, but that would be the case with petrol, bleach or oven-cleaner as well. They are all used, although they are subject to different standards.

***

One of the birds that had created a problem in the Department of the Environment was the Ruddy Duck. It had been imported into this country about fifty years ago by, I think, Sir Peter Scott. That was fine, except a number of them escaped and flew off to Spain where they found the White Headed Duck deeply attractive. As is the case with such emotions, the Ruddy Duck copulated with the White Headed Duck and produced a cross-breed. The trouble was that the White Headed Duck was the National Emblem of Andalucía.

At some international ministerial meeting, a well-meaning junior United Kingdom Minister said that we would control the Ruddy Duck. But how do you stop a duck from flying? Or from copulating? The hapless Minister had unwittingly opened up a can of worms and had dropped his successors in the cart.

Even the RSPB – the Royal Society for the Protection of Birds – came to ask what we were going to do. Why didn't we shoot them? they asked. I said, 'Why don't you shoot them?' Oh they could not do that because they are supposed to protect birds, not shoot them. Otherwise they would be called RSPSB – the Royal Society for the Protection of *Some* Birds.

Why did the government not pay people to shoot the birds? – so much per dead bird. You could not use a shotgun, as you would kill everything. So it would have to be a rifle. I pointed out that many people felt quite proud when they had shot a flying duck with a shotgun containing many pellets. People must be mad if they thought that you would kill a flying duck with a rifle.

Even so, the impact that you would make on the population of the Ruddy Duck would be minimal, the numbers would be back to normal next year, and the money spent would have been wasted.

Endless discussions took place, and the name of the duck gave cause for ribald comment and laughter. So much so that, at one meeting, John Gummer said: 'I will not have any more of this jocular reference to the Ruddy Duck. It is a waste of time and nobody is taking it seriously. You will have to find another name for it.'

The far-seeing and witty Mr Plowman entitled his next submission '*** Duck'. It was hilarious.

Ruddy duck

From: J P Plowman
Wildlife & Countryside
N14/16 2 Marsham Street
APS/ Secretary of State cc: PS/ Lord Ferrers
6 March 1996

Mrs McDonald

*** DUCK

In view of the Secretary of State's embargo on references to the *** duck, I cannot give you the full flavour of reports that have now reached us without photographic evidence of attempts to deal with the *** duck.

The attached photograph has reached this office recently. The correct caption is a snippet of conversation overheard on the banks of a West Midlands reservoir and picked up by the Wildlife and Countryside Directorate's high-powered scanner in Bristol, was something like this:

'Would you like the rifle Derek?'

'No thanks, Chairman. Our research people have come up with something rather better...'

J P Plowman

It was made to look like a duck about to be decapitated by a man in a boat with an axe. It fact, it was somebody trying to rescue a duck which had been trapped in the ice.

Some civil servants are wonderful – earnest, hard-working, loyal and fun. We were very lucky.

***

John Gummer had always been very keen on regulations for hedges. Some thought too many had been pulled up. I was never keen on yet more regulations, and the fact that far more trees and hedges had been planted over the previous ten years than had been pulled up – for some extraordinary reason – seemed to carry no weight at all.

Eventually, because hedges fell into my remit in the Department of the Environment, the civil servants produced the draft Hedgerow Regulations for me to approve. Well! They were hugely complicated. I found them almost impossible to understand, even with the benefit of being helped by officials. How were ordinary farmers, who would not have the privilege of such help, manage? I told the Secretary of State that I thought that we should not proceed. I even telephoned him when he was in Austria to tell him so. And what was his response? 'NO. We must have them. It was in our manifesto and we have done nothing about it. We cannot go into the next election having done nothing.'

I personally did not think that the result of the general election would depend on whether we had any Hedgerow Regulations or not – but I saw his point.

So the Hedgerow Regulations were introduced into the House of Commons. Then the general election was announced. When that happens there is what is called a 'wash-up': government and opposition get together and try to decide which Bills should be dropped and which should be given accelerated treatment before Parliament is dissolved.

Fortunately, it looked as if the House of Commons would not have time for the Hedgerow Regulations, or that they would be dropped. 'Don't worry, the Regulations are at the bottom of the list and the House of Commons will not be able to read them.' Hooray.

Then, two hours later, 'All the early business in the House of Commons has gone through far quicker than expected. They will now be able to take the Regulations.' Disaster.

I had a meeting in Robert Cranborne's room. He was the Leader and Tom Strathclyde was the Chief Whip. 'Do you want to take these Regulations?' I was asked. 'No. I hate them.' 'Well, we'll tell the House of Commons that we haven't the time and cannot fit them in.' I could not do that, and drop my ministerial boss and friend, John Gummer, in the cart. It would have been totally disloyal. I would never be able to look him in the face again. So we decided to take them.

The Hedgerow Regulations were the last business of all to be taken in the House of Lords before the Dissolution of Parliament, and it was the last business that I would ever take through on behalf of the government after eighteen years. I disliked it. But it all went off quite well and quite good humouredly. I remember seeing the Lord Chancellor, James MacKay, sitting on the Woolsack and roaring with laughter at something I had said. That was quite encouraging.

***

John Gummer became Lord Deben and he wrote a poem about me. I was tickled pink. It was this:

> *To a Recalcitrant Earl*
> *Earl Ferrers is a nobleman of very great renown*
> *A Minister who served his country well.*
> *He stood at the dispatch box, impeccably polite*
> *With charm he gave the Opposition hell.*
> *The trouble with Lord Ferrers is his failure to believe*
> *In the scientific methods we apply.*
> *He doubted that the gas which his shaving cream expelled*
> *Would rise and do such damage in the sky.*
> *The ozone hole was something that Lord Ferrers couldn't see*
> *So, like St Thomas, he denied the claim.*
> *And as for global warming, he thought it so much guff*

And treated health and safety much the same.
When it came to saving habitats Lord Ferrers, though polite,
Was full of righteous anger deep inside.
Beetles (stag) and Beetles (dung) he specially disliked
And protecting them he just could not abide.
Luckily Lord Ferrers had a Secretary of State
A believer in redemption for us all.
He set about conversion of this very noble Lord
So charming, so elegant, so tall.
He explained in simple terms how climate change was caused
With pictures, diagrams, and easy graphs.
But having had the benefit of all that science gave
Earl Ferrers turns around and simply laughs.
'You're telling me that you believe, the world is heating up
We're all at risk because of CO_2.
When I was young the summer was much warmer then than now
And we boiled alive in nineteen-forty-two.
The trouble with these scientists, they're not as old as me
They can't remember back before the War.
Most things have been the same for as long as I can tell
They'll continue much the same – of that I'm sure.
There are ups and downs in life and things will come and go
And we need not worry when we think they change
Just give them time and they'll come back to where they were before
Only Socialists attempt to rearrange'.
The patient S of S, returning to the charge
Explained the growing scourge of BSE
And why protecting hedges was a vital national goal
And the damage that was done by CFC.
It was only when discussion moved to ruddy ducks
That the two of them could heartily agree
That the people who could shoot those f***ing little birds
Were the ruddy RSP ruddy B.

***

I am not good at remembering statistics, but there is one set which I have always remembered and which I find quite alarming.

In 1960, there were 3,000 million people in the world. That was projected to *double* to 6,000 million forty years later, by the year 2000. And that figure was projected to *double again* within twenty-five years – 2025 – to 12,000 million. It is hideously on track for that.

All these extra people are going to require homes, schools, hospitals, trains and roads – as well as food. But much of the land will have been taken up by building the requirements for these people. Where is the food going to be grown? One day, not far off, there will be a major shortage of food, prices will rocket and disaster will happen again.

Do we make provisions for this? No. Why not? Because politics is short-term stuff.

***

One of the greatest compliments that I was paid in the Department of the Environment was when we were having a leaving party before the general election and one of the officials came up to me and said, 'Well, there is one thing which you have taught my Division.' I said, 'What is that?' 'How to write letters.' I was amazed and flattered. I had thought that, when I had so often altered the drafts of letters to my style, the civil servants would have been fed up. Apparently that was not so. I felt touched and humbled.

When the general election came, Labour won and the Conservative Party was removed from office. That is the way in which the political system works, and everyone understands that, but it does produce personal and emotional and financial problems for many of the people who are involved, which the good general public do not know about. And why should they?

All of a sudden, Ministers and Members of Parliaments are out of work. They have nothing to do after, sometimes, many years of working for their country in Parliament. Their income is cut off overnight – or almost. They then have to find another job – not very easy for Ministers who had, on becoming a Minister, been bound to sever their connections with their previous work. Going back is not all that easy because, when a hole is made in the sand, the sea soon comes and covers it up and you cannot see where the hole was. Firms who were happy to employ you before find that they have no need of you again, and anyhow you have got out of touch with what they were doing. It is easier for backbenchers because they have been able to keep their connection with outside firms.

Then the MP or Minister, who finds himself out of office and trying to find a new job, finds that he is in competition with about 250 of his colleagues all of whom are paddling around the same village square, bound on the same errand. There is a limit to how many empty slots there are in the business system. The fact that you have been doing your best to help to run the country during the past several years does not necessarily result in tycoons falling over themselves in gratitude and excitement that you are now available to help them.

That is why the government allows MPs and Ministers to continue to draw their salary for three months after the election – to tide them over whilst they reorientate their lives and hopefully enable them to get on the road to finding a new career.

The same happens in the House of Lords, too. Retiring Ministers could continue to draw their salary for a further three months – *except* for me and, I think, Baroness Trumpington, because we were over sixty-five. The Civil Service does have the most bizarre, and sometimes indefensible, rules. I asked why being over sixty-five should make any difference. 'Because you can draw the Old Age Pension.' I asked what on earth that had got to do with it? The Old Age Pension is paid to everyone once they achieve a certain age and has nothing to do with being financially inconvenienced because the general election has put you out of a job – 'and,' said I, 'it is presumably more difficult for an Old Age Pensioner to find employment than for a younger person to do so.' Of course, it made no difference. It was like talking to a brick wall. I had spent eighteen years in government and I felt it a bit rough to be told that the day you leave your pay ends, but that your young stripling colleagues, when they leave, know that they will continue to be paid for three months.

***

The government has been so determined to 'reform' the House of Lords that one is entitled, after ten years, to ask whether it is now better. I think that the answer is in the negative.

They have got rid of most of the Hereditary Peers. They have got rid of the Lord Chancellor. They have got rid of the Law Lords. They have changed the 'set-piece' debates from Wednesday to Thursday and they now start at 11 a.m. instead of 2.30 p.m. When these debates were held on a Wednesday, the House was full. Monday, Tuesday and Thursday were government business days when Committee Stages were taken and divisions occurred. So, people were there for Wednesdays. The debates were well attended. The subjects were interesting. People were interested.

In the 1970s when the daily allowance was £4-14-6, the House was well attended at 7 p.m. on a Thursday and sometimes to 10 p.m. and even much later. Now that the expenses are about £300 per day, the House is dead at 1 o'clock on a Thursday and closed by 7 p.m. Is that better? To answer the question which is always asked about everything, is that better value for money? I think not. Yet, when all the changes were being promoted, we said 'it will cost more'. The government's answer was always 'Parliament and the Law cannot be constrained by funds.' What we have now is the worst of all worlds – more expense and less achievement.

Why can government and legislators never understand that, when they alter the law to make things 'better', that does not always happen? They are sometimes made worse. They can argue until they are blue in the face that 'this' will happen, but 'this' often does not happen. Once you let a greyhound out of the trap, he can follow the route round the track. Fine. But, once he goes into the open, no one knows where he is going to go. This is not an argument for no change, merely a warning that, although you may be trying to alter the bad parts, you may find that, inadvertently, you are altering the good parts too. And watch what you write and say because events will often not work out in the way in which you expect, intend or say.

It is people who make life – the good, the kind, the intelligent, the careful, the gracious, the courteous, the hard working, those who think of others. In most of my House of Lords life I have had the wondrous benefit of having Margaret West as my secretary. I was not, of course, the only one to receive the benefits of her skills. She had other people for whom she worked too, but she has worked for me for about thirty-four years. Total discretion. Total loyalty. Wonderful at finding things that happened years ago almost immediately. And she even brings one letters to sign at 10.30 p.m. in the evening. She has been the most remarkable, efficient and gracious secretary.

I used to take all my letters from home up to London and give Margaret the responses to them, which she would type and let me have back – for filing at home. The filing took ages and wrecked quite a bit of the weekend, and what was more debilitating was that I could never find the correspondence when I came to look for it – and I had no one else to blame.

So for the last nine years, I have had the benefit of a secretary at home, Jane Wickstead, whose husband is a surgeon at the Norfolk and Norwich Hospital and who lives about two miles from us. She looks after my home affairs and all that goes with that. That takes ages – and it seems to get longer. She is also wonderful, thorough, meticulous and kind and keeps everything on an even keel. And she remembers where everything is.

It seems very spoilt having two people to help, one in London and one at home – and I expect that it probably is – but it does enable one to keep one's head above water. It is not just the typing of letters. It is all that goes on underneath the surface – rather like the swan going down the river looking resplendent and graceful, but paddling away like mad underneath.

I do dislike things being disorganised. I hate letters being unanswered or scruffily written or the English being bad or just the appearance of the letter being unattractive. Well-written letters reflect a well-ordered mind and a well-organised secretary. They are the shop window of one's organisation and of oneself.

Chapter 18

House of Lords Bill

IN 1999 THE government introduced the House of Lords Bill – the Bill that was to remove all the Hereditary Peers from the House of Lords. It was wildly controversial and hugely divisive. The two sides of the argument were basically quite simple. Why should people be in Parliament, making laws for the country, simply by the accident of birth? The contrary argument was why should people be in the House of Lords because of the patronage of the Prime Minister? From that everything else flowed – and it did, with passion. One quite simple – but I always found quite telling – argument in favour of the Hereditary Peers was that it is presumably no worse to be chosen to be in the House of Lords by the Almighty than by Mr Blair.

The Labour government of the day had a huge majority in the House of Commons and therefore the Bill sailed through there. In the House of Lords it was a very different matter. People were deeply wounded. Their families had been in the House of Lords for generations – and now they were all going to be tipped out on to the road, like a barrow-load of rubbish.

The House of Lords and its make-up, whatever you may think of it, was part of the Constitution, and the government was going to destroy it. Baroness Jay of Paddington was the Leader of the House of Lords and she was in charge of the Bill. Whatever her qualities may be, her handling of the House of Lords Bill was appalling. She said that those who were complaining of the Bill were like drowning sailors hanging on to any piece of wood or furniture which they could find. Well, why shouldn't they? You cannot get much more insulting than that even if you are changing the Constitution and, if you are changing the Constitution, there is no reason to be insulting in the process.

There was a good deal of patronage there, too. Her father was Jim Callaghan, an ex-Prime Minister who was now himself a member of the House of Lords. Over such a sensitive matter, one would have expected delicacy, courtesy and understanding despite the controversial contents of the Bill. But there was not a drop of any of it. Lady Jay said, with all the finesse of a bulldozer, 'It is time to say thank you and goodbye.'

During the course of the Bill's passage, it was clear that the total removal of all the Hereditary Peers would leave a huge gap in the House of Lords simply from the point of view of the running of the House, if nothing else. Hereditary Peers were involved in committees, sometimes as chairmen of committees. Others were Deputy Speakers. It would not be easy to find a replacement for all these people from the ranks of the Life Peers.

Then there were positions like the Earl Marshal and the Lord Great Chamberlain, both hereditary offices. Were they to be thrown out, too? Then there were ex-Cabinet Ministers and ex-Leaders of the House of Lords, who were Hereditary Peers, some very distinguished ones like Lord Carrington and Earl Jellicoe. Were they to be thrown out, too? – and all the knowledge and experience which they had, go disappearing with them from the House and from Parliament down the drain? As the debates went on it became perfectly obvious that the Bill was an absurdity and, as it was, it would not work.

The Bill, in fact, caused considerable problems both for the government and for the opposition. You do not make a monumental hole in the Constitution without having a whole host of side-effects, some of which are, at the time, unrealised by either the government or the opposition.

The opposition were in quite a difficulty. Some said, in a very bellicose way, 'Fight the Bill tooth and nail. Vote against it at Second Reading.'

The government had such an overwhelming majority in the House of Commons that the opposition could not do much. They could argue as much as they liked but, when it came to voting on an amendment, the opposition was always flattened. If there was any impact to be made on the Bill, it would have to be in the House of Lords.

There were many Conservative Peers who felt that this was a matter of principle and that the House of Lords should vote against the Bill at Second Reading. It was good warrior-like stuff. We will all go down fighting in the trenches together. That this did not happen caused a lot of Peers distress. They felt that they had been let down. But, if that course had been taken and if the government had been defeated, which was quite possible, there would have been an almighty political row – Lords versus the People and all that stuff – and the government would have re-introduced the Bill under the Parliament Act. The government would have got their way and all the Hereditary Peers would have gone at once – wiped out.

Cranborne, now the Marquis of Sailisbury, was Leader of the Opposition in the Lords. He had different ideas. His view was that, if we had been determined to vote against the Second Reading, it would be like telling all your troops to run up the hill and go over the top into a stream of gunfire. Everyone would be killed. It would be like the Somme. No Hereditary Peers would be left. But, if you could find a different alternative, there may be a chance of at least some Hereditary Peers being left and, if some are left, who knows? And for how long? The Cecils are nothing if not politically astute. Cranborne was.

Cranborne decided that the best tactic was to let it be known that the House of Lords would make as much trouble as it could with the Labour government's programme by delaying bills and by other tactics. The government's European Election Bill, for example, which contained the appalling 'list system' of voting, was delayed so much that the government had to push it through under the Parliament Act. All this frightened the government.

One day Lord Irvine of Lairg, the Lord Chancellor, said to Lord Cranborne, 'Would you like to talk?' Cranborne asked William Hague, who was the Leader of the Conservative Opposition and the Shadow Cabinet, and he agreed to it. So Cranborne said yes. I am bound to point out that this is my understanding of what happened and I cannot vouch for its total accuracy. I have no reason to believe, though, that it is far from the truth.

At the meeting the Lord Chancellor said, 'I think that we ought to keep some Hereditary Peers in order to enable the House to continue to work.'

'I agree,' said Cranborne. 'How many do you have in mind?'

'Fifteen,' said the Lord Chancellor.

'You must be joking,' said Cranborne.

'How many do you have in mind?' said the Lord Chancellor.

'One hundred,' said Cranborne.

'You must be joking,' said the Lord Chancellor. So they decided to go away and think about it all.

They eventually settled for ninety-two. Seventy-five – which was 10 per cent of the 750 Hereditary Peers from the different parties – to be elected by the Hereditary Peers of the party concerned. Then there were a further fifteen, who were servants of the House – Deputy Speakers etc. They were to be elected by all members of the House. Then there were the Earl Marshall and the Lord Great Chamberlain, too. That brought the number up to ninety-two. On top of that were the Hereditaries of First Creation, like Viscount Tonypandy and Viscount Whitelaw and the ex-Leaders of the House. That brought the numbers up to one hundred and six. Not a bad bit of negotiating when the original number asked for was one hundred.

These negotiations between Lord Cranborne and the Lord Chancellor were carried out with the knowledge and full approval of Hague.

Hague told Cranborne that he approved but that he, Hague, must get the agreement of the Shadow Cabinet. This frightened Cranborne. There were some twenty-six members of the Shadow Cabinet and it was as leaky as a sieve. Up to now not a word had got out.

At this point, the government had agreed to ninety-two Hereditary Peers – and further negotiations were necessary to bring them up to 106. As Cranborne feared, the Shadow Cabinet said 'Stop the negotiations'.

Having got this far, Cranborne wanted to finish the negotiations off. The idea was to get an amendment allowing for the extra Hereditary Peers to be put down by the Cross-bench Peers, led by Lord Tonypandy.

By now it was becoming very leaky. Alastair Campbell, who then comes on the scene, said to Cranborne, 'When are you going to tell Hague? Because we believe that Hague is going to raise it at Prime Minister's

Questions.' This was Wednesday and Cranborne had told Hague that morning. Prime Minister's Questions were on the Wednesday afternoon.

Cranborne could not believe that Hague would raise this, as it would give the Prime Minister the opportunity of saying, 'Don't you know what is going on in the House of Lords?', which is precisely what he did say. Hague might have hoped to say, 'So, by having these talks you are now watering down your commitment to remove all Hereditary Peers.' This was all good fiery, political stuff.

Then the inevitable happened. At Prime Minister's Questions, Hague asked the Prime Minister a question to which Blair replied, 'This has all been agreed. Does not the Right Honourable Gentleman not know what is happening?'

Well. Hague was acutely embarrassed. He was caught out on the floor of the House not being up-to-date. He was livid. Cranborne had let him down. Been deceitful. Acted behind his back. Hague demanded to come to a meeting which Cranborne was holding with the Association of Conservative Peers – the committee of backbench Peers. Everyone was there. In the Moses Room. Cranborne had spoken to us and had had a very sympathetic hearing.

In walked Hague. Not alone, but with the Conservative Chief Whip, his Party Secretary, Michael Ancram, Uncle Tom Cobbly and all. There must have been eight of them. They had, in effect, burst into a private meeting. The atmosphere was electric. Hague spoke. People tried to intercede to calm things down, especially the ex-Lord Chancellor, Lord Mackay of Clashfern. But to no avail. Cranborne and Hague, with Carrington, retired to Lord Cranborne's room to discuss the position there. Lord Mackay of Clashfern asked if he could come and help. He is a remarkably calm and unflustered person in a tense state of affairs. To the horror of many of us, he was excluded.

'Alright,' said Cranborne to Hague. 'I admit I have not behaved well. I have been like a spaniel running in at a shoot. I can understand you being cross. If I was in your position, I would be too. I shall resign – or would you rather sack me?'

'I would rather sack you,' said Hague. So he did.

Lord Strathclyde, who was the Conservative Chief Whip, succeeded

Cranborne, but only on the understanding that he could keep the agreements which Cranborne had made. This Hague gave.

Despite having technically 'done wrong', Cranborne felt that his loyalties to his country were greater than were his loyalties to his party. That's why he did what he did and why he persevered with the negotiations.

How right he was. It was expected that the remaining 100 Hereditary Peers, who were to be elected back to the House of Lords, would only be temporary until Stage 2 of the House of Lords Reform took place – which was expected in a year of two. But there was subsequently so much controversy of what Stage 2 should consist it has not, anyhow yet, come about. Now, ten years later, there are still Hereditary Peers in the House of Lords and, in a way, they provide the 'glue' to the House.

I put down an amendment to the House of Lords Bill to leave out 'A' and insert 'An' in front of 'Hereditary Peer'. The text, as submitted to Parliament referred to 'a Hereditary Peer'. I suggested that it should be 'an Hereditary Peer', and I enlisted the help of dictionaries to prove the case. It was a bit of fun really. Of course, it was turned down. Gareth Williams said that 'an' was right but it was 'a' which appeared in all the previous statutes. I thought that grammatically 'an' was correct. We had a division and I lost. The government brought all its troops in.

Interestingly, some three years later there was a television programme all about the House of Lords Bill and how it had progressed through Parliament. The programme showed a meeting with all the government front bench team and advisors. 'And now we come to the Ferrers Amendment.' After a general discussion the chairman said 'What do you think, Lady Jay (the Leader)?' 'I think it ought to be "an"'. 'What about Lord Williams (Minister of State at the Home Office)?' 'I think that it ought to be an "an"'. Lord Chancellor? 'an'. But the Parliamentary Draughtsman said that it should be 'a'. All the other statutes said 'a', and it would mean amending them all in order to ensure that there was no ulterior hidden meaning by the change.

Can you believe it? All the senior people in government thought that 'an' was correct, but they all lay down prostate in front of the Parliamentary Draughtsman. So 'a' it was. And so the poor Lord Williams of Mostyn and others had to eschew their own beliefs to say that which they thought was right was wrong. But it was not their belief that they were expounding, but the government's belief. It so often happens!

The Hereditary Peers had their election. The number of places to which Hereditary Peers could be elected was dependent on the proportion of Hereditary Peers who sat as Conservative, Labour, Liberal Democrat or Cross-bencher. The Conservative Party had 42, Labour 3, Liberal Democrats 12, Cross-benchers 41.

For the election, each candidate could write seventy-five words as to why Peers should vote for him. I said that I was against this, as it looked like each Peer writing his own election manifesto. I suggested, in one of the debates, that I supposed that some Peers would find it appealing to have a copy of their coat of arms emblazoned on the outside of their manifesto as well. Why not?

Many Peers said that they would not write a manifesto. I did not intend to do so – on the basis that it was somewhat vulgar and pompous. As the time of the election drew closer, people began to weaken in their resolve not to write their seventy-five-word manifesto. Annabel said it would be a pity not to write one and then fail to get elected. I said that I had been in the House of Lords for forty-four years and that people probably knew what they thought of me, and they would not take any notice of what I had written anyway. So I did not write one. But I began to get nervous.

By some extraordinary piece of luck, I came top in the election for the forty-two Conservative Hereditary Peers, but that was after a complex system of voting which nobody understood but which required something like forty different countings of the votes. There is nothing like proportional representation to make a whole election process totally incomprehensible. It is even more incomprehensible when one realises that each of the twelve or so different systems of proportional representation there are would provide a totally different result. So much for simplicity.

One of the happiest results of that election was that the Headmaster of my old school at Winchester, James Sabben-Clare, wrote to congratulate me. I was thrilled. I had never been top of anything in my life before and to think that I should be congratulated by the Headmaster of my old school for being top was unbelievable. No Headmaster had every congratulated me on being top of anything – and I had to wait until I was seventy for that. I think that there is a moral there somewhere. Like Nil Desperandum?

***

Question Time is always fun in the House of Lords, not necessarily because of the subject matter but because of the questions and the way in which Ministers answer them.

It is rather like school days. You don't always ask the question to elicit the answer, but in order to try and trip the master up. Short questions and short answers are always far better, and they are more fun. They keep it slick, and it all goes along happily. Ministers do not have time to think of a reply before they are on their feet.

An ex-Conservative and naval MP, the blind peer Lord Fraser, once asked a question. The government Deputy Chief Whip, a rather stolid and unexciting Labour Peer, Lord Bowles, answered it. 'No, my Lords', he said. That was unusually and unexpectedly brief – but the House loved it. 'Why not?' was the supplementary – total brevity. Everyone roared with laughter, and Lord Bowles was stumped.

Peter Carrington, as Secretary of State for Energy, was asked a question about North Sea Oil, as some people were worried that the EEC was going to take over our oil reserves. He answered several supplementaries on it, and then Lord Shinwell, who was nearing a hundred, came back and asked another. Peter's reply was a gem. 'North Sea Oil is British, and that's that.' End of story. No other questions.

On another occasion, Peter Carrington came down to the House of Lords to answer a question, having just arrived that morning at Heathrow from a ministerial visit to Australia, feeling pretty jet-lagged. A member of the Opposition asked him whether the report in *The Times* of what Peter had said in Australia was true. Peter's reply was on the lines of 'I only flew back from Australia this morning, and I have not had time to read the papers yet. But, if *The Times* said that I said what the Noble Lord said that it said that I said, then I didn't.' Game, set and match.

On one occasion, when I was in the Home Office, Lord Campbell of Croy, a Conservative ex-Secretary of State for Scotland, asked me a question. He was, understandably, very proud of having been Secretary of State for Scotland, and he had a habit of pre-empting many of his supplementary questions by saying 'When I was Secretary of State for Scotland...' which tended to irritate everyone. He did so on this occasion. 'Does my Noble Friend realise that, when I was Secretary of State for Scotland...' And then he asked the question. I replied, 'I know that a lot of things happened when my Noble Friend was Secretary of State for Scotland about which he is kind enough periodically to remind us.' The House fell about. I can see today Toby Aldington's laughing face. I did not mean to be horrible, but Gordon Campbell did not use that expression again.

Answering questions was always pretty alarming. One would brief oneself with officials for about an hour, write *very* brief notes for possible supplementaries. If the notes were too long, you would never find them in time. And then one would just hope for the best. I once had all the four questions of the day to answer – half an hour on different subjects.

John Boyd-Carpenter asked me why a prisoner had escaped. I told him that he was being taken to have tea at a hotel before he was released from prison in order to familiarise himself afresh with the outside world. He wanted to go to the lavatory. He was escorted upstairs and the prison officer waited outside the door. The prisoner did not emerge. There was a window inside. It had been left open 'and the prisoner scarpered'. Everyone thought that it was hilariously funny with the result that nobody asked any other supplementaries.

David Renton asked, as a supplementary on spittoons, whether, if a person spat at you in the street and, if it hit you, would it be an assault? Of course, I had not the slightest idea. I said that he might well be right but it reminded me of a little ditty which my mother had taught me when I was young:

Julius Caesar
Let a Greaser
Right across the street

And hit Agrippa
On the Nipper
And knocked him off his seat.

The House bellowed. Fortunately, I got away with it.

On one occasion, everyone was very excited because there was a piece of material flying around in outer space and it was coming down towards Earth and it looked as if it might hit England. I was asked, as the Home Office Minister, whether it would be likely to hit the Houses of Parliament. How much notification would there be likely to be before the thing hit the country. I replied that Black Rod was pretty certain that there would be enough time to say 'Cheerio Chaps'.

I then was asked whether it would be likely to hit the Houses of Parliament.

I replied that the chances were rather smaller than a No. 11 bus driving into the Victoria Tower. Whereupon the charming Cross-bench Peer, Lord Boston of Faversham, otherwise known as Terry Boston, who used to be Lord Chairman of Committees and is quite a dandy and always perfectly dressed, got up and said with the straightest of faces, 'Does the Minister realise that, if a No. 11 bus were to drive into the Victoria Tower, that would be very careless of it, as it would be going down the wrong road. It would be going down Millbank and it ought to be going down Victoria Street.' The House absolutely howled with laughter. I think that that was one of the best and funniest supplementaries that I have ever heard, certainly that I was ever asked.

Lord Mishcon, that charming Labour Peer and eminent lawyer, who was in charge of Home Office matters for the Opposition, once asked me a question on Comic Relief Day, which was a national day – several days in fact – for raising money for children. They raised millions of pounds. Everyone was supposed to wear an absurd big red blob on their noses to show that they supported the cause.

Lord Mishcon started his supplementary with 'Does the Noble Earl realise that my grandchildren urged me very hard to wear a red nose in the House today?' I replied that I did not realise that he wasn't. More good fun. Lord Mishcon enjoyed it, too.

Sometimes, when I was asked a question of which I did not know the answer, I used to say, 'I prepared myself for many possible supplementaries to this question, but not that one.' People generally understood.

Lord Mishcon made one of the most charming, gracious and correct observations when, after a BBC reporter had thrust a microphone under his nose outside Westminster Abbey after Princess Diana's funeral service and had asked him what he had thought 'of that', Lord Mishcon replied, 'If only things had been different, what a wonderful Queen she would have made.' A superb answer. So gentle. So understanding. So totally encompassing. So right.

I well remember the 'old' Lord Salisbury. Not the present Lord Salisbury. Nor his father. But his grandfather. He was a very powerful person in the political world. He was the driving force behind sending Archbishop Makarius, who was then President of Cyprus, into exile in the Seychelles.

He was described as the Kingmaker in the newspapers at the time of Macmillan's retirement when a successor had to be found and Butler and Hailsham were the most likely candidates. In those days 'soundings' were taken around the party as to who would be the most suitable person to lead the party, and a new leader 'emerged'. They did not have anything vulgar like elections. That would horrify anyone nowadays, but it worked in the context of those days. A 'Kingmaker' had a lot of influence. Lord Salisbury was one such.

He was a formidable leader of the House of Lords and, amongst other things, introduced the idea of expenses being paid to members of the House – of three guineas (£3-3-0) per day. Now it is £300. Before that, you were only paid your first-class rail fare – Norwich to London return, first class, was £3. Now it is £149.

I remember Lord Salisbury in a debate in the House of Lords, telling the story of how a man had died and woke up in a beautiful green field full of flowers. He looked around and saw on the horizon a huge colourful stone edifice, with a small black line in front of it which snaked around and grew bigger the nearer it got to him. Which it did. And he realised that these were the Pearly Gates and this was a queue of hopeful people, of which he was now a part, trying to get in.

All of a sudden there was a very soft noise which he strained his ear to try and hear. Gradually the noise became louder and he realised that it was cheering. And then the chap in front started cheering. The fellow tapped the man in front on the shoulder and said, 'What is all the cheering about?' He turned round and said, 'They have just decided, Adultery does not count.'

That would have been pretty avant-garde stuff for debate even in this day and age. It was very avant-garde stuff then. It was very funny, not least because it was such a surprising thing for a person of Lord Salisbury's stature to say. I have no doubt that it is hidden away in the bowels of Hansard, but I can see him making the speech now at the senior end of the Privy Council Bench on the government side of the House.

Chapter 19

Government Over

So ENDED EIGHTEEN years in government. What now? What next? Whatever next? One looked into the abyss. I was sixty-eight. Not many people, or firms, or businesses would want to take onto their payroll a character of that age. There was no point, therefore, in touting oneself around. I did make one or two enquiries, and put out a few 'feelers', but they all came to nothing. Anyhow, holiday first.

One of the things which Annabel and I did was to go out to Singapore, Malaysia and Thailand for five weeks. I love that part of the world and we had been lucky enough to go there from time to time for a short while. On each occasion I had always told Annabel that I would like to go there for a proper holiday. 'Well, you will have to wait until you are retired,' she said. Now that I was retired, we decided to go.

I sometimes think that the places to which you go when you are young make a great impression on you. I had, of course, been to Malaya when I was nineteen and we had called in at Singapore on our way there and back. But that was in 1949. Things were very different now. There was a great romance about Singapore and Malaya. Although it felt like much longer, it was in fact only four years after the end of the War when I was there and the place had all the hallmarks of the old colonial regime. I hasten to add that that is not meant as an insult or a criticism. Quite the reverse, in fact. I admire the colonial regime.

An example, which I was given many years later, was when the Bishop of Swaziland came to preach in Norwich Cathedral in about 2000. It is a country of about one million people. A friend of mine, John Miller, who lived in Norwich, had worked in Swaziland as a Colonial Officer as his first job after leaving university. When he returned to Swaziland a few years ago, he was standing in the street looking at a building and a man, thinking John was a tourist, came up and spoke to him. 'That building is the Secretariat building,' he said. 'Look at all the huge high-rise buildings around it. They are full of civil servants.'

In the old days, the country was run by thirty-two Colonial Officers of which John was one. Now it requires all these buildings full of people. One person even said to him, 'We wish that you were running the country now.' The colonial regime was good. It was not harsh or oppressive. How could it be with only thirty-two people there – and nobody to protect them?

Now, with our present-day attitudes, standards and opinions, it is easy to look at the past and criticise it with the standards of the present. That is the trap into which everyone falls, but one should never do it. We never seem to learn that fundamental lesson. The standards of the past were there and they reflected the conditions, the reasoning and the culture of the time. It was the past which created the conditions of the day for that day. It is too easy to say, 'That was all wrong.' Maybe some of it would not have found acceptance in the thinking and attitude of the present generation. But that does not matter. Their standards reflected their times. And who are we to say that that was wrong in the context of the thoughts, the standards, and the expectations of these days?

People sometimes say that deserters should not have been shot during the First World War, and that they ought now to be pardoned. How can we, one hundred years later, say that the justice meted out in those days was the wrong justice? Of course, much of what was done then would not be done now. But then was then and now is now. And, with all our complacent criticism, I am not sure that future generations will look back and think that we have made a great fist of the way in which we have dealt with our problems, and the standards which we have had, and the standards which we have pursued in the countries for which we were responsible overseas.

Anyhow, Annabel and I departed on 'the holiday of a lifetime'. We had a memorable stay in Singapore in a wonderful hotel – they really do have wonderful hotels in the Far East – and we had some dresses made for Annabel and some suits and shirts made for me.

We went by Singapore Airlines Business Class, which they call Raffles Class. It was superb. Singapore Airlines is the best airline in the world. It is clean, efficient and the cabin crew are both courteous and attentive – and the air hostesses are stunningly pretty. However much people may say in this modern day and age that that kind of thing does not matter, my reply is that it jolly well does. People say that they are only courteous and smile because they are trained to do that. My reply is 'Maybe, and thank Heavens that they are.' It is still a nice thing to do and, if you are going to be boxed up in a tin can for thirteen hours, it is good for it to be done in agreeable circumstances.

When planning our holiday, the Travel Agent said that she thought that we had put in too many places, and that we ought to cut one out. She suggested that we cut out the hotel where your rooms are on stilts overlooking the water. We said that we particularly wanted to go to the hotel on stilts, and so we kept it in. It was just as well because the hotel was at Pangkor Laut. We happened, by chance, to meet the owners, Hong and Kathleen Yeoh, at a dinner party in Kuala Lumpur beforehand. They have subsequently became great friends. We have visited Pangkor Laut frequently since then, as have most of our family, and it is our idea of perfection – a dream holiday. I am so glad that we kept 'the hotel on stilts' in our itinerary.

Peter Walker, who had been Minister of Agriculture, had let one of the people in his bank at Dresdner Klienwort Benson, Piers Willis, know that we were coming to Kuala Lumpur. Piers and his delightful wife, Cecilia, asked us to dinner. We then realised that we had met them before in Norfolk when Selina, our daughter, was younger.

Piers and Cecilia were so kind. They had asked about eight people to dinner. In came one hugely pretty and glamorous Chinese Malaysian lady with a figure like an hour glass and a white dress with red flowers on it. I shall never forget it. I was bowled over. I wondered who the lucky person was who was going to sit next to her. It was me.

She was Kathleen, and her husband was a young, very effective and very successful businessman called Hong, who was also charming. I told them how, on the way from Singapore to Kuala Lumpur, I had gone to sleep driving our hired car and woke up hitting the metal fencing in the central reservation.

Annabel, in one of her cool, typical-Annabel ways, said, 'What on earth do you think that you are doing?' I said that I had gone to sleep. There is always a bright side to every cloud and, in this case, about a mile further down the road, the metal fencing stopped and there was just a huge monsoon ditch, like an elephant trap separating the two carriage ways, and this was punctuated with the odd tall palm tree growing up from the bottom. I cannot think what would have happened if I had gone to sleep there and we had ended up at the bottom of the monsoon ditch, wrapped around a palm tree.

At dinner I happened to say what had befallen us on the way from Singapore to Kuala Lumpur. Hong said, 'You did not drive your-self? You must have had a chauffeur-driven car?' I said that it was a self-drive car which I had driven myself. 'You must never do that in Malaysia. If you have an accident and hit someone, you will be in the most fearful trouble. Where are you going tomorrow?' I said, 'Pangkor Laut.' 'Very well, I will send you my car with my driver and he will take you there.'

I could not believe such kindness from one who had been a complete stranger until two hours before. What I had not realised, either, was that Hong happened to own the one to which we were staying in Kuala Lumpur and he also happened to own the one the one to which we were going in Pangkor Laut.

It is a small world. That started the beginning of a great friendship between Hong and Kathleen and us. It also started our love of Pangkor Laut. We have been fortunate enough to go there several times since, as have Robert and Susannah and their children and Jonathan and Angela and their children.

This first time that we went to Pangkor Laut Annabel and I were sitting on the glorious beach called Emerald Bay. One of the senior hotel staff came up to us and said, 'The Manager would like to know if you would like to come on a sunset cruise. If so, could you be on the quayside at 6.00 p.m.?' Annabel and I talked about it and we did not feel like exerting ourselves, so we tentatively declined. The person from the hotel said, 'If I were you, I would go.'

We did. Well, it was stupendous. This was Hong's private yacht, *YTL Princess*. There were only a few of us on board, the Manager, Peter Bucher, and his wife, Irene, Annabel and me. We went around the island in the sunset, drinking champagne and eating canapés. It was glorious and dead romantic. When we returned to the quayside and were just about to get off, Peter Bucher said, 'You are not going to go? There is dinner now.' I could not believe it. It was the most memorable evening. Yet again, we were hugely spoilt.

We went to other places in Malaysia including Langkawi and Penang. They were lovely. It was all so different from forty years before.

Ben Blower, a great friend of ours at home, had once said to me, 'You really ought to go to the Oriental Hotel in Bangkok just once in your life.' I thought that that sounded fabulously expensive – but it was do-able. We went there. We had a personal butler to look after our requirements in the bedroom. He even ironed the *laces* on my trainers!

We were standing by the buffet one night at the Oriental, in preparation for dinner next to the busy river with all the boats lit up and going at great speed. I said to Annabel, 'Wouldn't it be funny if we met someone here?' The words had hardly left my lips before I got a touch on the shoulder, 'Good evening, my Lord!' It was Tommy and Nel Arran. Tommy, amongst other things had worked with me in the House of Lords and in the Home Office. It is such a small world.

We went to other places in Thailand as well as Chiang Mai and right up on the border with Burma. The people, as everywhere in the Far East, are so gracious. We in the West can learn so much from them.

We stopped at Chiang Mai and went to a silk shop. A very pretty Thai girl, in a long silk dress, looked after us. We bought some material, green shot-silk. Also very pretty. We asked if she could make a dress for Annabel. She said that she could.

She appeared at our hotel the next night with the dress beautifully made which fitted Annabel perfectly, so well that she has worn it at the Opening of Parliament on several occasions. Twenty-four hours and a perfect fit. How do they do it? Why cannot we?

The touching thing was that the girl had had her hair specially done because she was coming to our hotel. And she was wearing jeans which were supposed to be nice and modern and Western, but she was not nearly as attractive as she was in her shot-silk Thai dress!

When we returned home, we got stuck into our newly-found 'normality'. I am not quite sure what it was, and I am still not quite sure what it is. I continued, and still continue, to go up to London to the House of Lords for two or three days a week. We had our flat at 26 Warwick Square, and Annabel used to come up with me every week by car. It was lovely. I could not go back to farming. I was sixty-eight when government work came to an end and, although I love the countryside and our home, farming was always an anxiety and I just could not go back to running it. Anyhow, Robert was in charge, and I was happy for him to take over all the responsibility.

It was still fun to be part of the House of Lords and to take part when one felt like it or when one was particularly interested, instead of being told by the Chief Whip 'There is the Boot and Shoe Order tomorrow. You are to deal with it.' Been there. Done that!

I also had the best office in the House of Lords. We used to have Janet Young and Quintin Hailsham in it, but they died. It now consists of Bertie Denham, an ex-Chief Whip; John Wakeham, ex-Secretary of State for Energy and an ex-Chief Whip in the Commons, ex-Leader in the Commons, ex-Leader of the Lords (in fact, John is the only person in living memory to have been Leader both of the Commons and of the Lords); David Waddington, ex-Home Secretary and ex-Leader of the House of Lords and me. We are now joined by Peter Carrington. They are a hugely fun lot, and it is a very happy room to be in. Again, how lucky one is.

One of the things which I found totally upsetting during the Labour government's long period in office was that they downgraded everything of value – standards in life and behaviour, the composition of Parliament, the respect of and for Parliament, the police, doctors, teachers, the whole jolly lot. Of course, if you were to say that to a fervent Labour supporter, he would totally deny it. But influence is a funny thing.

You do not have to pass a law saying that the police, for example, should be respected less. Oh no. It is far more subtle than that. A law is passed and, as it were, the thought is let out of the cage. It runs like a snowball down the hill. It collects others bits which attach themselves to it, so that the original is hardly recognisable and, of course, the self-attached pieces were never deemed to have been passed by Parliament. It just 'happens'.

I will give you an example. The Labour government introduced an Equality Bill. The government love that kind of thing – making everyone equal and all that jazz. But, of course, it is not equality at all because, by making somebody 'more equal' than they were before, you make somebody else 'less equal'. You take away their rights and practices and therein live all the seeds of a big fat row.

The Equality Bill said something to the effect of 'There will be an Equality Commission whose duty it is to *create a society* in which … [various things happened].' I said you cannot put that in a Bill, to tell a Commission to *create* a certain type of society. That's what Hitler tried to do. Societies *emerge* over time. You don't wave a wand and create one. The government fortunately changed that wording.

Anyhow, who are these wonderful people who are going to form the Commission and who are going to have this great power and duty? Of course, they will have to conform to a cross-section of society to make sure that they are fully representative. There will have to be one-eyed people, black people, lesbians, single mothers, and many others. And they will all be paid. It is not as if they will all be the Archangel Gabriel and his friends. Who will choose them? The Secretary of State? Oh no. We will put that to an outside body of people, so that the Secretary of State will not be involved. Who chooses the outside body to choose the members? The Secretary of State. You cannot get away from it, government is involved all the way through. The idea may sound good, but it is gross interference with life and society.

The same idea went through the Gender Recognition Bill. It says that, when a male person later decides to become a female person – or vice versa – you can pretend that they were always of the gender of which they are now part, but of which they were not part when they were first born so that there should be no embarrassment. One gets hopelessly tangled up when one starts messing around with things like this and, before you know where you are, you are putting on to the Statute Book absurdities and laws which say you must *lie*.

How can you say that a person who has had a sex change and is now called Anna, was always called Anna when, in fact, she was born, and appeared on the birth certificate as, Peter? So, you now have to change the birth certificate to say that the person was born Anna – even though she was born Peter. The law now makes you lie.

The Gender Recognition Bill – curiously enough – had a part which excluded the Peerage from the provisions of part of the Bill. I thought that this was odd. If equality is so good, surely it should be applied to all – and not exclude one part of society. So, I made a speech. It was supposed to be a bit of a spoof, pointing out how absurd the Bill was. I did not think that it would be particularly funny. But apparently it was. Even the Clerk of the Parliaments said that one Peer had tears streaming down her cheeks, she was laughing so much. I said this:

> I would like some explanations to some serious points, and I hope the Minister will answer them. What happens if an earl has a sex change? In order to make certain that there is no duplicity, we will call him Earl Dodger and his son Viscount Chump. If Earl Dodger has a sex change, does he become a countess, in which case there will then be two Countess Dodgers? Or does he remain as an earl although he masquerades as a woman?
>
> As the earl has changed from being a male to a female, what happens to the title? Does Viscount Chump suddenly inherit the earldom and become an earl as the earldom is apparently vacant? That does not seem right because you would then have two earls. What happens if Countess Dodger, on the other hand, changes sex and becomes a man? What does she become? Does she become Earl Dodger, so that there are two earls? She cannot, because she was not appointed. What does she do?
>
> Let us suppose that Earl Dodger has a son and a daughter. Let us suppose that the daughter is older and that she has a sex change and becomes a man. Does she then become Viscount Chump instead of her younger

brother who, up till now, was Viscount Chump? If she does become Viscount Chump, does she inherit everything else? Does she inherit the title of earl instead of the proper Viscount Chump, and all the cash, if there is any? In my experience, earls do not have much cash nowadays, but they used to in the good old days. What happens to the proper Viscount Chump? There may be a trust fund under which it all goes to the holder of the earldom. Does the lady get that and, if so, will she remain friends with her brother?

Clause 16 (a) states that the Bill does not affect the descent of any peerage or title of honour. Of course it does – it goes to someone to whom it was not supposed to go.

I have read Clause 16 (b) six times and I cannot understand it. It says that the fact that a person's gender has become the acquired gender does not affect the devolution of any property unless an intention that it should do so is expressed in a will. In years gone by, quite a lot of these properties were expressed in wills by grandfathers and great-grandfathers who did not have the curiosities that exist nowadays.

If it is intended that the land owned by an earl should pass on to the next earl, and if Earl Dodger becomes a woman and vacates the earldom, does he have to pass his land on to Viscount Chump, who presumably becomes the earl? Of course, he cannot become the earl, because the earl is still alive. It does not seem very fair, and it happens to nobody else in the country. I hate to put it like this, but the Government are discriminating against hereditary Peers. They have always hated hereditary Peers but I think hereditary Peers are jolly good folk. It is a pity to see the Government discriminate in this way by suddenly saying that the Bill is wonderful, but the change must not appear to be part of the peerage.

The noble Lord, Lord Filkin, made an interesting remark in a letter to my noble friend Baroness Buscombe: 'The hereditary principle is hence untouched. However, this does mean that a person recognised in law as a woman may inherit a "male title". Clearly, a person in this position may wish to seek a change to the form of address.'

He said that the whole purpose of the Bill is to allow a woman to inherit a male title. Yet, earlier on, it said that there would be no change. In his letter, the noble Lord goes on to say that: 'Subsequent to these discussions,' that he had with the Garter Principal King of Arms, 'it is clear that a person in this position would be free to petition Her Majesty for a change in the form of address. Therefore, rather than making the detailed provision in the Bill to deal with every possibility, we believe that this issue should be dealt with on a case-by-case basis and that this discretion should rest with Her Majesty.'

Do the Government mean to say that they have introduced a Bill that is so complicated, and has made such a mess of everything, including the peerage, that the only way out is to get Her Majesty to resolve it? I find that quite extraordinary.

I shall remind your Lordships of what the right reverend Prelate the Bishop of Winchester said in Committee. He asked what happens if a female priest changes sex and becomes a man and said: 'It is an infringe-ment of her rights that *Crockford's* – or, as the right reverend Prelate also mentioned, *Who's Who*, *Debrett's* or *Dod's* – 'continued to contain details of the early stages of her ministry.'

If one removes the first part of a person's career from a professional directory, where does the editor stand in terms of the Trade Descriptions Act? I thought that that was a very trenchant point by the right reverend Prelate. The Government did not have an answer to that.

What happens if, as one does, one has a medical directory? Suppose there is a person who becomes a doctor, goes through the training, becomes a surgeon and decides to become a woman? Is the directory to cut all that out of a person's previous career? Would not anyone employing that person as a surgeon want to know where that person was educated, what medical school he or she went to and what happened to her career? That must all be cut out because she has changed sex and it must not be referred to.

One could say that if one looked in *Dod's* or in a similar directory, and saw that a person was educated, for instance, at Winchester and Magdalene College, Cambridge, even though she was a woman, one could discover that she was probably a man because those places usually educate men not women. No attempt has been made to answer these points.

The Minister who will respond to this amendment – I am not certain who it will be, but I have a good idea that it will be the noble Lord, Lord

Evans – may say that when people are in positions of importance, such as bishops, priests, surgeons, Peers, and anyone in public life, everyone will know that they have changed sex and they do not have to worry about it. It is only people lower down the echelons who the Government are worrying about. That is no way to produce a Bill. If the Bill is so good that it has to refer to these 5,000 who, regrettably, for reasons with which we all sympathise, have to change sex, it must refer to everyone; a group cannot be excluded.

The real answer is that the Bill is so bad because it is based on a deception. The whole idea is a deception. My noble friend Lord Tebbit, who regrettably is not here, has said this all along. It is based on a deception whereby you say, 'Here is a person who was born a female,' and then you say, 'We have decided forty years later that he was born a male.' That is a deception. It turns nature topsy-turvy. I hope that the noble Lord who replies to the amendment will provide perfectly clear and not complicated answers to these questions as the measure has turned nature upside down and we should like to know what the position is.

Lord Evans of Temple Guiting rose to reply. He said:

My Lords, I rise to speak in an attempt to match the extraordinarily funny and interesting contribution of the noble Earl, Lord Ferrers.

The Government do not hate hereditary Peers. I am a Member of the Government. My closest friend, who does not sit in this House, is a hereditary Peer. Without wishing to pre-empt anything that may happen later in the Session, it may be hereditary Peers sitting in the House of Lords who present the problem. However, we regard them as an endangered minority who have to be looked after and nurtured.

I replied: 'My Lords, the whole of this Report stage has been worthwhile just to hear the noble Lord say that.'

Quentin Letts wrote the following piece about the Gender Recognition Bill in the *Daily Mail*:

Tory Peer Earl Ferrers is worried about proposed new sex change laws.

What will they mean for the hereditary peerage? Toothbrush-moustachioed Robin Ferrers made a hilarious speech in the Lords on Tuesday when he wondered what would happen if the nobleman became a transsexual.

The Government, perhaps understandably, said it didn't really know. Civil servants are now working on an answer. Pip, Pip.

***

Lord Elton is a man of many parts. One of his talents is that he can draw cartoons. The other is that he can write limericks or rhymes as sport of what is happening. They can be very amusing.

I was going to have a 75th birthday party, so Rodney Elton produced the following letters purporting to come from a government office with horrible powers of control. He is a very talented man.

The Office for the Supervision of Individual and
Departmental Entertainment
(Offside)
99b Whitehall, London SW1PE 1T
Minute internal Date 1/4/04
From Director of Official Merriment (DOOM)
To General Liaison Officer, Official Merrymaking (GLOOM)
Subject Earl Ferrers

Ferrers is having too much fun;
It's time that he was stopped.
So, kindly see that this is done
- or else I'll have you dropped.
We know he plans to hold a binge,
A party quite unmatched.
Work out how his plans infringe
Our rules, and get it scratched.
Three-quarters of a hundred years
He's managed to enjoy.
Don't let him mark it with his peers,

Resort to *any* ploy.
Signed (Drew P Drawse)

The Office for the Supervision of Individual and
Departmental Entertainment
(Offside)
99b Whitehall, London SW1PE 1T
Minute internal Date 31/4/04
From Director of Official Merriment (DOOM)
To General Liaison Officer, Official Merrymaking (GLOOM)
Subject Earl Ferrers

Robin Ferrers in his early
Years was known as Master Shirley;
His retinue had scarcely learned
To call him this ere he had turned
To Tamworth as his proper style.
They naturally took a while
To say this right and without errors.
News that he'd become Lord Ferrers
Shocked all his liegemen to the core.
They asked 'What *are* these titles *for*?'
Though Ferrers answered with this view
That isn't something I'll pursue
In this memo. But with this rhyme
I shall assess the lapse of time
Cited as a valid reason
For this party out of season.
Five and seventy year *are* what
Have passed since *Shirley* used his cot.
But Robin *Ferrers'* been around
For rather fewer years, I've found.
So this function, in a sense, is
Being held on false pretences.

A simple warrant should suffice
To put this jollity on ice.

Signed (William E T Bland-Kytt)

***

I gave up being High Steward of Norwich Cathedral in 2007. I had
done it for twenty-eight years. It was not an onerous duty, but I loved it,
because I came to love that cathedral more than any other church, other
than the Chapel at Staunton Harold. The standard of everything was
always high – the standard of cleanliness, the standard of orderliness, the
standard of the clergy (they stand upright and, like pieces of china, they
do not move during the service), the standard of singing, the standard
of organ playing. It was all high, high, high – and still is. I thought I
ought to retire from being High Steward although I did not want to.
My legs were becoming less reliable and I thought how awful it would
be if I fell down the steps in the middle of a procession and, harking
back to Annabel's Deb days, I always remembered her saying that it was
important to leave a dance whilst you are still enjoying it. So I did.

I wanted to give the cathedral a memento in recognition of my time as
High Steward – which had been such a privilege. I did not know what.
Jeremy Haselock, the Precentor, said, 'What about a Chalice and Paten?'
I said, 'You have got stacks of those.' 'Oh no, not ones that belong to the
cathedral. We mostly borrow the ones which we use.'

So I gave them a Chalice (for the wine), a Ciborium (for the distri-
bution of the wafers) and two Patens – a six inch one and a thirteen
inch one so that there would be one for each size of Host – six inch for
weekdays, thirteen inch for Sundays.

They were made by a superb silversmith, Simon Beer. They were going
to be silver with a bit of gold to adorn them. I thought of that wonderful Communion Plate at Staunton Harold. I said to Simon, 'Silver is
lovely, but gold is glorious.' It is surprising how experiences of childhood
remain with you and make an impact on you for the rest of your life. So
they were made in silver and then gilded.

The engraving was quite beautifully done with the cathedral coat of arms and my coat of arms engraved on them and the words 'Do the best things in the worst times and hope them in the most calamitous', taken from the West Door of Staunton Chapel, and part of Sir Robert Shirley's epitaph.

Around the periphery of the Patens was inscribed, 'All Might Majesty Dominion and Power'. This was part of the doxology which Mr Parsons, the parson at Staunton when I was a child, often used in the Chapel at the conclusion of his sermons. It was 'And now to Him who is above all things be ascribed as is most justly due, All Might, Majesty, Dominion and Power, now henceforth and for evermore.' Lovely, lovely words. In those days, we stood when they were said at the conclusion of the sermon. They are used in the cathedral now from time to time. Thank Goodness!

So the effect of Staunton and one's youth continues to play a part, and even manifests itself at the age of eighty. But that is what happens. That is what life is about – learning, remembering, absorbing things by a process of osmosis. It is all good exciting stuff.

One of the greatest sorrows in the last ten years has been the way in which Parliament and the House of Lords has been de-bunked and vilified and lowered in the public esteem. If you constantly lambast something on the principle that it needs changing and therefore you ought to shout what you consider to be its shortcomings from the roof-tops, one cannot be surprised if others take up the clarion call and, like the proverbial snowball, it gets bigger and bigger and out of control.

When Tony Wedgwood-Benn was Secretary of State for Trade and Industry in 1964 – I think that that was its correct title then – he had the problem of Concorde. The Labour Party had lambasted it in opposition and said that it would be too expensive. Nobody would want to buy it. It would use too much fuel. The cost of fuel per seat mile would be too high. You will never sell it. On and on it went. When he came into government, he found that it was his responsibility to review the continued building of Concorde and, if necessary, to sell it.

So, what did he do? He set up a committee to review the whole of this vastly expensive, but exciting, innovation. It was decided that the project was alright. What happened? They could not sell it. Having discovered the drawbacks and having blasted them from the rooftops for three years, it was hardly surprising that all the potential purchasers got the wind up and ran for cover, preferring to keep their money in their pockets. Concorde was a beautiful and a remarkable aircraft but it was very difficult to sell.

The House of Lords was rather like that.

It has suffered enormously. We had the 1997 House of Lords Bill which threw out all the Hereditary Peers except ninety-two. That was bad enough, but the Labour government has now thrown out the Lord Chancellor and the Law Lords, on the basis that 'people do not understand how the Law Lords work'. That was the most ridiculous argument. The House of Lords, sitting in its judicial capacity consists of the highest court in the land which is composed of the most senior and most able judges.

Because 'people don't understand this', what did the government do? It got rid of the Law Lords, and it spent £50 million on renovating the old Middlesex County Hall Buildings 300 yards away across Parliament Square, which will then cost £12 million per annum to look after as opposed to the previous system which cost £800,000.

The title 'Law Lord' – a glorious title – goes, and it is replaced by a 'Judge of the Supreme Court'. They wear no wigs and when they come to the State Opening of Parliament, they wear an unexciting gown, with a badge on the back which says Supreme Court. It might just as well have said McDonald's. The whole thing is a vast and unnecessary and expensive change, which benefits no one. It is all cosmetic. After all, these new judges of the Supreme Court are the same people, the same brains, the same intellects, the same judgments as the Law Lords. It is just the place, the standing and the names which have been changed.

On 21 July 2009 – our Wedding Anniversary, but that was coincidental – we had in the House of Lords what is known as 'Tributes to the Law Lords' on their leaving the House of Lords. The motion is proposed, as these things are, by the Leader of the House, followed by the Leader of the other parties and the cross-benchers. It is then open to any Noble Lord to join in. I felt very strongly – and still do – that this is a terrible mistake, lowering the value of everything with just nothing on the plus side. I thought that there would be a number of Peers taking part, but I was – alarmingly – the only one. The chamber was packed. Virtually every Law Lord was there. Although people were querulous when I stood up, when I sat down, I received quite a cheer, which was encouraging. People liked what I said – even some of the Law Lords. Very few like this change.

I said this:

My Lords, might I be permitted to add my tribute, in a small way, to the noble and learned Lords, both past and present? They have been a remarkable feature of the House. They have been admired and respected by everyone, not only in the House but outside it. Their knowledge of the law, clarity of opinion and relative humility in projecting their views; their ability to transmit their views in a way that ordinary people can usually understand; and the charm with which they have done it, have left us all – both inside and outside the House – overwhelmed with respect for them. It is just such a pity that it all has to come to an end.

It must come to an end because it is said that people do not understand the difference between a political Lord and the Law Lords and, therefore, they should be housed separately. However, people never understand the niceties of other people's businesses in which they themselves are not involved. Not many people know how to butcher a pig. That does not really matter because, fortunately, a butcher does.

It is said that people who administer the law should not be involved with creating it but those, who have been involved all their lives in dealing with those who break the law, have their own particular contribution to make in suggesting ways in which the law should be tightened. The views of the Law Lords were always valuable and cherished.

When I had the privilege of serving as an ornament in the Home Office, and when we produced one of those frantically controversial Bills, such as the Home Office does produce from time to time, I remember the excitement which we all felt when it transpired that the noble and learned Lord the Lord Chief Justice was on our side and was going to speak in favour of what we were proposing. It gave the officials in the Home Office, not least the hapless Minister, great confidence that we might at least have been going somewhere near the right direction.

It seems a shame that this fine and select body of people should be excised from your Lordships' House to go across the road, to do the same work which they do at present – the same people, the same intellect, the same judgments but a different name and a different venue. That seems such a pity. The name 'Law Lord' was a glorious name. In future, there will be no such thing as a Law Lord. I thought that, in this mundane format in which we all seem to be operating, they would be called 'Administrators of Justice, Grade 1', or some such. Fortunately, the Powers That Be – I never quite understand who the Powers That Be are – have been more generous than that and have given them the more exalted title of Justice of the Supreme Court.

In grieving the passing of the Law Lords – I do grieve their passing – I cannot help but think that it is all unnecessary. The Government have overseen the removal of most of the hereditary Peers – well, you can say, 'That's all right, time for them to go' – the removal of the Lord Chancellor, with the shell of his office now being in the hands of a Member of Another Place, the removal of the Law Lords, and now, one gathers from the papers, that the poor right reverend Prelates are in the firing line. This is pretty drastic stuff by any standard. It is an assault on your Lordships' House and an assault on the Constitution.

When these huge constitutional changes are made, it is seldom for the better and very often it is for the worse. What has happened to our knowledge of history, our love of history and our respect for history? Why have we lost the ability of taking pride in the privilege of holding the baton of history for a while? Once these changes are made, it merely encourages others to do the same. Now we have a Speaker walking about in just a suit and a gown, like a preparatory school geography master, all on the altar of change.

The Lords of Appeal in Ordinary have had a unique place in the history of this country; a unique place in your Lordships' House'; a unique place in the affection and respect of your Lordships; and a unique place in the legal jurisdiction of the country. I join other noble Lords in thanking them for that. I wish them well in their new surroundings but I deeply regret their passing.

***

All during 2009, the *Daily Telegraph* carried out a fearful campaign against Members of Parliament and their expenses. They seemed to be oblivious to the fact that expenses were set up to provide exactly that – expenses for Members of Parliament. I dare say that some members might have tried to push their luck. But what I do not believe is that most Members of Parliament are a bunch of crooks. If there was anything wrong, it was the rules which were wrong. I do not believe – but I do not pretend to be an expert – that there is nothing which the rewriting of the rules could not have cured.

But the *Daily Telegraph* went systematically through the Members of Parliament doing intense damage to many of them, to Parliament itself, and to the public's view of Parliament. The *Daily Telegraph* was the prosecutor, jury and judge. However unfair a criticism may have been, the poor helpless Member of Parliament had not a chance of having his view or his explanation being given a hearing against the cacophony of abuse being hurled at him. Some were outrageously blamed for things which they had not done. Douglas Hogg was accused of receiving expenses for digging out a moat. There was no moat. Only a ditch. He received nothing for it. He agreed with the Head of the Fees Office the amount to be paid for his expenses. It was all down in black and white – and totally above board – until Sir Thomas Legge went and changed retrospectively the amount which could be claimed.

Sir Peter Viggers was lacerated for having claimed money for a Duck Palace in his garden. He did not claim anything for it. He received nothing.

But truth was not allowed to get its voice in against the Court of Public Opinion. Many members who had given years of good, hardworking time for their constituents and their country were made out to be untrustworthy self-seekers. This was deeply wounding. The atmosphere in the House of Commons was dreadful, and many decided to pack it in and not to stand again. What a terrible indictment of years of hard public work, and what a terrible way to treat good hard-working people who were mostly going by the rules, and what a terrible thing, in Parliament of all places, to introduce change retrospectively and so to turn honourable people into apparent cheats.

It was difficult for Members of Parliament to stand up for themselves, because no one took any notice. I tried to do my best in the debate on the Parliamentary Standards Bill on 14 July 2009 when I said:

I am glad that my noble and learned friend has tabled the amendment because it goes to the heart of the whole problem. As he said, this has been going on for thirty-five years. Why has it come to this fearful mess? Simply because the *Daily Telegraph* bought a disc for £300,000 and published its contents day after day. No one had any redress and, if they tried to find any redress, they were ridiculed. Good, honest Members of Parliament – and the majority of them are good and honest and work hard – have had their names blackguarded and their characters assassinated.

The noble Lord, Lord Foulkes, made a typical mistake – not typical of him but a mistake that is typical of many people – when he referred to moats and to duck palaces The two gentlemen to whom he has referred did not get a penny for either of those, but they are associated with having got money and, as a result of that, they are obliged to leave Parliament. I think that is an absolute tragedy.

If we have a House of Parliament which we value and like, we should consider how best to improve Parliament and not just say, 'This is a matter for the House of Commons.' It is a constitutional matter. Just because a few people down there may want such and such a thing at this time, it does not mean to say that in 18 months' time many of them will still be there. This will be passed on to the next generation and therefore it is right that it should be considered by both Houses. I hope that your Lordships will do so.

However, if this has been going on for 35 years – and it was not wrong; it was the method by which people were paid – it is because no Government would accept the opinion of the Senior Salaries Review Body. I remember Baroness Seear from the Liberal Democrats, who was a member of the Senior Salaries Review Body, saying, 'There is no point in being a member of the Senior Salaries Review Body when, whenever we suggest something, it is never accepted. What is the point of going to all the trouble?' Governments did not accept its recommendations for the good reason that they felt the public would not stand it, so they accepted instead the parliamentary allowances scheme.

The conditions of that scheme were wrong and it was unfair, when people, who took advantage of what they were entitled to, were then accused of being wicked, milking the system and having their snouts in the trough – all those ghastly expressions that were applied to them. The Members of the House of Commons are good, honest people and it is terrible to see them blackguarded like this.

As this has been going on for so long, for thirty-five years, why are we in such a hurry to get it through in two weeks? There is a problem and we have to try to get the solution right, but we do not get the solution right by doing it in such a hurry. I do not blame the noble Lord, Lord Bach, for saying, 'I'll take this back and I'll think about it'. The need to get the solution right is the reason for having three, good, set periods between the stages of the Bill as it goes through Parliament and not doing it all in a hurry, because, otherwise, we will come to the wrong view.

There are a lot of problems here, but my noble and learned friend has accentuated them by suggesting that if we pay people a proper salary and cut out the expenses, everyone will supposedly be satisfied – except, of course, the moment you pay them a proper salary, there will be such a rumpus in the newspapers and everywhere else because all the Members of Parliament have paid themselves more. That is an awful problem. However, we have got to be careful not to hurry this and produce an inadequate result.

And again in the debate on the Address in Reply to the Queen's Speech on 23 November 2009, I said this:

What worries me is that there has been a great crisis of confidence in the parliamentary system, which destabilises the Constitution. The country is lacking in trust. It is lacking trust with Parliament, with the legal system, with officialdom and with one another. That is bad and it is divisive.

On top of that, the Government seem to be encouraging not only the nanny state but the police state. 'Get out of the bus lane. Fine: £100. And I have a camera in the back of a bus to photograph you.' 'Sneak on your neighbour if you think that he is cheating on social security benefits, and

there is a hotline so that nobody need know that it is you who are ringing.'
'Watch what you put in your wheelie bin: otherwise we will photograph it
or weigh it.' All that is a sharp, bad turn for the worse. It really is the way in
which Society has been going for the past ten years. In that time, of course,
your Lordships' House has seen the removal of most of the hereditary
Peers, the Lord Chancellor and now the Law Lords. The remainder of the
hereditary Peers and the Bishops are now under threat. The noble Lord,
Lord Bach, gave us a whiff this afternoon of what might come.

At the moment, the two Houses have separate compositions, separate
rules and separate responsibilities. Each House has a different task and
each is complementary to the other. However, make them similar – with
the second Chamber saying to the other, 'We have been elected, too, and
we have just as much right as you do, House of Commons, to have our
way; our views on legislation have equal weight to yours' – and you will
end with bitterness and discord between the two Houses of an undreamt
of nature.

In common with most noble Lords, I am sure, it breaks my heart to see
what has happened, and is happening, to Another Place. No one approves
of Members of Parliament breaking the law. If they do, they are subject to
the law of the land just like everyone else, but many Members of Another
Place, who are at present being pilloried, do not fall into that category. I
was so glad that my noble friend Lord MacGregor of Pulham Market said
what he did about Members of the House of Commons because so many
of them are honourable people.

Most Members of Another Place are good, honest people. In my view,
it is largely the rules that have been at fault. If the rules say that you are
entitled to this or that, it is not good enough for someone to say, 'Oh
yes. You may be entitled to it, but morally you should not have claimed
it.' It is like saying that you are entitled to a first-class railway ticket but
you ought to have bought an economy one because the country would
have been better off if you had. I venture to suggest that, if there has been
improper payment, the Fees Office, which, like the Inland Revenue, is the
guardian of public funds in its area, should have had more control over
the disbursements.

Some chivalrous-minded gentleman decided to dig up – not dig – the garden of the honourable gentleman Mr Duncan. Some time later, in order to try and let bygones be bygones, the honourable gentleman asked his new friend to have a drink with him on the terrace of Another Place. Having gone through all the security, as he was removing his bicycle helmet, the new friend withdrew something from within the earpiece of his helmet and put it up his sleeve. With that, he filmed and recorded what was supposed to be a convivial private conversation. What was the result? The honourable gentleman was removed from the Shadow Cabinet. However, the significant point is that no one ever reprimanded the person – or even expressed disgust – for having engaged in one of the most dishonourable and despicable of all practices: entrapment. Justice seems to have become upended. With this virtual wall of water of public fury, people do not wish to hear the truth or even a defence. The fact is that, as we all know, a Lie gets halfway around the world before Truth has got its boots on.

The Speaker said that there had to be some rough justice. If I was on the receiving end of that kind of rough justice, I would think that it was grossly unfair. Most Members of Another Place are still honourable Members doing their best for the country and for their constituents and I salute them for that. The Powers That Be seem to have lost their judgement and their sense of direction over all this. The Government's answer is, as always, to set up another quango, the Independent Parliamentary Standards Authority, to control what Members are paid. The chairman is to be paid double what a Member of Parliament is paid. Is that right? It is unbelievable.

Some say, with justification, that this is the nationalisation of Parliament, but do we want Members of Parliament looked over by rules, commissions and quangos, theoretically cleaning it all up but actually creating more traps for people to fall into, more authorities to judge and more punishments to be dispersed? Do we really want to discourage Members of Parliament from having interests outside the Palace of Westminster and thereby being alert to what is happening in the mad world outside Parliament? I do not think that we do. Do we really want to know how much they are being paid for their outside interests? Do we really want to know how many hours of work they are putting in? Put in twenty hours, and it is bad for your firm; put in 200 hours, and you are not doing any work for your constituents.

There is no winner in all this other than the rigid manacle of bureaucracy. It is a convenient way of saying, 'No remuneration from outside Parliament from now on.' That will be hugely detrimental to getting the right people into Parliament and to Parliament itself. Members of Parliament were elected to run the country in the best way that they can and, if what they do does not have the approval of their constituents, they can be removed at the general election. They were never elected to be dictated to by some higher, better remunerated and unelected quango.

In my view, Another Place is making far more of a mess trying to get out of the mess than the original mess itself. If Another Place is going to clear itself up and be a place of Authority again, it needs to be led by a Speaker with authority, who speaks with authority, who conducts himself with authority and who dresses with authority. I am sure that I am not the only one feeling a sense of sorrow that the Speaker chose the majestic State Opening of Parliament, where everyone symbolically represents the office of which he is the temporary holder and not himself, to fall out of line and not wear ceremonial dress to represent the full panoply of one of the highest offices in the land. Perhaps I may put it thus, I hope not offensively: Mr Speaker means everything; Mr Bercow means nothing.

Parliament has not been assailed by such distrust and by such a demise of power over the Executive for 300 years. My fear is that the anticipated cure for it all is going in the wrong direction. It is giving less power and less independence to Members of Parliament when what is wanted is more power and more independence for them and more trust.

The *Daily Telegraph* had the House of Commons running like a herd of cows in front of a dog. The members were upset. The leaders – of all parties – panicked. Let us get over all this – 'move on' is the fashionable expression – and get back to relative normality as soon as possible. I think that they are taking the wrong course.

Because the House of Commons is being lambasted, everyone seems to think that the House of Lords should be one step ahead of trouble, and the Senior Salaries Review Body was, therefore, asked to look at the

House of Lords and make any suggestions which they feel should be made.

It was a bad report which did not seem to understand how the House of Lords worked. I contributed to the debate on 14 December 2009. I said this:

> My Lords, one can understand people getting worked up about expenses. The noble and learned Lord, Lord Lloyd of Berwick, recalled that when he was a member of the Top Salaries Review Body, the expenses were £11 a day. When I came here they were £3 a day; in fact, there was nothing to start with. All you got was a first-class rail fare, provided you attended a certain number of sittings. If you got flu during the fourth week of the month, you were not paid anything because the expenses could not be carried over. There was great excitement when the expenses were increased to £3. The newspapers went wild and said that the bluebloods – they were bluebloods in those days – would be taking their girlfriends out to London nightclubs on expenses. That was absolute rubbish.
>
> I am afraid that I do not think that mine will be a particularly helpful intervention. I hope that that does not matter, but sometimes it is a good thing to stand back and survey the scene from a distance. What does one see? The House of Commons is being destroyed, and why is that? Because a court ordered that all the files in the Fees Office should be published. It was too great a problem to be done in-house and so the task was, as the Americans would say, 'outsourced' to a contractor. There, the disc concerned was copied by an employee who hawked this property, belonging to someone else, around Fleet Street. No one wanted to touch it but the *Daily Telegraph*, which purchased a copy of the material that rightly belonged to someone else for, I understand, £300,000, and then published it drip by drip, day after day, rightly or wrongly – and so it continues.
>
> What a terrible reflection of years of hard work and pride – and what a reflection it is of what is happening to Parliament. Now Another Place is to be administered by a quango costing £8.5 million per year. The chairman is to be paid twice the salary of a Member of Parliament for a three-day week just to ensure that Members of Parliament are not paid too much. That is a good old mix-up. I think that people have gone off

their heads. The whole point of Parliament is that it should be separate from the Executive and not run by it. Members of Parliament are elected to run the country and to keep a check on the Executive, not to go to Parliament and be immersed in the web of the Executive's regulations. We certainly do not want it run by the media.

Your Lordships are going to be allowed to go first class in a train provided that they work. If you want to read a thriller, you will have to go Standard. But if you stuff a copy of *The Sun* in your pocket and go into First Class, you can have the pleasure of looking at the Page 3 girl if your Lordships like to do that. You are allowed to go first class because you will be reading up about what is going on in the world, and therefore you are working. I cannot think what the Senior Salaries Review Body was thinking of when it concocted that idea. A first-class rail ticket should be automatic. It always has been, ever since rail fares were first allowed as expenses in the early 1950s. Why has it got to be changed now?

If a noble Lord lives in Scotland, it has always been the practice that you can travel with your wife in a first-class sleeper. Now, it will be all right for the Peer to go first class but, as my noble friend Lady Shephard observed so graphically, 'the wife' has to go in the guard's van with the baggage. That hardly seems to be a delicate way of running expenses in your Lordships' House, and it is pretty insulting to the wives.

Recommendation 26 of the report proposes that the new quango, IPSA – it sounds like the People's Dispensary for Sick Animals – should extend its activities from Another Place to your Lordships' House. The noble Lord, Lord Tyler, wants that too, but then the Liberals always want something quite absurd and unsuitable. I hope that that will not happen. We must remain independent from Another Place and not become subject to this expensive and wholly inappropriate quango. Your Lordships' House and Another Place are different. This House is simply run and is inexpensive – indeed, it is the least expensive second Chamber in the world. It always has been good value for money. We must beware of the great temptation of being drawn into this spider's web of bureaucracy on the apparent altar of transparency and openness and accountability, which have nothing to do with common sense or the duties of Parliament.

Your Lordships might recall that Archbishop Fisher once said:

'There is no unreasonable argument which cannot be proved reasonable by reason.'

Payments should be simple: so much for a day or a night. If you claim an overnight payment and decide to sleep on the Embankment, that is fine. It should not be the business of the Powers That Be to inquire about that. If people cheat or break the rules, that of course is a different matter, and they should be subject to the appropriate discipline. However, I find it unacceptable that your Lordships, many of whom are very distinguished, who have contributed in a variety of different ways to the life of the nation, some of whom – unlike me – may not be in the first flush of youth, and who come here to continue to give their best without payment, should be treated like fifth-form schoolboys over expenses. Most people are upright. Not everyone is a baddy, and it is offensive to see proposals put forward which insinuate that this is the case.

Mr Speaker said the other day that Members of Parliament have never worked so hard. That may be so, as far as the social worker duties are concerned. But they work only three days a week in Another Place: Monday, Tuesday and on Wednesday mornings a football shouting match at Prime Minister's Questions, and then home. The real job of the House of Commons is to look at legislation to ensure that what gets on to the Statute Book is right and reasonable, and to keep a check on the Executive. But Another Place only looks at 10 per cent of each Bill which comes in front of it.

The rest of the Bill passes to your Lordships' House from Another Place just as the parliamentary draftsman had drafted it. It is here, in the unpaid House, where the whole of every Bill is subject to scrutiny on which the country depends for the integrity of its legislation. If it were not for this House, much more bad legislation would appear on the Statute Book than is the case now. I therefore find it extraordinary that the Senior Salaries Review Body can produce such a nit-picking report.

As if that is not bad enough, we are asked to approve the architecture – that famous word – of the report. What on earth does that mean? I agree with my noble friend Lord Strathclyde that architecture normally refers to houses. You might just as well ask you Lordships to approve the 'general drift' or the 'building blocks' of the report, but you cannot use that kind of language when dealing with Parliament. In this case, architecture is a dilettante word which does not fall easily from the lips of the noble Lord the Lord Chairman of Committees. Your Lordships are normally asked to 'take note' of or 'approve' a report, not to approve its architecture. I do not know what it means – except that it insinuates something fishy – and, like the noble Lord, Lord Barnett, I do not propose to vote for something which I do not understand.

In all this rumpus about Hereditary Peers continuing in Parliament, I felt that it was important to put the value of Hereditary Peers into the equation. It is too easy to say 'get rid of them' or, more enticingly, 'The House of Lords needs modernising and bringing up to date,' which will mean the gradual demise of the Hereditary Peers. I happen to think that Hereditary Peers, have their value, are an important part of the House of Lords and, if all the fuss is at one end of the pool, it is important to throw a stone right up the other end.

I did an article on the subject for the *House Magazine* in 2002. It said:

Anyone want an Hereditary Peer? Not many, it seems, nowadays – anyhow in Parliament. They have become almost outcasts of the political scene. They seem to see political opprobrium not because of who they are but of what they are.

The House of Lords Bill decreed that all Hereditary Peers were to go, like the housewife brushing all the rubbish out of her hall and putting it on to the pavement. Then the government wanted 100 of them to stay. Now they want them all to go again. It is not a very elegant method of reforming Parliament. It is odd that the only members who have been in any way elected are the ones who are to go, whereas those who have not been elected are the ones to stay. The fact is that the government are in a mess over their House of Lords reform. They started out not knowing what the final objective was to be, and they are no nearer to knowing that now.

Have the Hereditary Peers no part to play in the House of Lords of the future? Are they so tarnished with the fact that they are what they are that they should be excluded from any participation? In any other sphere of life this would be called discrimination but, in the political world, this is good red meat.

Hereditary Peers have always been good whipping boys. If they did not participate, it was considered disgraceful that they should show no interest and should not 'do their duty'. If they came and took part, it was considered disgraceful that they should participate just because they were the sons of their fathers. If they came and did not speak, it was considered disgraceful that they should be just lobby fodder. They could not win.

For the last 100 years the reform of House of Lords has been like a continuing song. But it was Attlee who said, 'It is aristocratic, indefensible, quaint and historic. But it works rather well. Leave it alone.'

Now, half a century later, his successors have tried to bite the bullet, and they have come to realise that the process is not as straightforward as they had imagined.

Do we want an elected second chamber which can ride roughshod over the House of Commons on the basis that 'we, too, are the product of Vox Populi'? Of course there is a case for election but, if that were to form the basis of the composition of the Lords, much of the variety and independence of the place will be lost.

Some say that the House of Lords should be more professional, whatever that may mean. But do we want a more professional House? It is true that, if we were starting afresh, we would not be starting from here, but we are not starting afresh. Six hundred years of continuity and experience should not be disregarded as if it is of nothing – although it may not be everything.

The duty of the House of Lords is to scrutinise, revise and improve bills. The qualities needed for that are not necessarily just to have been successful at the ballot box. It needs a variety of people, with different backgrounds, different careers, different knowledge, different skills, different expertise. That is why Hereditary Peers have much to offer.

After all, they are there by chance. They do not owe their place in Parliament to anyone living. They have never asked to be there. They have never begged for favours. They cannot be 'deselected'. They have a truculent distaste for the power of the whips. They provide youth and, because they come from a basically non-political background, they have outside interests, whereas those who are appointed are those who have usually made their mark in life and they are not likely to be young. It is reasonable to argue that heredity should not be the basis of a place in the House. It is unreasonable to argue that it should have no place.

It is not for nothing that people have frequently referred to the excellence of debates in the House of Lords, stating that: 'You would never get a debate like that in any other chamber in the world. Certainly not in the House of Commons.' We should be careful to retain that remarkable quality in which Hereditary Peers have been contributors, and not to dispose of it all on the altar of so-called democracy. The will of the people can be found in actions and attitudes and opinions as well as in going through the mathematical hoop of public approval.

A Christmas pudding consists of many ingredients. They all react with each other to contribute to the excellence of the whole. The yeast may be only a small part of the contents, but to dispense with it entirely would provide a very different result.

***

Sending in people to tape conversations clandestinely and without their knowledge is becoming more frequent and, in my view, it is most regrettable.

Having ruined the stature of the House of Commons and the standing of many members of the House of Commons, the *Daily Telegraph* recently made an announcement with pride. They were supported by the BBC – the media are as thick as thieves – who announced with equal pride that undercover reporters from the *Daily Telegraph* found that Vince Cable, the Business Secretary and Liberal Democrat Cabinet Minister, had said this, that and the other about the Coalition in a way in which the newspaper thought was an unhelpful nature. They scented blood.

Frankly, it was not what Cable said that shocked me but the really despicable manner in which he was tricked into talking to two people who masqueraded as being his constituents, but who were in fact undercover reports from the *Daily Telegraph*. They recorded the private interview, and then emblazoned it across the newspaper with all the force and pride of having discovered a band of terrorists.

This was not journalism. It was entrapment. Where has the integrity, pride and honesty of being a journalist gone? How can anyone say with pride, 'I masqueraded as someone else, and got a person to say things that he would never have said if he had known to whom it was that he was talking?'

I regard this as shocking journalism, and I despise those who practise it and those who authorise it. Its sole purpose it to create trouble. And, when you see the trouble which you have created, you get hold of a few more Members of Parliament and do it again. Using the same clandestine, cheating method, you ask them for their views on what was said by the original person. Then there is more trouble.

Journalism was, and should be, a proud profession. It should despise, and dispose of, these disreputable methods.

Chapter 20

Order of St Lazarus of Jerusalem

ONE DAY, LORD Mowbray and Stourton – alias Charles Mowbray – asked me if I would be prepared to take on a post from which the Duke of Westminster had just retired and which he himself had filled prior to that. This was Grand Prior of the Order of St Lazarus of Jerusalem in England and Wales.

Charles was not succinct in explanation and, although he had many characteristics of which friendship was one, I did not always feel a natural contentment with his judgement. 'I will think about it,' I said.

Shortly afterwards, when I was disrobing in the vestry in Norwich Cathedral after the morning service, Canon Haselock, the Precentor, approached me and talked about the Order. He said that he knew that Charles Mowbray was going to approach me. I said, 'As a matter of fact, he already has, and I was thinking of saying no to it.'

Jeremy, who was then the Chaplain General of the Order said, in a delightfully courteous manner, which always characterises his approach to things, 'Well, do give it a bit of thought. Don't dismiss it out of hand because it really is a good organisation, doing good work with good people – and it is quite a lot of fun, too.' I realised, then, that he was part of the Order, as well. I went away to think about it. I respected Jeremy and I admired what he did. So I agreed.

I have always found that, if you take on anything connected with a charity, there is usually a row attached to it. If you take on anything connected with a religious charity, there is usually a big fat row attached to it. So there was in this case, but not when I took it on.

The Order of St Lazarus of Jerusalem is a Military and Hospitaller Order. It traces its roots back to the fourth century. Initially, the Order was run on military lines when the Crusaders were then fighting the Islamic hordes who were trying to prevent Christians from getting to the Holy Places. Then they contracted skin diseases and thought that they were going to get leprosy so the bravest of the Knights put themselves in the front rows of the battles, in order to be the first to be killed. That sounds to me to be the height of bravery, honour, integrity, selflessness – call it what you will. They had great standards of conduct in those days. I think that I would have just run away.

The Order is non-political and it is ecumenical, its membership being open to men and women who practise the Christian faith and who are in good standing with their church. It consists of Anglicans, Roman Catholics, Orthodox, Methodists and other Christians.

In England, there were two jurisdictions. The Grand Priory of England and Wales of which I was the Grand Prior, and the Grand Bailiwick of England and Wales of which Lord St John of Fawsley was the Grand Bailiff. Both Lord St John of Fawsley and I were equals in different organisations. Great efforts were made to bring these two into one.

We decided, though, to continue on our own with a new young Grand Master, Prince Charles-Philippe, the nephew of the Comte de Paris, who is the Head of the House of France with the previous Grand Master, the Duc de Brissac, having retired.

Prince Charles-Philippe was tall and good-looking, and a man, by nature, of considerable integrity. Unfortunately, he chose as his right-hand man, and as the Grand Chancellor, Count Piccapietra. Count Piccapietra was a Swiss of German extraction. He was a great organiser and with plenty of character. He had his hair cut in a most telling way, straight up and down at the sides and straight across at the top. It looked aggressive. It had all the countenance of the French Foreign Legion.

I found that the appearance of Count Piccapietra reflected the man. He wanted to run everything and to boss everyone around. He reminded me of a sergeant on the Barrack Square. You shouted. Everyone stood to attention, and then ran off to obey your command.

The Grand Master – and Piccapietra – regrettably failed to realise one essential thing: that all the different Grand Priories in different countries were individual organisations. They were drawn together by a bond of unity to the Grand Master, but they had their own different ways of doing things, which had been passed down through the centuries. They had their own histories, their own ways of conducting their religions, their territorial organisations for running their Grand Priories. Some of it was, of course, old fashioned and, maybe, needed renewing and modernising, but each country had its own problems in trying to organise its Grand Priory to run in the best possible way.

Piccapietra expected to tell all these different foreign organisations what to do, some of whom do not even speak the same language. They did not like it. Not only did people get dismissed from various positions, but countries were discharged from the Order.

I told the Prince that was intolerable. People in the Order had as much right to be in the Order as he did. His duty as Grand Master should be to cultivate, help, encourage people in all parts of the Order, to draw them together, to promote and project unity, not to throw them out because he did not happen to approve of what they were doing or the way in which they were doing it. I told him that his tenure of office was quite small in the totality of 800 years or so of the Order, and that it must be used to harmonise and not to destroy. Regrettably, it had little effect.

The Grand Priory of England and Wales was going to have an Investiture which was to take place in Norwich Cathedral in May 2006. We wanted it to be an all-embracing, new-look-to-the-future kind of occasion. There was still a rumbling of disharmony, so I said that I must go and see the Grand Master, Prince Charles-Philippe. I was advised against this. The situation is too delicate. You will find yourself jockeyed into a position which you will regret. Things you say will be held up against you. I said that if there was a row of this nature, I must go and see the Grand Master to see if it could be alleviated.

The Grand Master agreed that I should come and have a talk on a one-to-one basis at the Ritz in Paris.

I took the Eurostar in the afternoon from Waterloo and was met by a charming lady in Paris who took me to the Ritz. It was a sumptuous and glorious place. The Grand Master was not there. He was at a meeting

and would be late. She asked me if I would like a drink. It was very hot,
so I asked for some cold water. Ice cold Perrier came – very good it was
too. Later, she asked if I would like another drink. I said, 'Yes, please.'
Another ice cold Perrier came. When the Prince arrived, he said, 'What
are you drinking?' I said, 'Perrier.' 'Good idea. I will have one too. Would
you like another?' I replied, 'Yes, please.' Another ice cold Perrier came.
And then we had a long conversation. The Prince is a charming person
whom I like.

I asked him to come to Norwich, as it would be a wonderful
reconciliation of everyone's differences. He indicated that he would
like to, but that he would have to ask others first. That was entirely
understandable.

I explained that we lived in a bungalow and that Annabel was not too
well, but we would love it if he came to stay with us. He might, though,
find a 5-star hotel in Norwich more convenient. He said, 'No, I would
like to stay with you.' It was a happy, delightful meeting between two
people who were trying to find a way through a problem.

I returned to London that evening by Eurostar, content that I had
done the best that I could. I could not help wincing when I thought that
I had gone from London to Paris and back in one afternoon and had
gone to the Ritz – all on three glasses of Perrier water. Somehow, I had
always associated the Ritz with champagne!

As it happened, it was all to no avail. The Grand Master did not come,
nor did any of the members of the Grand Magistry. I could only conclude – with sorrow – that Piccapietra had slammed the door shut on the
whole thing for everyone.

We had a lovely Investiture at Norwich Cathedral in May 2006. The
service was excellent. The organ was excellent. The Bishop of Norwich
preached. Then they all came back to lunch at Ditchingham Hall and
afterwards went around the gardens. The only sad part was that it poured
with rain the whole time. There were representatives from many other
jurisdictions there – Ireland, Austria, Germany, Scotland and the United
States. It was a happy occasion, tarnished only by the fact that it was a
wonderful opportunity for reconciliation and reunification which had
been eschewed.

From then on relations between us and certain other jurisdictions on the one hand and the Grand Magistry on the other went downhill.

The Irish got sacked because they had come to the Investiture in Norwich when they had been told not to. Many of the other Grand Priories were sacked, too: Austria, Germany, Hungary, Ireland, Liechtenstein, Romania and New Zealand. Eventually, it was our turn – a bland formal document saying that we were sacked. Of course, unpleasant words like that were not used. More delicate and refined words were used. The document said, 'The Grand Priory of England and Wales is thereby suppressed as an independent Jurisdiction.'

What were we all to do? We were like a whole cluster of boats bobbing about in the sea, not attached to each other and no welcoming port of call but, nevertheless, with a common cause. So we decided to join together to see if, collectively, we could find a way forward. I was asked to be the chairman. Our small federation of countries became known as the Norwich Group. Later, Slovakia joined us.

There is a silver lining, though, to every cloud, and this one had one too. Everyone, being tipped, as it were, into the sea at the same time created great friendship and a corporate determination to get over the problem.

Each country, which was a member of the Group, continued as it had done before with its own investitures and other functions to which we were all invited. They were always fun. The Irish were great attenders. Sometimes 15 or even 20 of them would come to another country. They had a bubbling bonhomie which was infectious. The Grand Prior of Ireland was Bernard Barton, a charming, articulate, successful barrister. Dr Alex Mittelstaedt, a German, had been responsible for setting up the Grand Priory in Rumania, at the request of Princess Tatiana, a fine and much loved lady, whom, regrettably, I never knew and who had been Grand Bailiff of Germany. Dr Mittelstaedt was a quite delightful man, who spoke English well.

Then there was Johannes Mühllechner who was very tall and wore some wonderful clothes, which I think the Austrians would call lederhosen, which were like plus fours. They made him look as if he had just marched down from the mountains like something from the *Sound of Music* leaving his horn and sheep behind him.

On these international events, the host country always, understandably, pushed the boat out for its guests. At our Chapter-General in
Vienna we had dinner in the Imperial Hotel. It was sumptuous and
gracious. In the Austrian custom, before sitting down to dinner, you
are entertained by singing or dancing – or both. We had both – in true
Viennese style.

We went to Mass in the cathedral next day which was packed. Each
week they have a different, but full, choral Mass with choir and orchestra
– Haydn, Mozart, or some such. It was out of this world. Later in the
afternoon, Jeremy Haselock, Gareth Vaughan, Vincent Keaveny and I
went to the Café Sacher where we had some of the superb well-renowned
Sacher Torte. And champagne. And Café Viennoise. Jeremy said afterwards that it was a bit of a 'decadent' afternoon. I dare say that it was,
but it was very good.

At Venice, we, the jurisdiction of the Norwich Group, voted for the
Marqués de Almazán, to be the new Grand Master. The following week
those votes were added to others at a Chapter General of the entire
Order at Manchester. The result was that the Marqués de Almazán was
confirmed as the Grand Master of the Military & Hospitaller Order of
St Lazarus of Jerusalem. Horray. Unity, at last.

Great efforts had been made to bring us all together, and at last we
succeeded in September 2008 when we pledged our allegiance to the
Marqués de Almazán.

It is easy to portray these kind of happenings as trivial occurrences
caused by a few idiosyncratic and self-important, possibly even pompous, people. But it is not that. The Order of St Lazarus of Jerusalem is
an international Order with parts of it in many countries. Each part is
the product of its own country, its own religion, its own people and its
own history. History is important and that must never be forgotten nor
be idly dismissed. It is that with which we have all become involved.
We have not created the Order – or the Grand Priories – but, just for
a short period of time, we can put our own oar into the water and try
to help propel the boat forward. It is a responsibility – in fact, quite a
responsibility. It is not for us to dictate or to dragoon – but just to do our
bit in whatever part of the boat we happen to find ourselves.

Friendship has become one of the fundamental ingredients of the Order and, as is so often the case, it is also one of the prime movers. Our Grand Priory has been stuffed with friendship between people of all sorts of different backgrounds and interests as well as with people in other jurisdictions.

Jeremy Haselock is one of the prime movers of our organisation. As Precentor of Norwich Cathedral, he is a great intellectual, a man of a huge variety of knowledge and skills and a wide spectrum of interests, not just religious, as well as being an understanding Pastor. He has been one of the leaders. He can see where we need to go and how we can best get there. The art is to take people with you and not to dragoon them. He was the Chancellor and then became the Bailiff of the Grand Priory (i.e. the Chief Executive, in quite inappropriate lay and commercial terms).

Gareth Vaughan is the Secretary and was secretary to the whole Norwich Group. He is a great person – very efficient, and great fun. Laughter is never far away from him. He is an actor and an opera singer. Large, jolly figure which goes with a large, jolly personality. He is a good organiser.

When we were staying in Vienna, a few of us were having a drink at the end of the evening in the Hotel Regina on the veranda near the garden, and we prevailed upon Gareth, I cannot think how, to sing a piece of opera. We knew that he would not do this – but, much to our surprise, up he stood and out it all came louder and louder – full helden tenor. It was superb. I think that he must have been heard three or four streets away, but no one complained. No bedroom lights were turned on. No hotel manager came. No police came. But then it was Vienna and they love music. We did, too.

One of our other great stalwarts has been Vincent Keaveny, a young, clever, successful lawyer, who, with his wife, Amanda, enjoys life and people to the full. He loves detail and is superb with it. He is now the Chancellor of the Grand Priory.

On one occasion we were having an investiture in Aldershot. I always love these investitures. They are beautiful services. All the priests, of whatever religious denomination they may be, dress up in their finest

– birettas, black ones with black pompoms, green pompoms or pink pompoms, and pink birettas, too. Plenty of incense and beautiful music and organ.

I love the words of the service, particularly the description of the Order's Cross. It takes one back to reality and makes one realise that what one thinks of as 'just a star' has a far deeper meaning to it. The prayer says this:

Brothers and sisters, consider this Cross, our badge and inspiration.

It is of gold, symbolising charity, to teach you to love God and your neighbour.

It is coloured green to symbolise hope, which consoles the afflicted and inspires us with courage to perform good deeds.

It has eight points to exhort you to exercise those virtues which are called the Beatitudes, namely:

- Contempt for riches of this world,
- Gentleness of spirit,
- Christian sympathy and compassion,
- Ardent zeal for justice,
- Mercy and pity,
- Purity of heart,
- Peace of mind,
- And the bearing of persecution for righteousness' sake.

This Cross is pointed on all sides to teach you always and everywhere to defend the faith and to fight against the onslaughts of your foes, both visible and invisible.

Each point bears a golden orb, representing the fruits of the Holy Spirit, the reward for the great and good deeds which you will be doing.

A lovely prayer.

At one point in the service, I, as Grand Prior, go up to the steps near the chancel. It is then necessary to promote the people from one rank to another and to dub with a sword, as the Queen does, those who are promoted to the rank of Knight. Other decorations or honours are also bestowed.

The candidates stand in the centre aisle as their names are called out one by one by Jeremy Haselock. I noticed that the line of candidates in the aisle had come to an end, but Jeremy was still continuing. Then I realised that it was … for me.

I could not believe it. I stood there in front of everyone looking down at them. I could not understand how or why I was being given any honour, whatever it was to be. I knew nothing about it. It was only at the end of the citation which Jeremy read out that I realised what a huge honour it was. It was the Gold Cross of Merit. He said, 'It is the highest distinction that the Order can bestow.' It was deeply humbling. I felt that I had done nothing. It was all the others who had done the doing. The citation was beautiful. It was this:

For: Outstanding leadership of the Grand Priory of England and Wales and inspirational presidency of the Governing Council of constitutional national jurisdictions during a time of international difficulty and disruption in the life of the Order.

Above the door of the church in the grounds of Staunton Harold, the ancestral home of Lord Ferrers in Leicestershire, is the following inscription:

'In the years of 1653 when all things sacred were throughout ye Nation either demolished or profaned, Sir Robert Shirley Baronet, founded this church, whose singular praise it is to have done the best things in ye worst times and hoped them in the most calamitous. The righteous shall be had in everlasting remembrance.'

When Lord Ferrers consented to succeed the Duke of Westminster as Grand Prior of England and Wales he can little have known that the qualities so evident in the life of his direct ancestor would be required in great measure from him in the years of leadership that lay before him. His qualities as Grand Prior are clear to all the members of our Orders who have met him as he has unfailingly attended all major functions both national and local. Only those who have had the privilege of working with him behind the scenes in trying to resolve the international tensions and difficulties of the last few years can appreciate how perfectly appropriate the Staunton Harold words are to our own Robert Shirley. Throughout this time he has gone to great lengths, at considerable personal inconvenience, to do 'the best things in the worst times' and however depressing and calamitous the situation may have seemed he has never failed to hope for the best. For this reason the Grand Priory, with the full consent of our international partners, awards him the highest distinction the Order can bestow, the Gold Cross of Merit.

Sir Antony Reardon-Smith then fixed the Gold Cross on to my morning suit. I was astounded and shattered. How could I have been given this most remarkable decoration when I had done nothing? I took the meetings, it is true, but it was the others who had borne the burden and heat of the day and who had negotiated tirelessly. I was deeply touched. I loved it and I loved what it meant, and I just felt hugely grateful.

It is, really, a very happy organisation.

I shall shortly be standing down as Grand Prior of the Order when the Grand Priory of England and Wales joins up fully with the Grand Bailiwick of England and Wales. Like so much in life, it has been a great privilege and it has been a great experience, and it has brought one into contact with so many glorious and fascinating people. What fun life is.

Chapter 21

Nuggets

A NUMBER OF funny things happen during one's life. One often remembers the occurrence or the saying but not necessarily the context in which it appeared. The following are some nuggets which I have drawn out of my life.

Some twenty-five years ago, my sister, Betty, thought that I was doing too much – a rare occurrence! – and sent me this piece. I had it framed and it has been in my study ever since.

Slow me down, Lord!

Slow me down Lord! Ease the pounding of my heart by the quieting of my mind.

Steady my hurried pace with a vision of the eternal reach of time.

Give me, amidst the confusion of my day, the calmness of the everlasting hills.

Break the tensions of my nerves and muscles with the soothing music of the singing streams that live in my memory.

Help me to know the magical restoring power of sleep.

Teach me the art of taking minute vacations – of slowing down to look at a flower, to chat with a friend, to pat a dog, to read a few lines from a good book.

Remind me each day of the fable of the hare, and the tortoise, that I may know that the race is not always to the swift,

that there is more to life than measuring its speed.

Let me look upward into the branches of the towering oak, and know that it grew great and strong because it grew slowly and well.

Slow me down, Lord, and inspire me to send my roots deep into the soil of
life's enduring values that I may grow toward the stars of my enduring
destiny.

Anon.

Then there is the following piece which contains perceptive and sparkling advice on how to live life. I dwell on the simplicity of 'listen to others', and 'avoid loud and aggressive persons'. It is all good, simple and pure advice – and beautiful English.

Go Placidly Amid the Noise and Haste

Go Placidly amid the noise and haste, and remember what peace there may
be in silence. As far as possible without surrender be on good terms with all
persons. Speak your truth quietly and clearly; and listen to others, even the dull
and ignorant they too have their story.
Avoid loud and aggressive persons, they are vexations to the spirit. If you
compare yourself with others, you may become vain and bitter; for always
there will be greater and lesser persons than yourself.
Enjoy your achievements as well as your plans. Keep interested in your own
career, however humble; it is a real possession in the changing fortunes of time.
Exercise caution in your business affairs; for the world is full of trickery. But let
this not blind you to what virtue there is; many persons strive for high ideals;
and everywhere life is full of heroism.
Be yourself. Especially, do not feign affection. Neither be cynical about love;
for in the face of all aridity and disenchantment it is perennial as the grass.
Take kindly the counsel of the years, gracefully surrendering the things of
youth. Nurture strength of spirit to shield you in sudden misfortune. But do
not distress yourself with imaginings. Many fears are born of fatigue and
loneliness. Beyond a wholesome discipline, be gentle with yourself.
You are a child of the universe, no less than the trees and the stars; you have a
right to be here. And whether or not it is clear to you, no doubt the universe
is unfolding as it should.
Therefore be at peace with God, whatever you conceive Him to be, and

*whatever your labours and aspirations, in the noisy confusion of life keep peace
with your soul.
With all its sham, drudgery and broken dreams, it is still a beautiful world.
Be careful. Strive to be happy.*

* * *

When I was in King Edward VII's hospital, having had a hip operation, Lord Elton (alias Rodney Elton who is married to the stunning
Richenda) wrote a poem about my absence from the House of Lords. He
is a dab-hand at poetry and writes beautifully. He wrote this:

*'We want Lord Ferrers back', they said
In chamber, bar and Colmondeley room.
'Lord Ferrers' back is in his bed;
It's broke', they answered, full of gloom.
'We want Lord Ferrers back', they cried
On terrace, stair, in left and hall;
'Lord Ferrers' back is bust', replied
The Powers that Be – who know it all.
'His bust is none of our concern',
Rejoined his friends, on the attack,
'What we demand is his return
at once, complete; please give him back'.
'His back's too stiff', they said, 'to bend
Enough to kiss his lovely wife;
And further more it hurt no end.
No wonder he preferred the knife'.
In chamber, gallery and bar
The Peers grew crosser by degrees;
You know what those old codgers are,
How finicky and hard to please.
In volume not to be ignored
They offered their assured advice:
'We want Lord Ferrers back', they roared,*

'No understudy will suffice'.
Down corridors and up the stairs,
So loud it was, the message soared
Until it reached the failing ears
Of one remote and greying Lord
Who downed his pen and with a smile
Embarked upon the winding way
That led him down from loft and tile
To carpets red and light of day.
And so at last the message fled,
Printed on white in solid black,
To Robin's hard and lonely bed:
'The House of Lords wants Ferrers back!'
(Their Lordships have, what's more, agreed
They want his back back well as well
though how to punctuate that screed
Hansard alone, I think, can tell.)
I started out on this poor verse
To say we hope you'll swiftly mend.
Reading longer might make you worse;
So there, I'll have to make an end!

20.vii.95

When I had another hip operation – these things seemed to have happened every twenty-four months or so – Rodney wrote me another poem. He is a prodigious fellow at this kind of thing – and highly entertaining – especially if there is a bit of distress about. This was his letter:

Dear Robin

Hippity, hoppity, hippity
Lightly poor Robin did trippity
Trippit so lightly he slippity
Slippit and brokeit – his hippity

Hoppity, hippity, hoppity
The poor fellow surely did coppity;
All his activities droppity
Now must in hospital stoppity

Hippity, hoppity, hippity
A turn up but not serendipity
His plaster and crutches exhibity
Poorfellow, poorfellow, is suchpity.

Hoppity, hippity, hoppity
Send him a bottle of poppity
Into his tumbler then sloppity
And drink to his walking, not hoppity!

Yours ever
Rodney

I always thought that the following was a preface to *Stemmata Shirlieana*, a book which has depicted our family history. It might well have been and it certainly applies, but I cannot find it there. I do not know, therefore, where it was that I saw the quotation nor can I remember the exact words but, in taking pride in one's own family which most people tend to do, some more modestly than others, it is no bad thing to remember:

Rejoice in the past and all which your forebears have done. But, remember, the achievements are theirs. They are not yours. Use them as a standard for your own conduct.

When I was fifteen or so, if my father thought that we ought to go to bed, he would come into the room and say 'Shadrach'. This was an abbreviation of the biblical three, called Shadrach, Meshack and Abednego. This in turn was translated to Shadrach, Meshack and To-bed-we-go. This in turn got translated to Shadrach, Meshack and Off-we-pop, i.e. Time to go to bed.

My father had a number of succinct phrases which I remember well and which said a great deal. Some of that which follows are his. Others are others':

- Water your friendships for they grow like flowers and they die like flowers.
- On a less than perfect holiday – A change, even for the worse, is nevertheless a change.
- Bank your praises. (When everyone is cursing you, it is nice to remember that someone once praised you).
- You will be blessed in this life for the things which have cost you nothing. You will be cursed for the things to which you have given your all.
- Annabel and I used to dance to a jolly little number with a perky, bright theme, called 'Enjoy yourself. It is later than you think'. It is so true. I have used that as a motto all my life.
- One of my maxims has always been, 'If you have something in which to rejoice, wallow in it.'
- The road to Hell is paved with good intentions.
- Rudyard Kipling's *If.* ('If you can keep your head when all about you are losing theirs and blaming it on you.' All of it.)
- My grandfather, as a justification for a long lie-in in bed used to say, 'I sleep slowly'. I use that expression frequently.
- Some people say, 'Good Health is the most important thing after life'. I do not agree. You can have good health but deep unhappiness at home. The result, misery. You can have bad health, but a hugely happy home. The result, happiness. If you are happy, you have the greatest gift which God can offer.
- A simple guide towards success in the Domestic Budget:
  Income £1, Expenditure 95p, Result – Happiness
  Income £1, Expenditure £1.05, Result – Misery

My advice to a couple getting married.
Do three things:

1. Make a Will.

2. Share a double bed – not for any sexy reason, although that might be a perfectly good reason for it – so that, at the end of the day you can touch each other. It is like the Gadarene Swine. The stresses of the day go from one to the other and are lessened.

3. Go for a holiday for two weeks every year. The definition of a holiday is the two of you away, alone, together. Everything else may be fun and interesting and relaxing, but it is not a holiday. You marry a person because you love them a lot and, if you are not careful, thereafter you do not spend any time alone together. It is very important. Rekindle the original love.

- Love is like a furnace. It will give off a lot of heat with no attention, but then it will begin to get colder. But keep fuelling it, and it gets hotter and hotter.
- My father's advice on having a title: 'Remember, people will always think that you are better than you are, or worse than you are. They will never take you at your face value.'
- I have always consoled myself, when trying to resolve a problem, that you cannot hope to do the right thing. All you can hope to do is the least wrong.
- When things go wrong – and they constantly do – it is always a comfort to know that there is a Better Opportunity Tomorrow. And there is. So don't fret.
- Most people are infuriated by those who pontificate and say that you cannot do this or do that. 'It doesn't work. I have done it myself.' But, remember, the qualities which, in others we call Stubborness and Obstinacy, when found in ourselves we call Knowledge and Experience.
- I once said to my Private Secretary about a submission, 'I cannot understand this.' He said, 'Nor can I.'
- On another occasion I was reading a draft speech on a technical subject, and I said to the civil servant, 'I can't understand this.' He replied, 'Oh don't worry, Minister, everyone in the audience will know what you are talking about.' I said, 'If I cannot understand

what I am talking about, what makes you think that anyone else can be expected to understand what I am talking about?'

I usually tried to add something to draft letters to Members of Parliament to 'personalise' them. Equally, when I received letters from Ministers, I would always go through them with a tooth-comb to see if I could find anything personal about them, or whether the Minister had just topped and tailed a civil servant's script.

Douglas Hogg thought that letters were an unproductive expenditure of time. I thought that they were the shop window between the Department and the public, and were very important.

At one of our morning meetings in the Home Office, I complained about the length of time that the Department took to answer letters. It was a silly thing to do, as I was then made Minister in charge of Correspondence. When I had a list of the time each Minister took to answer his letters, I was always at the bottom – the worst. 'Why?' I asked. 'I am always very careful about my letters.' 'Well, you see Minister, you always insist upon seeing the drafts first and then altering them. Most other Ministers just sign them as drafted.'

One civil servant, on going through a draft speech with me, said, 'You are the most difficult person to write a speech for.' 'Me? Why?' 'You always alter them.' 'But don't most Ministers?' 'Oh no, they usually just read them out'...!

***

The following is a correspondence which I had with Vodafone.

August 2007
E Ferrers
Park Lodge
Hedenham
Bungay
Suffolk NR35 2lE

Hello Earl

We want to make sure you're absolutely happy with the value you're getting from us. So we'll be sending regular updates that show exactly what you've been getting. We don't want to take up too much of your time, so we've kept it short and sweet.

That's it Earl.
We'll send you another update in a few months.

I replied to Vodafone:

17 September 2007

Dear Sir,

Thank you for your cheery letter, a copy of which I enclose, telling me how many free minutes I have received on the Vodafone Stop the Clock. I am, indeed, grateful to you for letting me know that I have received some free minutes.

It is clear from the manner of your address that you must think that I am an American or some such with a Christian name of Earl, and that you feel it is appropriate to start and end your letter by using my Christian name.

I am not, in fact, an American and Earl is not my Christian name. It happens to be an English title – very unfashionable, I know, but it is just one of those irritating facts of life.

Of course, at Vodafone you must do so much of your work by telephone that you probably have lost the art of writing letters, which is the sorry fate of many children. Letters do not naturally start with 'hello' and end with 'That's it, Earl'. They are usually signed by the person responsible for writing them and have the address of the sender attached. Neither of these appeared on your letter.

If I might respectfully so suggest it, it might be a help if letters were to be properly written – if only to encourage others to do the same.

Please do not trouble to send me 'another update' in a few months. They do not seem to be of any particular benefit.

Mr The Earl Ferrers
Park Lodge
Hedenham
Norfolk
NR35 2LE
21 Sep 2007

Our Reference Number is C2727100

Good morning Mr The Earl Ferrers,
Thank you for contacting us. I'll be glad to assist you.

Mr Ferrers, I understand that in the letter which we have sent to you your name was not addressed in an appropriate manner. I'd like to offer you an apology for any frustration that this issue may have caused you. I would like to assure you that this matter will be thoroughly investigated.

Rest assured that this letter is recorded on your account as a permanent record of the information I have provided you with. If there is anything else I can help you with, please feel free to contact me.

Best wishes,
Dolly Mehra
Vodafone Customer Services.

I replied:

24 September 2007

Dear Madam,
Reference C2727100

Thank you for your letter of 21 September.

It is so kind of you to apologise for having addressed me in the incorrect manner, and I am deeply grateful. I am glad that you have recorded the error and that there is an amendment on my account.

Unfortunately, your letter has still not retrieved the position entirely.

Despite the possibility of being considered pedantic, perhaps you will allow me to point out the three still prevailing errors:

1. The style of address is shown as 'Mr The Earl Ferrers'. It should be 'The Rt. Hon. The Earl Ferrers'.
2. The letter begins with 'Good Morning Mr The Earl Ferrers'. It should be 'Dear Lord Ferrers'.
3. The letter ends with 'Best wishes, Dolly Mehra'. It should be 'Yours sincerely, Dolly Mehra'.

I hope that you will forgive me giving what may appear to be an elementary course in letter-writing, but computers are inanimate, obstinate beasts which indulge in neither natural courtesies nor correctness unless dragooned into doing so.

Badly written or wrongly written letters convey an adverse reflection both on the company and on the writer. I hope that you will be kind enough to redress this by further amending my account accordingly, thereby resolving both the errors and the reflections together.

I did not receive another letter of acknowledgement – but I received a telephone call!

Four years later in 2011, I received an account from Vodafone addressed to 'Mr Earl Anonymous Ferrers'. Can you beat it? How a computer can have worked that out, and how it could have appeared to no one in the company as a bit odd, defies imagination.

So the absurdities and inaccuracies continue. So much for computers – and so much for their handlers.

A company wrote out of the blue and sent me a biro, all beautifully inscribed down the barrel, as it might be suitable for promotional purposes. Unfortunately, there was an error. I pointed it out to them.

26 August 2009

Dear Sir,

Thank you for being kind enough to send me a Delane pen. I was delighted to receive it.

There is, however, one problem which I thought I should draw to your attention. As the purpose of the pen is to remind recipients of the name of the firm which gave them the pen it is clearly important that the wording on the pen should be correct.

In my case, I am referred to as 'The Right Honourable the Ear'. This is quite obviously a computer shortcoming but it might have been helpful if the accuracy of the wording had been checked before the sample was sent. It should have been 'The Right Honourable the Earl Ferrers'. But I dare say that that would have been too much for the computer to stomach!

I am enclosing the sample for you to see. This is meant to be helpful and not to be overtly critical. I am very grateful to you for sending me the original but do not trouble in sending me a replacement.

There was no reply. Double bad marks.

***

On a ministerial visit to Burma, when I was in the Ministry of Agriculture, we used to go out each day in a cavalcade of cars and with three policemen in front on motorbikes. They shoved people off to the left with their left hand and off to the right with their right hand, but the pièce de resistance was when they removed both hands from their motorbikes and dispersed people by waving both their hands at them. The motorcycles never wobbled. It was rather like the sight of an eleven-year-old riding his bicycle with no hands.

On a visit to Saudi Arabia, I was taken out to the desert where they irrigated crops with water drawn from huge underground reservoirs from a great depth. In order to explain the depth of the reservoir, my host picked up a stone and dropped it down the pipe. I put my head over the pipe. Waited for a long time, and there was an almighty bang as the noise ricocheted all the way up the pipe.

I got hold of the official from the Ministry of Agriculture, Brian Camp, who was with me. He was a very nice, slightly dour person, but with a great sense of humour. I said, 'Look at this. It shows just how far down the reservoir is. I will drop a stone down and you put your head at the top of the pipe. Put it nice and close, otherwise you may not hear the noise and tell the distance. He did. There was a long pause. Then an almighty bang. He emerged rubbing his ear and saying that it was worse than a 25 pounder going off!

On the same visit to Saudi Arabia I was taken by a very elegant gentleman to see his Arab horses. He was proud of them and obviously loved them. He had his own private ring where the horses were shown off whilst we sat like royalty in comfortable seats. 'Now, Minister,' he said. 'You must try a horse. Which would you like?' I about died. Annabel's father would have been in his element as he was always riding and playing polo and he rode in the Olympic games, but his son-in-law was not cast in the same mould.

'Well that is very kind of you, but I am afraid that I am not very good at riding.' He was persistent. 'Oh you must. They are very gentle animals.' I could see that I was rapidly getting shoved into a corner, and then I suddenly had a flash of inspiration. 'Quite honestly, I am just not very good at riding. I am too tall and lanky and it is not fair on the horses, but Mr Camp, he would love to ride one of them. He is very good at riding.' (I had not the slightest idea whether he was). Brian Camp gave me a sly look and agreed to have a go. What a wonderful gesture that was. I think that my host was slightly disappointed that I would not sample his lovely animals – and even a novice could see that they were lovely animals – but, oh what a blessing it is to have officials, especially when they are kind and fun!

On a Commonwealth Parliamentary Association visit to Singapore in 1964, about three weeks after Singapore had separated away from Malaysia, we had met Lee Kwan Yu, the Prime Minister of Singapore, and had heard his side of the story. We thought, therefore, that we must go to Kuala Lumpur to hear the Malaysian side of the story. This was not part of the prearranged schedule. The High Commissioner, Sir Anthony Head, met us at the airport in Kuala Lumpur with about six cars. The idea was that, after we had been briefed and had had a discussion with the High Commissioner and others, two people would go in each car and see what they wanted to see about Kuala Lumpur.

I went with Tam Dalyell (pronounced Deeyell), a young old-Etonian Labour member of the House of Commons who was, many years later, to become Father of the House. He had radical views and was quite determined that we were being shown only things which those in charge of the country wanted us to see and not things as they really were.

Tam and I set off around Kuala Lumpur. Tam kept stopping the car and taking photographs. That is the Sultan of Brunei's house with three huge domes painted with gold leaf. Click Click went the camera. And then we passed some Tamils who, in those days were the scruffiest members of society – and their houses really were scruffy. Click Click went the camera. You could see what Tam was up to. Back in his constituency in West Lothian, he would be able to say, 'This is how the Sultan of Brunei lives. And this is how the workers live.'

We got back to the airport late. Everyone else was there. The High Commissioner was waiting for us. It was getting dark and the airport had no night-flying arrangements, but it was being kept open for us – and we were late. Tam and I thanked the High Commissioner and apologised to him for being late.

We then went into the aeroplane. Silence. Deathly silence. We found a pair of seats. Silence. The aircraft took off and then there was unleashed a barrage of criticism from all the others (ten altogether, five Conservative and five Labour). Dan Jones was a Labour MP, a lovely Welshman, an ex-miner who was always very clearly spoken, and said 'Tam, Tam. It is a bloody disgrace. Do you realise that you were late? And you kept the High Commissioner waiting? And the airport had to be kept open especially to let us leave?' On and on it went. We sank into our chairs – at least I did. Tam was fairly robust at these kind of things. 'Throughout this trip', Tam said, 'we have only been shown the things which people wanted us to see, and not things as they really are.'

At that, Dan snapped and, in a state of rage, said to Tam, one of his own side, 'Well, good God, man. If I was having guests in to my house, I would want to show them into the Drawing Room and not the bloody tool-shed.' It was too much. I just burst out laughing, and the atmosphere gradually got back to normal.

Dan was a lovely man. I did not see him much afterwards but, whenever we did meet, he always gave me a fulsome welcome, 'Well, good God, man. You do look well.' That vignette of Dan Jones and Tam Dalyell will remain with me for the rest of my life.

On a later visit to Singapore, I was a Minister, and I was shown around a new yoghurt factory. Singapore did not have any cows, so they imported milk and then made it into yoghurt. I found that I had to creep underneath all the very smart stainless steel pipes, as they were about the same height from the floor as were my shoulders. I could not understand why the pipes were all installed so low, until I was told that it was installed by the Japanese, and that the pipes were the right size for the Orientals!

Certain expressions irritate me enormously. They are often started off by civil servants, picked up by Ministers and blown across the ether so that everyone then uses them. They feel that they are really 'with it' in using them and they feel that they are talking with the smart crowd, the 'in' crowd, using technical language.

I give below a list – only a partial list – of words or expressions which make me wince. Ministers often use them when answering Parliamentary questions (because the civil servants have prepared the answers). I find it is like pressing Button B on the old telephone boxes. Out it all comes, but it means nothing.

Efficient
Effective
Coherent
Cohesive
Overarching
Underpinning
Transparent

Raft of measures
I have to say
Meaningful dialogue
Full and frank discussions
To sum up
Package of measures
At this moment in time
I know where you are coming from
Let us move on
Let me share with you

I hate the use of acronyms. You always have to stop reading the narratives in order to think what it means – 'AR spoke to PW.' You have almost to translate it. The point of notes or submissions is to get your views across. This is principally done if the reading is easy. The only people whom acronyms help are the typists – and that is not the purpose of typing.

I once read a submission all about BSC. As I was in the Ministry of Agriculture, I naturally assumed that it was about the British Sugar Corporation, which was then a formidable entity. When I got to the end of the submission, I realised that it referred to the British Steel Corporation. So I had to read the whole thing over again. I chuntered.

I once had a submission which referred to UKCICC – pronounced UC-Chick. I wondered what on earth this was. I supposed that it must have been a company which specialised in exporting high quality chickens. In fact, it referred to the United Kingdom's Commander-in-Chief Committee. Who on earth would have thought that? That is the military for you. They love that kind of gobbledy-gook.

Champagne
We never used to drink champagne much – too expensive, too extravagant, too this, too that. I now realise that it is the best drink in the world, and I drink it on every possible occasion. Particularly lately. It occurred to me that there might not be any champagne in the next world, although my clerical friends advise me – I am not sure on what authority – there will be plenty and that it will be very good.

However, just to be prudent and on the right side, I have taken the view that it is best to drink as much champagne as you can whilst you are in this world – just in case there is not any in the next world.

Chapter 22

And Then

IN 2001 ANNABEL and I decided to move out of Ditchingham and to move to a smaller house, but we did not know where to go to. Robert said, 'Why don't you go to Park Cottage?', which is where Annabel's parents lived. We thought that it was a horrible little house – small, pokey and unattractive. We asked Patrick Bradley, who is not an architect but who is a Chartered Building Surveyor, and who lived in Bungay. if he could have a look at Park Cottage and see if he thought that he could do anything with it. Some thirty years earlier he had transformed a house for Aunt Kit which was so decrepit that it was literally about to be knocked down, but Patrick came in, rejuvenated it and made it quite beautiful. We have always had a great respect for him and for his abilities since then.

Patrick looked around Park Cottage and said that he thought that he could do something with it and that he could make it lovely. He did. I said that everything must be on one level as one of us, one day, would probably end up in a wheelchair, knowing full well that it would be me. I never expected that it would be the poor, lovely Annabel. But it is now all on one level – no steps inside the house or going outside the house, where there used to be three steps going from the front door to the garden and three steps from the conservatory to the garden.

The wonderful Enriquetta Crouch (who was always called Queta), was a superb interior decorator. She had been a friend of ours at Cambridge when she was married to John Lindsey-Bethune. Like Annabel, Queta was an undergraduate's wife when we were there. Our lives then drifted apart, but she came to help us decorate and furnish Ditchingham Hall, and later our flat at 26 Warwick Square and my ministerial office in the Home Office.

Can we have Queta to come and help us do up Park Lodge? For us, it was a must. We asked her and she said that she would come and help. She had that wonderful ability to see what places can be like when they are all drawings on a piece of paper or when they are partially constructed and consist of walls of dark grey concrete blocks. She used her ingenuity, and she has made it a simply lovely place. How I do envy other people's abilities.

When we had moved into Ditchingham, Annabel was appalled by the enormity of the responsibility of furnishing and decorating. I had said to her, 'Look, Ditchingham is a lovely place. You really cannot furnish it with fabrics from a sale at Peter Jones. Get Queta to help you and a huge weight will be lifted from your shoulders.' It was. So it was with Park Lodge. We 'upgraded' the house from Park Cottage to Park Lodge.

Then, what about the garden? We did not know where to start. Part of the garden used to be the field. And so we asked Mark Rumary to help us. He used to be the chief landscape designer at Notcutts, but he was now retired. He had helped us hugely at Ditchingham. He made the garden at Park Lodge wonderful. The drive was moved from the front of the house to the back. There were flowers, blossom, colour everywhere. When I saw his proposal for some rose-beds around the Dovecote I swooned and said, 'That will be terribly expensive.' He just said, 'I thought that it would be lovely to wake up in the morning and to see a blaze of colour out of your bedroom window.' We had the roses. He was right. I think of what he said every time that I open the curtains. Some people have the wonderful ability to see what could be right. He did. I cannot.

One final extravagance of all extravagancies was to put a little borehole down so that we could water the garden. Angela was horrified. 'Look, Daddy. You just can't do that,' she said. I replied that the garden was costing a lot to do and that there is no point in waiting for fifteen years for a mature garden and that these plants have all got to grow.

The shrubs all grew like mad and flowered like mad. In about three years, we virtually had a mature garden.

I have been reminded, hauntingly, of something which somebody once said to me. 'When you move house, spend as much as you can. And when you have spent your limit, then spend a bit more.'

It sounds like a recipe for extravagance, but it is not. When you move house, you spend a lot on rewiring, and then you cover all the wires up. You re-plumb it all and cover all the pipes up. You realign the floor levels, and then cover up all the discrepancies. So, when you come to decorating and furnishing – the part that you are going to enjoy every day – you say, 'Help, I have spent so much, we must cut down on something.' So you cut down on the kitchen floor over which you are going to walk every day.

It happens to everyone. It has happened to us – frequently. Whenever we said to Queta 'That is too expensive. We really cannot afford it. We must have something cheaper,' we were *always* wrong. There is a moral there and each person who reads this will have to work out for him or herself what that is.

We started work on Park Lodge in September 2002. We moved in June 2003. Robert and Susannah moved into Ditchingham in July 2003.

I was always conscious – and still am – of the danger of living too close to one's children. It is too easy to criticise, to go over uninvited, to be irritated by changes which a new generation inevitably makes whether it is to a house, or to a garden or to a farm. We try to adhere to the principle that we will only go over to them when we are asked – or if we telephone first – but that all of their family are welcome to come to us at anytime. We love seeing them. We do not want, as it were, to 'catch them out' in their own home by appearing unexpectedly.

It was a year after we had moved into Park Lodge that Annabel went into King Edward VII to have a knee replacement. Annabel was not very keen on this, to put it mildly, but she was having increasing difficulty with walking, and everyone said that she really must get it done.

The surgeon who had done my knee replacement eighteen months earlier, which had been a great success, was duly booked in to perform the same operation for Annabel's. He always said that the problem which Annabel had was more than just an awkward knee. But the knee was wrong and so we decided, and he agreed, to do it.

The procedure went fine but something happened afterwards which, as we found out later, had given her TIAs (Transient Ischeamic Attack) – in other words, mini strokes. I often wonder whether this was her body's reaction to the surgical invasion of the operation, whether it was due to the impact of the anaesthetic, or whether it was due to the fact that, when Selina died, Annabel never cried at all. She had bottled it all up.

Annabel adored Selina, but the lovely, gentle, generous Annabel was a staunch buttress when Selina died and she never gave in at all or had a real good cry. I often wonder whether the bottling up of all these emotions did not find its escape at the time of her operation because, afterwards, she could not walk. The knee was alright but the body said, 'No'. She used to walk with a walking frame and that helped for a while, but it got worse until she had to be in a wheelchair the whole time, and now she has to be helped in and out of bed with a hoist. Curiously enough, her mother was in a wheelchair and had great difficulty in walking and speaking. So was her sister, Tony Lothian.

This has made fearful incursions into our life. We have to have two carers, and not just one with which we started. I remember Patricia White, whose Agency we used, saying, 'If you want to take Lady Ferrers out of hospital on Tuesday, I can supply you with a carer but, if you can wait until Wednesday, I can supply you with the person whom I think will be really right for you.' Thank Heavens we waited until Wednesday.

Jennie Bleier came to be with us when Annabel left hospital and she has, except for holidays, been with us ever since – at the time of writing over six years. Her home is in New Zealand, but she loves England and has been here on and off for ages. She was a Matron in a hospital in New Zealand. She is very competent – medically. But she is kind, loving, understanding and deeply caring and she will do anything. She is full of fun and has a huge sense of humour. There is always laughter in the house when Jennie is about and we just believe that we have been so unbelievably lucky to have had her – *and* to continue to have her.

I have always had my anxieties about continuing to go to London and whether one should not stay at home the whole time to help Annabel. 'For better for worse, in sickness and in health,' haunts me. But so many people, including Annabel in her enormous generosity, have said, 'You must keep going to London, seeing people, doing things, otherwise you will sit here and fret and do nothing.' Even the doctor said the same, rather poignantly, when he said, 'In my experience, husbands and wives looking after each other is not usually successful and it does not lead to marital harmony.'

So, having my wonderful, generous, understanding Annabel, I continue to go to London. There is no normal pattern, but coming home is not a case, regrettably, of sitting down and reading a book in the garden. I cannot think why it isn't, but it just isn't. But then I doubt if it is, really, for anyone.

After six years, our garden really has become mature and it gives us great pleasure. Cliff Hart looks after it. He came to us forty-five years ago. His real love is machinery. He can mend, make, create, repair, devise anything, and he looked after all the machinery on the farm for years. But he can turn his mind to anything. He is kind, deeply responsible, courteous. How lucky we are. But I bet, when he originally came to work for us, he never thought that his life would end up this way!

His wife, Rosemary said, 'Cliffy is wonderful with the vegetable garden, but don't let him anywhere near flowers. He does not know anything about flowers!' I often think of that remark, when I look at the garden resplendent with colour.

One of our hobbies in our dotage has been ducks. When we came to Park Lodge, there was an appalling mess about 150 yards from the house. It looked as if it was an overgrown pond into which had been dumped every conceivable object – metal fences, whole oak tree trunks and any rubbish from the farm which had to be dumped somewhere. We cleaned it out and found that there were two ponds – one small one for the tiddlers and one larger one for the carp. These had kept Hedenham Hall supplied with fish in Victorian times and before.

Having dug the ponds out, we thought that we would put a few ornamental ducks on them and plant some trees. Over the following four years or so, we planted more trees and shrubs, and we put more ducks on the ponds and fenced them off against rabbits and anything else which might want to have a go at them and planted a hedge all round them. It looks lovely. And now we have a little hut there so that Annabel and I can go and sit in it, be cosy and watch it all. It is very peaceful and relaxing there.

It is a funny kind of life, really. Most people retire at sixty-five and settle down to a peaceful life, sometimes in the country, going for walks, reading books, visiting the many places in the world which they have always longed to visit.

Our life has not quite planned out that way. I have never regarded myself as a politician, but as a farmer who got caught up in the slipstream of politics. Even at eighty-one, I still go the House of Lords. Why? Partly because I have been there for fifty-five years, partly I suppose because I love it, partly because I have been elected, partly to see my friends, and partly because in this ever-changing world, it is good that some of the older people who have had the good fortune to have witnessed some of it earlier are, like a Christmas pudding, still part of the mix. And Annabel is gloriously generous to say, 'Keep going. You will miss it, and it interests you.'

There is an astonishing bond of friendship, care and love in the House of Lords which crosses all parties. You are cocooned in an atmosphere of kindness which I find more remarkable as every day goes by, and so many people have become personal friends.

When, in June 2009, I reached the dizzy age of eighty, we decided to have a party. Robert was putting up a marquee at Ditchingham for a dance to celebrate Susannah's fiftieth birthday on a Saturday and so he suggested that we use the same marquee on the Monday for a lunch. We did. It was huge fun. It was supposed to be for people locally, but we asked a few others from further afield knowing that they would not be able to come. But they did. We had over 200 people. They came from London, Devon, Belgium and even America – just for a lunch. It was very touching. The weather was unbelievably perfect. The sides of the marquee came down so that you could see the flowers, the house, the lake. There was a hugely happy atmosphere.

I worried in case this was a crazy extravagant personal indulgence, celebrating one of my own personal attainments for which, of course, I was in no way responsible. I concluded No. I was very lucky to have attained eighty. Life is wonderful. There are so many things for which to be grateful and friendship is one of the greatest. Most people have fearful dramas in their lives, about which most of us know little, and that to go out, have a wonderful lunch in the most perfect of settings, surrounded by one's friends, is a day of great happiness in which they, not just I, could indulge. If you can make other people's lives lighter and happier, just for a bit, what a huge pleasure that is and what great fun it is. I do not think that that is being selfish. There are so many miseries, disasters, sorrows in life that, if one has anything to be grateful for, then wallow in it.

Richenda Elton wrote a touching paragraph in her thank-you letter. She said, 'My grandmother, when asked about the After-life, used to say that she thought Heaven would be a place where she would see all her favourite friends, untouched by time, dressed in their best and surrounded by flowers. If she was right (and that distinguished congregation of clergy would certainly have a view) yesterday's celebration was such a glimpse of Paradise.'

It was lovely – just lovely. Some people have a majestic touch with words.

My father always used to say, 'Water your friendships, because they grow like flowers and they die like flowers.' It is not a question, necessarily, of doing a lot. It is merely a question of keeping in touch – periodically. Christmas Cards are a wonderful way of doing that.

We have always been bad at having people in and having people to stay. We should have done more of it. It was not that we did not like it, but there always seemed so much to do and, very stupidly, we found it difficult to fit in unless, as it were, it was 'predestined' for you like a shoot or a wedding. Once you go to a person's house, once you have enjoyed a meal there and, better still, once you have spent a night there, you are much closer to that person.

Ben Blower once said to me 'Remember, life is for enjoying too.' I liked the word 'too'. If you say that life is for enjoying, you are virtually promoting the lifestyle of a playboy, but if you work all the time that there is, then you risk becoming boring. Ben also said, 'Would it not be awful if, when you go to the next world, and you meet your Creator and he says to you, 'Do tell me. Did you enjoy yourself when you were down in my world?' and you replied, 'I did not have the time. I had so much work to do.' Would it not be just too awful?

It is always said that it is important to have a hobby, particularly so that you can have something to go and do when you are retired. Much to my eternal shame, I have never really had a hobby. I used to say in those directories which ask you what are your hobbies, 'Shooting. Music. Travel.' That's fine, but they are not what you might call everyday hobbies like tying flies or growing tomatoes or taking photographs. Shooting probably takes thirteen days a year. Music I have loved from Winchester days, but we have never been too good at the formal occasions like operas, ballets and concerts. Travel is something which most people do, but it tends to be very expensive and you usually only do it for about fourteen days a year.

So that has been a great lacuna in my life, and I have only myself to blame for it. Bertie Denham, despite being Chief Whip in the House of Lords for many years, was a Master of Foxhounds and told me that the great thing about hunting was that, when you were out, you forgot everything else – your work, your worries, your bank statements, the lot. Your entire concentration was given off to the hunt – the chase, the next hedge to jump, the next ditch to avoid falling into, the effort just to hang on. It was mentally and physically exhausting – and then you had a good sleep. It was a total switch-off and that is so good for everyone whatever they are doing in life.

For myself, in which – although I do not like to admit it – one is, I suppose, in the evening of one's life, I look back and think how hugely and undeservedly lucky I have been. I have been married to the most wonderful girl in all the world. I never thought, when we were first married, that love would not only blossom out but would spread its base wider and wider as the years go by and, oddly enough, even more so as mobility becomes more restrained. Kindness, generosity, understanding, total friendship and fun have marked our days. I am just totally indebted to, and inundated with love for, Annabel. To have had loving children and grandchildren, and now a great grandchild, has been another source of huge pride and contentment.

Of course, we have had the downsides, too. Selina, that lovely beautiful and glorious daughter dying at thirty-nine took its toll, and we always have the problem of Sallyanne. The one worldly and selfish thing which

I feel sorry about which has spoilt all the fun is that, throughout life, I have been constantly worried about money. I feel ashamed about this because, to others, we must seem to have little about which to worry. But everyone seems to worry about money whatever their position or responsibilities.

My real worry is that I have failed. I should have had a job – been an accountant, financier, lawyer or some such – which gives you the cash on which to live, to save and to have your holidays and is a ladder up which to climb. Instead, I have relied upon the most uncertain and volatile of all sources of income – agriculture. And then politics.

It has all been a huge privilege to be involved with the land – Annabel's land – and with politics, but I constantly berate myself for not having taken more personal command of my life and for not having provided better for Annabel and for the children. My gnawing grievance is not that things have not turned out well. They have – unbelievably, superbly well, better than anyone could ever dare to wish or to think – but, in the inner recesses of my mind, I sometimes think that I, Robin Ferrers, should have provided better for Annabel and the children rather than leaving so much to chance.

But life is a lottery, and chance has been overwhelming generous to me.

My father used to say, 'Remember that there is always someone saying "Gosh he is a lucky man – I wish I was him".' I merely feel that, considering how supremely lucky I have been, I should have contributed more myself.

Annabel and I have had a wonderful life together – mutual happiness and friendship in a big way and, in Annabel's case, great, great beauty. We have been mercifully spared so far – I cannot think how or why – some of these terrible illnesses, operations, and even death to which so many people are subject.

How much is there to rejoice in? Oh, stacks. Friends. Lovely home. Wonderful children. Glorious Annabel. Fascinating job. Interesting people and the realisation that most people, in whatever walk of life they happen to be, are good, honest, kind, courteous, loving and nice. It goes on and on. I have been smothered in good fortune.

Yet, I cannot help feeling tormented by those words in the Apocrypha in the Wisdom of Solomon, about Life. It says that Life is like an arrow which 'is shot at a target, the air, thus divided, comes together at once, so that no one knows its pathway'.

One's life, one's pathway, is gone. Invisible. Finished. Was it never there? All that work – schooling, learning, working, creating a home, bringing up children, living in the un-understable world – Finished? Nothing? Never there? It cannot be. It does not make sense. There must be a purpose behind this magnificent world – and this remarkable Life.

Yes, it was there. But, if it was there, what was there as the air which was once divided has come together again? It was the contribution which each of us makes to this thing which we may not, and cannot, understand properly, called Life. Like the Almighty, you may not see Him, but Life is there, and it is all hugely puzzling.

Whatever next? I don't know. No one ever knows, but I am just thankful that it was the one who did who won the race and not one of the other six million or so participants.

What an experience life has been, and still is. How lucky I have been, and how indescribably grateful I am to the Almighty for such an experience. May one never forget to say, 'Hooray' and 'Thank You'!

Index